The Memory of Soun

MW00782909

This book explores the connections between sound and memory across all electronic media, with a particular focus on radio. Street explores our capacity to remember through sound and how we can help ourselves preserve a sense of self through the continuity of memory. In so doing, he analyses how the brain is triggered by the memory of programs, songs and individual sounds. He then examines the growing importance of sound archives, community radio and current research using GPS technology for the history of place, as well as the potential for developing strategies to aid Alzheimer's and dementia patients through audio memory.

Seán Street is Emeritus Professor of Radio at Bournemouth University. He is author of *The Poetry of Radio: The Colour of Sound* (Routledge, 2013). He is also a regular broadcaster on BBC Radio 3 and Radio 4 and a poet, with nine published collections. He lives in Liverpool, UK.

Routledge Research in Cultural and Media Studies

For a full list of titles in this series, please visit www.routledge.com

The Memory of Sound

Preserving the Sonic Past

Seán Street

Routledge
Taylor & Francis Group

LONDON AND NEW YORK

First published 2015
by Routledge

2 Park Square, Milton Park, Abingdon, Oxon OX14 4RN
711 Third Avenue, New York, NY 10017, USA

*Routledge is an imprint of the Taylor & Francis Group,
an informa business*

First issued in paperback 2016

Library of Congress Cataloging-in-Publication Data
Street, Seán.
   The memory of sound : preserving the sonic past / Seán Street.—1 Edition.
      pages cm. — (Routledge research in cultural and media studies ; 65)
   Includes bibliographical references and index.
   1. Memory.   2. Sound—Psychological aspects.   3. Senses and sensation.
4. Radio.   I. Title.
   BF371.S8397   2014
   153.1'23—dc23
   2014007187

ISBN 978-0-415-71398-6 (hbk)
ISBN 978-1-138-69916-8 (pbk)

Typeset in Sabon
by Apex CoVantage, LLC

To Jo

Music, when sweet voices die,
Vibrates in the memory . . .

—Percy Bysshe Shelley

Contents

Preface

The Greek poet Simonides is said to be the founder of the art of memory. Born at Ioulis on the island of Kea (Ceos in Latin) in or around 556 BC, he was an orator in an age when the spoken word was the carrier of text and the transmitter of stories, before the reliance on the written word to preserve witness and experience. The story goes that on one occasion, Simonides was performing a poem created by order of a nobleman of Thessaly, called Scopas, at a great banquet. Part of the poem included a passage in praise of the gods Castor and Pollux, and Scopas, irritated that the focus had been shifted from his event, suggested that as these deities had been included in his commission, they should pay half the fee. The legend says that shortly after the performance, a message came telling Simonides that two men were waiting outside to meet him. On leaving the banquet, he found no one there, but at that moment, the roof of the building collapsed, killing everyone within and mangling the bodies to the extent that when relatives came to claim them for burial, they were beyond identification. Castor and Pollux had more than paid for their half of the poem, but Simonides was able to provide another service to the grieving families. By remembering where each of the guests had sat during his oration, he was able to identify the bodies; from this he inferred that selecting places in a room or within a building and forming mental connections with people, things or ideas that can be stored in those imaginative places enables the recollection of those memories when the picture is summoned to mind. In other words, the images come to denote the things themselves.

Simonides' art of memory was passed down and developed across numerous cultures, and adapted itself in the concept of memory palaces through the teaching of—among others—the seventeenth-century Italian Jesuit Matteo Ricci. A trained memory before the invention of printing was vital to the Romans as well as to the Greeks, and so later moved in an adapted form into this European tradition. With the coming of a set text, some mourned the resultant decline in memory, just as today there are those who suspect that the reliance on the accessing of facts and information through the Internet will lead to a further reduction in our mnemonic powers. Those seeking a history of the art of memory from the Greeks onwards can do no better than to read Frances A. Yates's superb *The Art of Memory*; Yates, through her long association with the Warburg Institute, has unlocked many mysteries, and her unique writings continue to inform the study of aesthetics and psychology and to contribute to our understanding of philosophy, science and literature. The voice of the poet Simonides will come back to us through this work, as will, I hope, the voice of our own memory.

This book has no need to retrace the steps of a path so elegantly taken previously; works, both theoretical and historical, have explored memory, its art and science from many angles and from a great number of perspectives. Instead, I seek to pursue a journey of my own, using Simonides' principles of imaginative physical pictures, and suggesting that by applying them to sound we have the potential for taking possession of a powerful aid to the recollection of things past. In the coming pages I shall try to explore personal recollection through sound, music, stories, roads and buildings. I shall discuss the memory palaces we create to preserve the sounds that have themselves been saved from time by recording, and I shall ask how much we can do to preserve sonic landmarks within ourselves, to help the saving of that self before the individual library that is in every human being on earth moves beyond time.

*

In some ways, this book is a sequel, growing as it has from ideas that began their formation in a previous work, *The Poetry of Radio—The Colour of Sound*. As with that text, this writing owes itself to friendships, discussions and ideas generously shared. To name those who have shown interest in many ways, and who have offered insights from fields of expertise far beyond my own, is to take pleasure in publicly acknowledging a debt that I have already underlined privately between us and within the main body of the text.

Among those whose insights—in the fields of academia and specialist knowledge—have been indispensable, and without whom I would have found myself alone in complex and fast-flowing currents, have been Jacqui Attwood, Carolyn Birdsall, Emma Brinkhurst, Stephen Deutsch, James Donald, Alison Gopnik, Bridget Griffen-Foley, Anthea Innes, Julie Kirkby, Peter M. Lewis, Justine Lloyd, Mary Mittelman, Helena Muller, Jonathan Peelle, James Reilly, Colin Robinson, Jacqui Taylor and Julia Taylor. They have shown patience, support, advice and understanding in all sorts of ways.

Sound specialists have shared their skills and knowledge, not to mention their motivation and thinking, from a diverse range of fields with characteristic support and I thank them: Mark Barber, Kevin Brew, Chris Brookes, Edwin Brys, Billy Butler, Charo Calvo, Janet Cardiff, Gill Carter, Andy Cartwright, John Cotcher, James Cridland, Gill Davies, Stijn Demeulenaere, Paul Easton, John Escombe, Nina Garthwaite, Vincent Hazard, Kari Hesthamer, Clare Jenkins, Michael Ladd, Kaye Mortley, Francesca Panetta,

Tony Phillips, Piers Plowright, Rony Robinson, Mathieu Ruhlmann, Simon Scott, Robert Seatter, Julie Shapiro, David Sonnenchein, Tony Smith, Adrian Stewart, Hans Stucken, Matt Thompson, Chris Watson, Emma-Louise Williams, Gwyneth Williams, Soo Williams, Anne Wood and Roger Wright. I am grateful to you all.

Cultural historians, consultants, poets, musicians, writers, teachers and artists have been key to unravelling some of the mysteries of memory and how it communicates a sense of self through sound, and I am grateful to them for their help, gifts and support: in particular, Nick Buchanan, Elizabeth Darrell, Tim van Eyken, Paul Farley, Sally Goldsmith, Jeremy Hooker, Stephen Isserlis, Stephen Kovacevich, Richard Mabey, Joe Musker, Noah Pikes, Katrina Porteous, Robyn Ravlitch, Dmae Roberts, Michael Rosen and Pascal Wyse.

From the American Folklore Centre at the United States Library of Congress, Ann Hoog and Bertram Lyons have been generous with answers to many questions. From the British Library Sound Archive, the Director of Sound and Vision, Richard Ranft, and his ever friendly and helpful colleagues Rob Perks, Jonathan Robinson, Cheryl Tipp, Janet Topp Farjeon and Paul Wilson, have shared and discussed aspects of their work that have greatly enhanced this work, as has Virginia Millington, Recording and Archive Manager at *StoryCorps*.

The online survey produced some fascinating insights, and I am extremely grateful to everyone who took the time and care to share their thoughts and memories from around the globe; in particular I would like to thank Mel Bray, Rob Bridgett, Ian Buckley, Mike Chapman, Shane Elson, James Ewing, Laura Ginters, Martin Hadlow, Magz Hall, Mike Hally, Quentin Howard, Margaret MacDonald, Anna Robinson, Helen Shaw, Nigel Starck and Colin Thornton. Their recollections—and those of many more who took the trouble to respond to the questions I posed—have been not only fascinating and informative, but also in many cases moving and heartwarming. I am also grateful to Julia Taylor for her help and expertise in setting up the survey, in addition to her knowledge and passion for the world of radio history. Thanks as always to my wife, Jo, for her patience.

While I gratefully acknowledge my thanks and admiration to all who were part of this journey, I fully accept errors and omissions as my own. In doing so, I would like to emphasise that while this book does not set out to comprehensively provide answers to the many mysteries relating to sound and memory, I hope that in some way it may stimulate interest, debate and discussion relating to those questions.

Seán Street

1 Introduction
Echoes and Shadows

The first sound is the roar of a huge rocket engine, deep, full of terrifying power, danger and possibility, evincing an image of something pulling itself almost painfully away from the earth's gravitational hold. There is an amber glow above me now, in September 1953. I am in the giant spaceship as it flies into the future of 1965, where Jet Morgan and his team are beginning *Operation Luna* in the first series of Charles Chilton's *Journey Into Space*, the last BBC radio series to win the ratings battle over television.

I am seven years old, listening on a pre-war valve radio (a Cossor 484 Table model from 1937, now old and relegated from downstairs, but still capable of booming sonorously enough when aerial and earth are set up correctly) in the rear bedroom of my grandmother's Portsmouth terraced house on the south coast of England. I know there are pictures on the wall, out of sight in the near darkness, images of nineteenth-century rural land-scapes that once belonged to my great-grandfather on his tenant farm in central Hampshire. My pictures tonight, though, are made by sound, as I lift off with Jet, Lemmy, Mitch and Doc towards the eerie twilight world of unknown space.

The memory of that radio, the golden light from its dial reflected on the ceiling over my head, opens other peripheral sounds. One road away there is a railway line. If I were to look out of the window now, I would see the silhouette of a footbridge across the line. Lying here as the radio story unfolds, I hear the sounds of trains shunting, the crash and clatter of wagons being pushed backwards and forwards seemingly arbitrarily, without pur-pose. Then I hear the soft complaining of my grandmother's bantam hens, disturbed by the noises on the line. I remember now that although we are in an urban street, my grandmother was born a farm girl from Liss, and she never lost the habit of keeping animals.

The sounds are layered; below me and under the immediate *musique concréte* of trains, hens and radio, there is the low murmur of adult voices coming from the living room downstairs. My father is talking with my grandmother and my aunt and uncle. I know they are smoking, because they always do: Player's Navy Cut. My grandfather is there, but I do not hear his voice. He has said very little since returning from Passchendaele in 1917, almost forty years before. But I remember now that before World War I shell-shocked him into silence, his trade was as a French polisher, working for a Portsmouth firm that sold grand pianos. I remember he always gave me half a crown. I remember the stubble on his cheek.

The next sound that emerges from memory is projected by a widening circle of experience and stimulated suggestion borne of recollection around the house. In the morning, there will be the sound of slow hooves, the iron wheels of an open cart. The greengrocer, Mr Madgewick, will come slowly down the road with his seemingly always tired horse, pausing outside every house to sell. My grandmother will walk down the curved, pastel-coloured, crazily paved front garden path and buy vegetables for the weekend. Then on Saturday afternoon, my Uncle Les will sit intently by the living room radio—the family's new Ultra 'Coronation Twin', (in honour of the year) model R786—as *Imperial Echoes* announces *Sports Report*, as he poises himself, roll-up cigarette on his lip, pen in hand, football coupon on the table, and listens for the escape from labouring in the dockyard that never came.

This is as far as I take this sound journey into my childhood for now, but I could go further. The important point is that all of this comes back when I hear the opening moments of a radio programme that seized my imagination as a young boy. Sound—like smell—is a significant trigger to memory. In this book I will explore the connections between sound—in particular radio—and recollection. How do we remember? What do we remember? Do I *really* have an auditory memory of those family sounds from the 1950s, or am I remembering them by association? Have I unconsciously applied a form of the ancient art of memory, a form of audio memory palace as originally conceived by the Greek poet Simonides sometime in the fifth or sixth century BC? If so, does that make the memory less valid? We shall interrogate this later in the book. In the meantime, the question remains: What is it about sound and its links with emotion that is both memorable and recoverable through our historic imagination? Why should it be that it is more accessible mentally than most moving images? Are we in danger of damaging long-term memory by the ability we now possess to access information within seconds on a 'need-to-know' basis via the Internet? These are important questions, because in an ageing society where we increasing treat large numbers of patients suffering from various forms of memory loss, the ability to learn or absorb a fact, feeling or theory, and then retain it mentally, is a significant issue.

I am writing here about radio, but my subject is sound in the broadest sense, so I will move laterally through various media in this writing; radio, though, is a starting point because it is so much about memory. As the Australian poet and radio producer Michael Ladd has so well articulated:

> It's a paradox; radio draws on sound archives, but its own sound is always disappearing. Radio's audio memories return, only to be erased again. Non-verbal sounds and the spoken word are always being born

and always dying. They exist in space, in the ear, in the perceiving mind, and then, fairly quickly, just in memory, or, if they have been recorded, lie dormant in the recording medium. They don't live unless they are being heard. While you can play back a track on a CD, or via a computer download, broadcast radio is a medium of continuous disappearance. It is simultaneous in the community but ephemeral, giving multiple listeners a unique experience of the passing moment. I was writing and publishing poetry before I began my radio career. Time passing, ephemera, were always key concerns of my writing for the page, so sound, and particularly the transmission of it by radio waves, was a natural place for me to investigate further.[1]

Given changes in recreational habits amongst the young, and the demise of the idea of a 'Children's Hour' or traditional listening form for infants and children, (something that many previous generations remember fondly), we should ask, what will be the long-term effect on memory of instantly sourcing information and entertainment through computers and electronic games? My memory of *Journey Into Space* will be, I suspect, typical of a generation of youthful listeners to 1950s BBC Radio. Others will recall tuning in 'under the bedclothes' to Radio Luxembourg or pirate radio. A pre-war generation could still recall into great old age the theme song to *The Ovaltineys Concert Party* from an earlier incarnation of Radio Luxembourg, which may give this advertising jingle the greatest longevity of any British-known brand. We may argue that given a society in which short-term attention does not necessarily mean that the capacity to store and preserve information is lesser, memory and its evolution will adjust in ways appropriate to that developing society. Equally, by considering nationalities and societies where oral traditions and traditional storytelling remain active, we may come to sense that as a modern society we are losing more than we are gaining.

The original context of hearing the sound is very important, however, because sound memory unlocks other senses. In doing research for this book, responses to questions about audio memory of radio in listeners born in the 1940s produced a shared, common recollection among British audiences associated with Sunday lunchtimes and afternoons. The playing of the tune 'With a Song in My Heart' created in many British listeners of a certain age a sense memory of the smell of gravy and roast meat cooking. Why? Because in the years immediately following the Second World War, and well into the 1950s, the BBC Light Programme broadcast 'Two Way Family Favourites', in which the BBC linked with British Forces broadcasters—usually in Germany—between 12pm and 1.30pm on Sundays, and the theme tune of the programme was 'With a Song in My Heart'. It may be true—as some respondents have said—that smell and taste are in some cases even more evocative than sound, (Proust would probably agree), but frequently it is sound that provides the first trigger. Likewise, many people of the same immediate post-war generation (remember radio was intensely important to this group, just before the advent of television) recalled clear mental pictures of their family front rooms (the best room for many UK families, often only used for special occasions and Sunday afternoons) linked to the sound of the radio's broadcast of variety programmes such as *The Clitheroe Kid,* which starred the child impersonator Jimmie Clitheroe, *The Billy Cotton Band Show,* and other comedy programmes from the era of British variety, always broadcast in the same time slot, in the early afternoon of a British Sunday. *Beyond Our Ken,* starring Kenneth Horne, and its sequel, *Round the Horne,* were favourite memories, as was the comedy series *The Navy Lark,* one of the highest audience rating programmes from the 'golden age' of post-war UK radio. Poignantly, one respondent remembered listening with the family to these programmes and then going out of the house to spend the rest of the afternoon with school friends. For him, the sound of laughter from the radio audience contrasted sharply with his memory of the quietness of an English summer Sunday in the mid 1950s. The sound world of childhood included the radio, but the broadcasts lay at the centre of a sonic pool, and the ripples of memory spread out from that centre: programme scheduling, family custom and the comforting habit of stability, however illusory, fuelled the post-war British appetite for a sound world of entertainment.

MELODIES SUNG AND SPOKEN

I want to examine the tools we use to plant sound into the human mind; rhythm, repetition and rhyme in poetry, song and oratory. Poets and playwrights have understood this from the time of Homer, as well as the itinerant balladeers and travelling storytellers who projected their images into the mind of audiences before there was a printed word. Shakespeare and his contemporaries used oral devices with great skill. As Hamlet hatches his plot to play on the conscience of Claudius through drama, he says:

> I'll have these players
> Play something like the murder of my father
> Before mine uncle: I'll observe his looks;
> I'll tent him to the quick: if he but blench,
> I'll know my course. The spirit that I have seen
> May be the devil; and the devil hath power
> To assume a pleasing shape; yea, and perhaps
> Out of my weakness and my melancholy,
> As he is very potent with such spirits,
> Abuses me to damn me: I'll have grounds
> More relative than this: the play's the thing
> Wherein I'll catch the conscience of the king.

—[*Hamlet*: Act II, scene 2]

The subtle blending of rhythms follows the pace of the human heart; much of Shakespeare's text moves in pentameters that mirror the natural average speed at which a human being walks. It is an aid to the actor remembering the lines, and at the same time it places the ideas into the brain of the listener in a memorable way. Likewise, we can observe here the device of the rhyming couplet to end the speech—and in this case, also the scene, as Hamlet exits, full of new purpose. This works in several ways; firstly, there is a sense of finality in the rhyme; delivered well, it will earn the actor a round of applause from the audience, because it provokes a response. It also tells us that this part of our experience is over, like the punchline in a joke. Even within the short span of a rhyming couplet, there is much to learn about sound and recollection; the end of the second line of the couplet is a sound memory of the end of the first, an echo. Shakespeare used the trick sparingly; he knew when to employ rhyme, and when not. Rhyming couplets and a strong rhythm are aids to learning, but without due care they can sink into doggerel. Hence, when we reach the player king's performance in the same play, we have the rhyme scheme and rhythm of a much lesser writer than the Bard, although it is still he that contrives this:

> I do believe you think what now you speak;
> But what we do determine oft we break,
> Purpose is but the slave to memory,
> Of violent birth, but poor validity:
> Which now, like fruit unripe, sticks to the tree;
> But fall, unshaken, when they mellow be . . .

> —[Ibid.: Act III, scene 1]

Rhythm and rhyme play an important role in our ability to remember offstage too. My father-in-law lived to the age of 97. Towards the end of his long life, he suffered from vascular dementia. There were times when he found it hard to recall his own family, or what had happened a few minutes earlier, but until the day he died he could recite from memory Prince Hal's speech from Agincourt in *Henry V*, and Tennyson's *Charge of the Light Brigade*, which he had learned as a schoolboy almost a lifetime earlier. He grew up in a time when learning by rote—be it poetry or multiplication tables—was a norm in school. The act of writing—as well as reading or learning a poem—can be critically influenced and affected by sound and structure in a similar way. Memory may be fleeting, but a shape can hold it, as the poet Katrina Porteous has said:

> For me a poem begins and ends in memory. The sound-patterning from which a poem is composed is a way of fixing a thought or feeling in the memory, a stay against loss. So poetry orders something in sound and in time, in order that it might be revisited, like a place. For me, writing a poem does not feel like an act of innovation but like one of

remembering, of listening, of being as true as possible to something which already exists: a translation of emotional resonance into physical sound and architecture.[2]

Rhythm and rhyme were and are powerful reference points for our daily audio memory, speaking, or thinking important numbers and passwords in certain rhythms. If the rhythm is wrong, often the number will not come. It can be subliminal, and often is more easily recalled for that very reason. Radio is memorable because it too works subliminally on the senses as we lead our lives, move about our homes or drive our cars. We hear a tune once on a music station and may be impelled to buy the record or download the song, because it has made a positive memorable impression on our mind, often through rhythm, rhyme and repetition, combined with a capturable melody. It may linger unwontedly too, the song we cannot bear, but will not leave us alone: 'Earworms'. There is melody in the spoken word too. The question remains: *How* do we listen? Just what *is* the connection between listening and memory?

SAVING SOUNDS

In his introduction to the film sound theorist Michel Chion's book, *Audio Vision: Sound on Screen*, the great film sound designer Walter Murch recalls the acquisition of his first tape recorder as a boy. He remembers one evening after school, coming home and turning on the radio to hear sounds that were, in their strangeness, like nothing he'd experienced outside his own imagination. As fast as he could, he set up his tape recorder, and began to capture this strange 'music':

> It turned out to be the *Premier Panorama de Musique Concrète,* a record by the French composers, Pierre Schaeffer and Pierre Henry, and the incomplete tape of it became a sort of Bible of Sound for me. Or rather, Rosetta stone, because the vibrations chiseled into its iron oxide were mysteriously significant and heiroglyphs of a language that I did not yet understand but whose voice nonetheless spoke to me compellingly.
>
> —[Chion: xiv]

Whether or not we have access to the actual audio memory of the recording ourselves, we have here Murch's human memory of its effect on him at the time, and its long-term significance in his subsequent life and work. Surely one of the key phrases in that extract is the phrase '*a language that I did not yet understand . . .*'. If we are imaginatively captured by a sound before we understand it, we remember it; that experience of wonder before understanding is in itself the beginning of true understanding. If we understand through imaginative engagement, we are much more likely to remember: passion persuades. For me it was the experience of hearing Stravinsky's *Rite of Spring* for the first time as a young boy. I had no idea what it was, it seemed to belong to no musical laws or conventions I knew, and yet I was excited, terrified and amazed by it simultaneously. Later, when I learned its story—on and offstage—it retained the power to shock and astound. To this day, it still does.

The tape recorder that preserved Walter Murch's experience was itself a memory machine, born out of a long and continuing line of devices by which we preserve the past mechanically and electronically, part of the dream to make at least a part of ourselves immortal. As far back as 1888, Edison had said: 'The phonograph knows more about us than we know ourselves'. [Milner: 35] Yet at its inception, the device—like the wireless that was yet to come—was conceived as a utilitarian instrument, its purpose being mostly limited to such tasks as teaching speech and language, recording the famous or dictating. It was also used as a *record* (the origin of the word in audio terms) of a precise event, and was therefore extremely useful as witness to testimony in a court of law, holding the precise words for ever more: 'As it may be filed away as other letters, and at any subsequent time reproduced, it is a perfect *record*.' [Ibid.]

That said, there have been occasions when the recording of fact has been misleading. When the BBC was establishing its sound archive in the early 1930s, it appealed to the public to loan any recordings from private collections that might be historically significant. One of the most interesting results proved to be the voice of the great British stateman William Ewart Gladstone. It had been Edison's policy to record testimonials from the great and famous for his invention, so it was no surprise to hear Gladstone, in stentorian tones, endorsing the 'product'. What was more surprising was what happened next; a number of other cylinder recordings arrived at the BBC, all declaring themselves to be Gladstone, all with the same words spoken, but all with a different voice. How could this be? And which, more importantly, was the real Gladstone? The answer came when a number of people who could remember the great man were played the recordings. Unanimously, they proclaimed one of them to be the 'winner'. It would seem from this that while Edison had recorded the 'real' Gladstone, a number of other recordings were made of actors reading his words for the *record*, the significant point being that it was the memory of the *words* that was important, rather than the *voice* that uttered them, just as words are used in a book or a speech as a quotation.

We have today reached a quite different perspective with regard to historic recordings in that we now venerate the true *voice* of history equally or above—in some cases—the actual text; for example, the British Library Sound Archive holds a recording of Florence Nightingale, near the end of her life, giving a message to veterans of the Balaclava campaign. The recording has been digitised and restored as best can be done, but it remains almost indecipherable. Still we treasure the sound because the thin tones of the old lady, the rise and fall of the cadence and the breath of life in the audio recalls not just her, but also, in our imagination, the room she sat in to make the recording, the era and so on, all by inference and suggestion. Above all, *that*, we tell ourselves, is what she *sounded* like. Likewise, so much do we venerate the actual object itself, the fragile carrier of these signals from another age, that the cylinder is on view in a glass case in the library, an artefact to be saved and viewed like any other museum object, part of the composite memory of society apparently. A chapter in this book will explore and celebrate the growing role of media archives as repositories of societal and historical memory, a place in libraries undreamed of by previous generations, showing that, as with all learning artefacts, the provenance remains vital and authenticity must be rigorously interrogated. After all, every kind of memory can be fallible.

*

The surviving daguerreotypes from the earliest days of photography often show us familiar streets peopled by shadowy ghosts, as the time exposure betrayed movement. These images are all the more touching for this, their unposed and spontaneous catching of the moment. For similar reasons, location recordings for radio carry a power in the memory that studio-based discussions do not have. When Herb Morrison recorded the Hindenburg disaster on May 6, 1937, at Lakehurst, New Jersey, for the Prairie Farmer Station affiliate of NBC, he left one the most famous pieces of audio reportage ever made, in which what stays in the mind is the emotion and horror of the commentator. Often he is overwhelmed by the trauma of the event, so we lose a lot of facts that a calmer, more controlled reporter might have given us. Yet Morrison's 'live' record of the crash is immortal. I have heard the broadcast hundreds of times, and one phrase of just three words rings through it all in my memory: 'Oh the humanity!' So much of an impact did this famous report have at the time, that Orson Welles was to use it as a reference in his notorious *War of the Worlds* broadcast on CBS by the Mercury Theatre on October 30, 1938. Listen to the reporter describing the Martian cylinder at Grovers Mill, and you hear an echo of Morrison, a sense of the media not being in control of the situation it is communicating. Perhaps even more significantly, it converted the traditionally 'live' radio policy of the network to the newly devised portable recording machinery that Morrison was testing at the time of the accident.

Morrison's early outside broadcast facility did not allow for any considered actuality recording—there are muffled voices and cries behind his commentary, and even the airship's explosion comes over as a dull thud, undramatic until we hear through his tears the cause of the sound. We are left with a series of impressions which in themselves carry little significance without a commentary, and indeed the narration is almost as chaotic as the event itself, which is what makes it so memorable, aided, it has to be said, by the poignancy for our time of the crackling, hissing 'sepia' of the actual disc recordings.

As the partnership between narrative and technology has developed, we have gained the ability to allow places—and their memories—to speak through pure sound, such as in the GPS-driven *Hackney Hear* project and others. We will explore the memory of place, and our growing opportunities for capturing the ghosts and stories of our past, as well as the responsibility of conveying true pictures of reality and the world those ghosts inhabit. The past, history and memory exist right up to the present second. This is where all the factual stories are, the stories that grow from memory. The next moment is unknown, a chaotic jumble of possibilities, and therefore food for science fiction and imaginings. Human memory begins with the sound of a closing door as we leave home for work, or the kettle switching off at the end of its boiling; the simple daily sounds of our lives are recollectable through sound before there is a picture.

On the day of the 9/11 tragedy, we were transfixed by the images, with almost a sense that we were watching a movie, so great was the enormity of the scenes and our disbelief at what we witnessed. Television gave us those pictures: I remember watching the event unfold and hearing a reporter on a US news channel, covering it in real time, saying sadly but quite calmly, 'There are no words' as one of the towers fell. Certainly at that moment, there were no words. Yet, numb as the broadcaster was, there almost seemed to be no emotion either. How would Herb Morrison have reacted? The next day, and through subsequent days, weeks and months, we needed words that helped explain the pictures, we needed the stories of the survivors, we needed to grasp at some understanding of what this had meant for *people*. So we turned to radio, and the simple sound of a human voice remembering created feelings in us that gave us pictures through stories on another level altogether.

The human voice, the power of it to convey emotion through recollection and the moment it becomes poetic through that emotion remains one of the glories of speech radio and audio, to the extent that our fundamental need to tell and be told stories is a root part of all sonic experience. Be it the humour of recognition or the consolation of knowing that others feel similar pain, we are as a species made of stories through our memories. National Public Radio has led other broadcasters through the *StoryCorps* project, involving conventional transmission, downloads and webcasts, supported frequently by printed texts. These are testimonies of ordinary people, recalling, often in conversation with a loved one, a time, an event or a person from their past. A transcription of the spoken word does not go close to conveying the emotion of a voice transcended by passion in the very grain of its sound.

I will discuss other international examples of the extraordinary, recalled from the apparently ordinary in these pages, analysing the background, principles and practice of projects such as the BBC's ongoing *Listening Project* (working with the British Library Sound Archive).

Radio producers around the world have explored memory both from their own experience and others through documentary programme making. Among them, Robyn Ravlitch and Kaye Mortley, both Australian by birth (although Mortley has lived in Paris for many years), have frequently used memory sounds instead of words to convey a poignant sense of the past. In particular it is a feeling of Place communicating a nostalgia through sound that comes across strongly in their work. Nostalgia is an important part of this study; often discussed pejoratively, it is nevertheless a significant part of the brain's processing of past experience. Sound, be it (frequently) music and song, the spoken word or the raw audio of the world around us provides direct entry to a lost or forgotten experience, and can be almost devastatingly potent because of this.

Nostalgia is not something we consciously seek or access, although it can be used as a cynical tool by film and programme makers. At its most sincere, it emerges out of recollection naturally, often when the mind is allowed to run free over the past. Community radio stations and 'micro' stations have few funds but enormous capacity for reaching an audience that is both contributor and listener at the same time, in a way that even NPR and BBC local stations cannot quite match in traditional ways. The nearest to come to this has been *StoryCorps*' 'Listening Booths' in the US. Likewise, small stations, often run by volunteers, retain a huge opportunity to tap into the community memory of their areas through mutual trust. A centralised community radio archive within a nation would pool experience and demonstrate kinship between apparently disparate places and people, a commonality of memory where we would find ourselves more alike than perhaps we ever knew. A society that can remember preserves a sense of justice and—often if not always—common humanity. Put simply, if a story is shared sincerely, verbally from the recollection of the teller, it is communicated to the listener or listeners, and thus to their memory; be it fact, fiction or folklore, it is preserved and disseminated. As a species we come out of an oral tradition, and radio—audio—remains the 'pen' through which that tradition can be perpetuated and enhanced.

That said, audio memory is about more than speech or even music, as we have seen, and circumstance, combined with a growing appetite among young producers to experiment, takes us to new areas of exploration. Increasingly, the traditional 'radio' outlets, linear broadcasting transmissions of speech, societal witness or 'art' programmes as part of a conventional schedule have been reduced or even taken off air due to funding cuts; web outlets provide in this climate important and global opportunities for such artists as the Spaniard Jorge Marredo, whose sonic work *De Ópera a la Plaza de San Jerónimo Pasando Por Sol* used actuality on location in

Madrid for a sound work published in late 2012 by the Republica Iberica Ruidista Netlabel. It is a sonic journey into the birth of the Spanish revolution, a real-time walk from the Plaza del Sol, the heart of Spanish public protest, to the Congress. In other words, it moves from public dialogue to institutional silence across time and space, thus taking us beyond personal memory to the collective memory of community through location sound. In this context, another word for memory could be 'conscience'.[3]

Our capacity to remember stories, as we have seen, is a key part of our human make-up. Some years ago, I had a personal experience of this while making a radio programme—about memory—for BBC Radio 4. For the programme, I recorded an interview with the theatre director Sir Peter Hall, who was at the time working at London's Old Vic theatre. For the interview, which was about his recollections of directing the first performance of Samuel Beckett's play *Waiting for Godot*, I had prepared a number of questions; in fact, in the event, I only asked my first, which was: 'Tell me your recollections of that first production'. Half an hour later, Hall ended his answer, which was a perfect description of the entire process, including the circumstances. I left with my producer and returned to Broadcasting House in London, only to discover that the tape was blank: not a word had been recorded. Confused and embarrassed, we contacted Sir Peter, who graciously agreed to a second recording, in which he gave virtually the same answer, word for word, and apparently spontaneously, without notes of any description. It can be argued, of course, that it was a question he had been asked on numerous occasions, and this was his stock, rehearsed answer. Nevertheless, it was a powerful demonstration of memory, and an equally powerful expression of the potency of the original event, the profound impression it made on him, its importance in his life and its continuing significance for him as a director more than fifty years after it occurred.

Not all memory is helpful or healthy of course. Each year the seaside town of Bournemouth on the south coast of England holds an air festival along its waterfront; every kind of aircraft show off its ability to holiday crowds: the Red Arrows display team, wingwalkers and warplanes such as the Eurofighter are favourites amongst the displays. It is an event that thrills thousands, coming as it does at the height of the holiday season. A few years ago, a local care home took some of its male residents to the beach to watch the display. It seemed to be a wonderful idea, to give these men a glimpse of the spectacular show and for them to take in the sea air and sunshine at the same time. All went well until a fly-past of World War II aircraft: a Lancaster bomber, flanked by two of the few remaining British fighters of the time, a Spitfire and a Hurricane. The crowd loved the sight, but for the elderly men, all of who had served in the military during the war, the sound of the aircraft placed them back in a time of great danger. For them, at that moment, the Nazi invasion of Britain, the blitz on UK cities and the years of conflict were happening again. They grew distressed, panicked, and what had been conceived as a special treat had to be swiftly curtailed.

For many people sound can evoke memories they have been trying to forget. The victims of post-traumatic stress can be transported to a place and time that damaged them, purely by the accidental hearing of a sound and the memory it triggers. Even gentle nostalgia can be very moving, so it follows almost without saying that painful memories evoked by sound can be almost unbearable, although sometimes cathartic. The connection is very profound, and the purpose of this writing is to celebrate the positive possibilities of this linkage and to advocate its potential to help us to retain and enhance a sense which, when understood and developed consciously, can release a dimension in ourselves that is too often forgotten, or at best taken for granted. As with every kind of potent stimuli, however, care and thought as to cause and effect are always necessary.

THE ARCHIVE OF THE MIND

This writing does not seek to explore in depth areas of neuroscience or cognitive psychology that have been extremely well documented and that continue to be researched within those specific academic, medical and scientific areas of expertise. Nonetheless I am grateful for the guidance and discussion from experts within those fields who have informed certain aspects of this book. The human brain is extraordinarily complex, controlling everything our physical being engages with, from the coordination of movement and speech and keeping our heart working to storing memory. That said, its deepest workings continue to hold many mysteries. A piece of our physical bodies weighing approximately 1.5 kilos is the link between the material world and the strange, intangible energy fields that interpret and remember that world as we move through it. It—or the mind for which it is the representative—*is* our being, steering us through the use of appropriate cerebral hemispheres contained within its structure—our grey matter processing centre—linked by the white matter of wiring.

Before proceeding further, we need to understand in simple terms the nature of the relationship between the various units within this amazing piece of technology. The brain can be divided into four main sections: the cerebral hemispheres, the limbic system, the cerebellum and the brain stem. The cerebellum—or 'little brain'—controls basic movement, posture and balance, whereas the brain stem governs and monitors our vital living functions such as breathing, heartbeat and blood pressure. As part of the machine, our cerebral hemispheres can in turn be divided into four separate lobes, each performing different functions. The frontal lobe governs behaviour, whereas the parietal lobe works on tasks such as spelling, calculation and complex movements; the occipital lobe is responsible for vision, and the temporal lobe is crucial for language, emotion and memory. The processor within the computer is the limbic system, and its structures are key in many of our emotions and motivations, significantly those that are related to survival, feelings such as fear or anger and sexual behaviour. Importantly for this study, some structures of the limbic system are involved in memory, and two of these, the amygdala and hippocampus, play very significant roles. The amygdala determines what memories are stored and where the memories are stored in the brain, determined by the scale of the impact of an emotional response or an event. The hippocampus sends memories out to the appropriate part of the cerebral hemisphere for long-term storage and retrieves them when necessary. Damage to this area of the brain may result in an inability to form new memories. The brain itself is made up of billions of nerve cells, elongated with tentacle-like 'dendrites' that link to surrounding cells and form a complex network between cells and white matter; signals are passed around this network through minute electrical impulses and chemical messages. When something prohibits a cell from performing its function, it may contribute to dementia.

To retain the capacity to remember is a crucial part of our identity as human beings. To lose that capacity—through brain injury, Alzheimer's or dementia—is to lose an important piece of the essence of Self. Devoid of a past, we exist in a temporal vacuum. Richard Ranft, director of the British Library Sound Archive in London, has noted that the uses of sound are increasing in the treatment of this and related areas: 'There's certainly increasing interest in the use of old music recordings to treat dementia, while the very act of interviewing itself has therapeutic benefits'. Likewise, on a national or societal level the library has been involved, as in Uganda, 'in cases of restitution of cultural memories, for example of the pre-Idi Amin era of musical heritage in the country.'[4]

More than ever before, our auditory memory—like a muscle—needs to be maintained as strongly as possible, and sound is the most important key to unlock and preserve this potential. Interestingly, for many, as we have noted, the sense that rivals sound as a major key to memory is smell; frequently however, it is sound that remains the primary key from which other sense memories flow. In the first volume of Marcel Proust's great work, *À la recherche du temps perdu*, the narrator speaks of a moment in childhood, the glimmer of his father's candle on a long gone staircase wall, and the voice of the man, now gone, calling to his mother, 'Go with the boy.' The moment, the place and the people are beyond physical recapture but for the memory of sound. Proust understands—as we should—the difference between voluntary and involuntary memory. In this case, given the right circumstances, the sound of the past can be caught by the memory like a photograph:

> For a little while now, I have begun to hear again very clearly, if I take care to listen, the sobs I was strong enough to contain in front of my father and that did not burst out until I found myself alone again with Mama. They have never really stopped; and it is only because life is quieting down around me more and more now that I can hear them again,

like those convent bells covered so well by the clamour of the town during the day that one would think they had ceased altogether but which begin sounding again in the silence of the evening.

—[Proust: 1, 39–40]

In his commentary on *À la recherche du temps perdu*, David Ellison underlines the importance of this beautiful passage, both for understanding Proust's great work and, incidentally, for preparing the way for the exploration on which this current writing is engaged:

> If one listens well enough, one can perceive even the most distant echoes of the past. But do these resonances occur only fleetingly, only when life has "quieted down" sufficiently for the listener to become aware of their existence? Or could there be a way to search them out actively, to make of these barely perceptible sounds the retrieved meaning of a life. . . .?

—[Ellison: 37]

Radio, as it approaches its centenary, is as old as some of its earliest audience members. This can only ever happen once: that a generation that heard the medium born has grown with it for more than ninety years, to witness the changes it is going through in the first decades of the twenty-first century. Their movement across time, and the mnemonics of that voyage, is also ours, and the future of memory, personal, communal and technical, and the use of sound for its most important purpose, namely to preserve that memory, experience and mental capacity to its fullest and richest degree throughout the human lifespan, is the ultimate destination of the sound journey upon which we are about to embark.

NOTES

1. Michael Ladd, Editor, *Poetica* (ABC Radio National, Australia), communication with the author, 2013.
2. Katrina Porteous, communication with the author.
3. Marredo's work can be experienced through this link: http://satisfaccionlab. bandcamp.com/album/de-pera-a-la-carrera-de-san-jer-nimo-pasando-por-sol (accessed April 2013).
4. Richard Ranft, Director, British Library Sound Archive, London, interview with the author, 2012.

2   Tell Me a Story

THE VOICE OF THE STORY

Stories are a major conduit of memory, be they ancient myths, personal experience narratives, urban legends, religious texts or the allegories of prophets taught in parables. To understand the stories of a culture is to understand its people; further, to absorb the meaning of a story is to learn from it. Aesop's fables are teaching tools as well as entertaining fantasies. The tales and romances of King Arthur gave—and still give—their audiences moral instruction. Stories began with sound; the making of a fictional tale starts with a voice and a premise: *supposing that . . .?* or *what if . . .?* These are the words that unlock all imaginative acts. The voice is always the key to the story, be it written or spoken, and the premise is encapsulated in the familiar words, *once upon a time . . .* The *sound* of the voice, heard by the ear and then the mind, or transported straight to the mind by the imagination or memory, governs the nature of the story. We absorb the narrative of our lives through stories: news, advertising, gossip, opinion—a babel of sound that assaults us from the moment we regain consciousness each morning. When we read, be it the morning paper or a book on the train or the bus as we travel to work, we are absorbing stories silently through an internal sound—usually the writer's voice—within our minds and imaginations. Beyond that there is the narrative of the world, the music of cities, the murmur of the countryside or the flowing of water, all combining to create a soundscape that tells the story of our personal environment as we pass through it, the story of our journey. Even the infinite possibility of the future, the unknown next moment, carries its own story through expectation, fantasy, fiction and prophecy. Without stories we simply would not exist; they—and their memory—are the proof that we are living.

This sound heard through all stories, implicit or explicit, heard or imagined, external or within us, is—most directly and dynamically—the human voice or voices, engaging us physically with where we are, the grain and timbre and dialect of the place, itself the genetic memory of streets, towns, counties, states, regions, countries and continents. Dialects are the subtexts and symptoms of language, the variants that make us human and unique.

Even within a single place, there are as many of these variants as there are people, and the sound of every person's voice is a gateway to the sharing of stories—memories. On visits to Newfoundland in Canada, I have encountered voices and accents I have recognised from England's west country. On one occasion, while I was taking part in a 'phone-in programme' on CBC Radio 1, St. John's, a caller rang to discuss storytelling in the province. I immediately recognised the sound and the culture from which the voice came. 'You're from Dorset, aren't you?' I said. 'That's right, West Lulworth.' he replied.

> 'I know it! It's a lovely little village.'
> 'So I'm told!'
> 'You've never been? How long have you been in Newfoundland?'
> 'Two hundred and fifty year.'

The man had never been to England, nor had his kin as far back as his great-great-grandparents, who had travelled the Atlantic in search of the rich pickings from the Grand Banks, when the Newfoundland cod trade was at its height. He had brought with him the stories of England dating back to the eighteenth century, and could add to them through the oral history and storytelling traditions of the place in which he and his family had grown, in his 'New Found Land'.

It is remarkable that within a relatively small geographical area such as Newfoundland or the UK there can be so many variations of dialect and linguistic 'memories'. That said, within the British Isles linguists such as Jonnie Robinson at the British Library have been observing a decline of distinctive styles of speech for about a century, particularly in the south-eastern part of the country, the area near London. Here the rate of change has been dramatic. 'Listen to a recording of speakers from the south east of England made in 1960, and compare it with today's speech from the same area, and it will be clear that a major shift in accent has taken place. The further away one moves from this area, the more stable the language.'[1] In some areas, such as Liverpool or Hull in Yorkshire, the dialect has also changed, but if anything it has actually become more locally distinctive rather than homogenised. At the same time, within major cities such as London, changes are occurring due to *inward* migration, leading to a bewildering range of sub-dialects, carried by British Caribbean and British Asian voices influencing—and being influenced by—the prevailing accent. To say therefore, that a general homogenisation of speech is taking place would be inaccurate; while shifts in such social influences as education—changes in the school-leaving age, higher education and so on—will have a levelling-out effect, change across a country will happen at different rates, in different ways, according the complex circumstances of society within a place.

Added to this, speech memory links us to our roots; there are codes within us that operate often at a subconscious level, responding to situations through the recollection of previous situations and habits. A person moving away from home may return years later and be told that he or she has lost or changed the sound of his or her speech. Conversely, that same person, when returning to familiar circumstances and social situations, may after a time relearn his or her dialect and speech traits.

A story begins with a single sound: a phoneme, the very basic unit of speech, as a note is to musical language, and with the same potential power to move or trigger feeling when heard individually. Verbal music plays on our ear even when we 'hear' it in the imagination, as when we are reading silently to ourselves. Put another way, the eye picks up the signal and the mind translates that visual cue into imagined sound that rings on in the memory. 'The music of words is . . . made up of internal sound-effects, rhythmical symmetries and patterns of variations within sound-families that support or make manifest the local context, whilst recalling other key lines, the key moments that provide the true music of memory.' [Piette: 24] It is this quality that makes the storytelling of writers such as Charles Dickens so attractive to stage and screen directors, recitalists and actors; the language clamours with sound on the page in a way that begs to be vocalised, as in the "bawling, splashing, link-lighted, umbrella struggling, hackney-coach-jostling, pattern-clinking, muddy miserable world' [Dickens: 344] that Dickens describes in *David Copperfield*. Piette here makes the point that dense prose, as in such passages, 'will tend to demand the help of the listening ear, if only to help pick out the sense—a crowded sentence will slow the eye down to listening speed.' [Piette: 15] Rhythm, onomatopoeia and alliteration allied to the sound signals sent by the words themselves condense the prose and make it more dense to the eye, directing it to the ear, where, once absorbed, it concentrates the words into the sound—read and heard—that is so much an essential part of Dickens.

TRUTH AND FICTION

Dmae Roberts is an Asian American independent public radio producer, writer, actor and playwright working in the United States. Much of her work focuses on cross-cultural issues or personal storytelling. Born in Taipei, Taiwan, living in Japan until the age of eight, subsequently growing up in the US from the age of ten when her family moved to Oregon, Roberts' work was as a multidisciplinary artist even before the term found common usage. In 1989, her documentary, *Mei Mei, A Daughter's Song*, for National Public Radio (NPR) wove two highly personal stories together: that of her compassion for her Taiwanese mother, who as a child suffered abuse, starvation and the horrors of war, and her own frustration at not living up to the ideal of being a perfect Taiwanese daughter. For this work, she was able to record her mother's voice, although her father had died a year before she began her career in radio and so was not present vocally in the piece.

Notwithstanding, his presence in terms of memory remains strong, as she says: 'I still regret not having recorded his tales and the southern spirituals he'd sing in his big bass voice. Now the only way I have it preserved is in my memory. And by telling you my story, I've passed on a piece of my history to you.'[2]

This act of telling is a key part of the preservation of memory. Because many of the world's greatest cultures share themselves through oral history, the voice is for many the only way to pass on a tradition, or family history. It becomes doubly important in the case of immigrant families who are separated from their own indigenous cultures. Expressed in a foreign language, and divorced by distance from a homeland, the fragility of preservation becomes all too evident. As Roberts adds, 'Even though people may have the ability to write, many people do not write about their history. It's up to the descendants and loved ones to capture those stories. To me that's the single most important function of a radio producer. By the act of interviewing and recording someone's story, we are preserving their story in that capsule of time.'[3]

We shall explore this aspect of personal archiving in more detail later in this book. It is important to stress here, however, that a story can take many forms, and its exploration in different media may not only present itself to many diverse audiences, but also show multifarious aspects of itself that may be exposed and enhanced by those media. This has certainly been the experience of Dmae Roberts in her work across various disciplines:

> I've turned *Mei Mei*, the radio documentary, into a two-act multimedia stage play; that experience inspired me to write a stage play about my early family life called *Breaking Glass*. When I received funding to do my first radio series, *Legacies*, 13 half hour autobiographical multicultural documentaries with dramatised material (what I call "docu-plays"), I adapted the stage play *Breaking Glass* into a half-hour docu-play. A few years later I created *Lady Buddha*, a multimedia stage play about the goddess Kuan Yin, and that play turned into a one-hour documentary called *The Journey of Lady Buddha*. When I produced an 8-hour Asian American history series, I adapted three of the pieces into short films.[4]

The process continues, with Roberts working to adapt *Mei Mei* as a series for the web, the approach remaining fluid, the content dictating the style of documentary or play within whatever medium offers itself as the conduit. At times Roberts has found herself asking questions, not so much of herself, but of others' responses to her work: 'Many times I've wondered if colleagues have not taken my personal explorations seriously because my own memories and stories seem like paths already taken. But one colleague told me that some people have such one big epic story to tell, and that's why I've sought out different mediums to express my personal history. I found that statement profound.'[5]

The poet David Jones, in his preface to *The Anathemata*, wrote one of the most significant essays on cultural memory, much of it encapsulated in the phrase 'one is trying to make a shape out of the very things of which one is oneself made . . . '[6] Of further importance, both in relation to the work of Roberts and to the impetus for preservation at the heart of this present writing, is Jones's opening to this preface, and the source he quotes there:

> "I have made a heap of all I could find." So wrote Nennius, or whoever composed the introductory matter to the *Historia Brittonum*. He speaks of an "inward wound" which was caused by the fear that certain things dear to him "should be like smoke dissipated". Further he says, "not trusting my own learning, which is none at all, but partly from writings and monuments of the ancient inhabitants of Britain, partly from the annals of the Romans and the chronicles of the sacred fathers, Isidore, Heironymus, Prosper, Eusebius and from the histories of the Scots and Saxons although our enemies . . . I have lispingly put together this . . . about past transactions, that [this material] might not be trodden under foot."[7]
>
> —[Jones: 10]

Stories here move beyond the personal into the cultural fabric of a people, hugely important, but heartbreakingly as fragile as the individual human voice and memory.

*

Oral tradition by its very nature has the potential to be factually variable; if a song or a story is not committed to paper or to electronic recording media, it is inevitably subject to change (some would say that this is its glory), and the process of gradual evolution, often over generations, means that time and circumstance alter the recalled essence, rather as weather changes climate. In 1979 and 1980, BBC Radio 4 ran a series of programmes with the title *I Remember He Remembered*, in which the limits of human oral memory were tested. Among the speakers of one of the programmes was a contributor whose great-uncle was drummer boy at the Battle of Waterloo, a recollection handed down by a great-grandfather seeing Napoleon on board a ship for St Helena, and stories of highwaymen.[8] The tales are absorbing; the sense of 'I was there', even when passed down through two or more generations, makes for compulsive listening, full of poignant detail: in one episode an ancestral memory of watching Napoleon's army, immaculate in peacock-like colours, marching past the family's inn, ten miles outside Warsaw, on its conquering road towards Moscow in 1812 is contrasted with the terrible aftermath of the broken retreating remnants. Told in 1980 by the grandson of the child who had witnessed the scenes, the imaginative pictures evoked by the words remain extraordinarily powerful. We are, as it were, just two voices away from the original witness; the contributor had the story from his father, who remembered *his* father's recollection of a scene observed when he was six years old. The child had grown to a man who lived to be 107, dying in 1913. By sharing the memory, the story is preserved. In the programme, a remarkable amount of detail survived; the colours of the uniforms, the mood and the awe of the event. It remains an eyewitness account, and it is as valuable as it is flawed—as all such recollections must always be.

*

In his memoir, *Who's Been Talking?*, the Sheffield writer and broadcaster Rony Robinson recounts an idyllic moment from his schooldays:

> Once upon a time, Miss Freeborough took us on a nature walk to the curly river in the big field . . . between the Crown and the Akky. We dangled in the curly river and she read us *Tom Sawyer*. That was the happiest I ever was at any school ever.
>
> —[Robinson: 38]

It is the perfect childhood memory, but how accurate is Robinson's memory of the event, recalled almost a lifetime later?

> I don't know. Was it true? It seems *too* perfect now, looking back, so I wonder if it *was* true. The perfect book about childhood being read to us on a perfect childhood day as we dangled our feet in the water and Miss Freeborough read to us about the Mississippi? I don't know. Perhaps it wasn't, but that's my memory of it. I've often been in that same field since then, it's where I walk the dog these days, so subsequent memories have come in on top of that day now. But if you said *Tom Sawyer* to me, I'd probably go back to that memory. Does it matter if it's factually wrong? No, I don't think it does, but the chance to tell your story—your life—in your own way—is crucial.[9]

There is something much more profound about the function of memory than simply a facility for storage and retrieval; later in this book we will explore the role of electronic media—in particular radio and other sound tools—for the transmission of memory through the imagination. As has been illustrated here, a story can be fact or fiction, or a hybrid; a parable or a fable may use imaginary circumstances to illustrate a universal truth, and images from our personal past, whether imagined, recalled accurately or otherwise, or transmitted verbatim from the page, retain an essence of self that becomes heightened when communicated through the voice, or the implicit voice transmitting silently through the written word—mind to mind. 'Memory is more a crucible of meaning than a vessel of truth.' [Olick,

Vinitzky-Seroussi & Levy: 310] The radio producer Clare Jenkins takes the same view; faced with the criticism of some social historians that oral history is not validated, that human memory can be treacherous, she responds: 'I wonder if it matters? If it's their memory, why does it matter . . . if that's the truth to them?'[10]

On the other hand, for our memory to be validated beyond the personal relationship we have with it, truth might matter if it is to form part of the historical fabric by which future generations form an image of what life was like in our time. It is after all possible to have memory shaped by the power of suggestion, or even to have false memory planted in the mind. There are strategies by which the oral historian can verify, to some extent, the reliability of personal memory, whether it is related to sound or not. Let us return to the sequence of recollection starting with *Journey Into Space*, the memory with which this book began. That chain of sound started by unlocking the images in the dark bedroom with the amber glow from the radio. It moved through association to the railway line, my grandmother's bantam hens, the voices of my family in the room below, outside again to the front of the house, into the next morning when the greengrocer's horse would plod down the street. All this happened, and somewhere in my consciousness an echo of it all remains, but how much of it is applied, and how much has subsequent knowledge and the desire to make a coherent narrative shaped that story? It is all deeply subjective; in summary, how much is pure sound memory, and 'does it matter'? It is after all a family story to be passed on to children and grandchildren, a flavour of my particular childhood. The answer must be, in this context, a somewhat equivocal 'yes'. Set against the 'crucible of meaning/vessel of truth' argument, we must consider the personal and also the broader role of memory as a building block of history. History is not just a paper-based document or marks literally carved into stone. We may consider the physical artefact to be oral history transcribed; in this sense, the Venerable Bede was one of the first oral historians, and history—in some parts of the world more than in others—is as strong, or stronger, in its oral form than in its manuscript tradition.[11]

The British Library in London has recognised this, and its Lead Curator in Oral History, Rob Perks, was moved in a recent restructuring operation from his original place within the Department of Sound and Vision to the Department of History and Classics, while retaining a presence in both departments. Taking my *Journey Into Space* story, and applying to it the rigours of the oral historian, makes the relationship between what is *actually* recalled as real sound and what is circumstantial and more tenuous much clearer:

> I would want to examine all that in detail, and discover how much of it is actually coming from the auditory memory, and how much of it is coming from things you were subsequently told, that have become family stories, and how much you're projecting back into things that are not auditory memories at all, but are part of other memories that you've

got, that you're reprocessing and then representing. Whether they were *actually* auditory memories, or whether you're recreating them retrospectively, is the issue. I would want to ask you a lot of supplementary questions about how the narrative was constructed, and whether or not it is actually an auditory memory.[12]

The golden glow evoked by the apparent memory of those sounds starts to fade in the cold light of day, and I question the authenticity of them, in a way that perhaps I would not had they been musical recollections. Later in the book we shall discuss music and memory in detail. In a sense, however, in the context of this case study, whether the life sounds recalled by the audio of the radio programme are the *actual* reproductions or not, on a personal level the fact remains that by starting with the radio drama I listened to in 1954, I have found small fragments of childhood I might otherwise not have been able to retrieve. These recollections are perhaps best described as a form of echo; when we hear an echo we are hearing a reflection of sound coming back to us through a transformation by its contact with surfaces across distance. In doing so, the echo may be changed, but these alterations do not render the original less valid. Carolyn Birdsall has suggested that 'the echo . . . offers a useful metaphor for describing the re-sounding of the past in embodied practices of remembering. Sound memories are not necessarily predicated on the exact reproduction of past sounds, nor does the ear-witness account reveal "how it really was" to the researcher.'[13]

Nevertheless, for the oral historian working on projects that are larger than individual personal memory, perhaps (as in the British Library's case) on specific areas of industry or business across a range of interviewees, from management to office cleaner, detail and accuracy *do* matter. Recent projects have involved the *Oral History of British Science* and the *Oral History of the Electricity Supply Industry in the UK*, and in such archival collections there may be as many as forty-five interviews conducted across the strata of the workforce. This is one extreme within the oral history movement, and the process adopted for the British Library's *National Life Stories (NLS)* series, which in 2012 celebrated its twenty-fifth anniversary, is a particular example. *National Life Stories* has as its mission statement: 'To record the first-hand experiences of as wide a cross section of society as possible, to preserve the recordings, to make them publicly available and encourage their use.'[14] An average *NLS* interview is 12–15 hours in length and is a full biographical life story, augmented by material relating to earlier family members and peripheral information that may have a bearing on the audio interview itself. A chronological life course will be followed over perhaps five 2–3 hour interview sessions, through a period which may be weeks, months or, in some cases, even years. This exploring of memory over time is important; after each session and before the next, the interviewer will create a written summary, using this to review the content so far, commencing the next session with a recapitulation of what has been said, sometimes going back over material where more detail is required or where clarification is needed. Gradually the chronology moves forward and a life unfolds.

Working in this way, the *NLS* project has become part of one of the largest oral history collections in the world, with in total some 35,000 recordings housed in the British Library, of which 2,517 are long in-depth biographical interviews made by the *NLS* through the process described. Among the projects recorded have been oral histories of the oil and steel industries, computing, aerospace, art and photography, architecture and design, horticulture, banking and finance, Jewish Holocaust experience, publishing and authorship, theatre design, fashion design and the press. Once completed, all such projects are accessioned and catalogued, with detailed content summaries and in some cases transcriptions. Content is increasingly available online.

It is clear that in such projects there must be consistency and a set of criteria that fulfill test conditions, ensuring reliability and parity. Elsewhere in this book we discuss how we define our selves through a performance that varies according to who we are with and the circumstances in which we find ourselves. Likewise, the version of a story we are telling will differ depending on whom we perceive the interviewer to be or the context of the conversation, a phenomenon known as style shift. An experienced journalist will be aware that interviewees will initially communicate what they consider to be either what is required or what they wish to share. It is through digging down during the process of supplementary questions, or in the more aggressive forms of news investigation (what might be called interrogation), that a truth is reached or at least approached. The nature of the perceived relationship between the interviewer and the interviewee dictates the version of the narrative communicated. We adjust our performance according to our audience, and if they are interested—if, for example, they demonstrate their interest through a series of supplementary questions or non-verbal signals such as smiling, nodding or visibly reacting in other ways, we may expand or change our narrative. The basic account may remain the same, but other elements or people may enter the memory picture, leading to a multi-layered versioning of a story that can vary on different occasions.

*

The folkloric aspect of an oral tradition—the passing on of stories through generations, the retelling of fictions and fact from numerous cultures, is part of the enrichment of national cultures. In the US, with its long tradition of immigrant absorption, there is the opportunity for the gathering and study of storytelling traditions that link both time and place through memory. One such significant collection, held in the American Folklife Centre at the Library of Congress, is the archive of the International Storytelling Foundation, an organisation based in Jonesborough, Tennessee, founded in 1973. Including as it does eight thousand hours of audio and video recordings, as well as manuscripts, publications and photographs, and covering every national storytelling festival since the early 1970s, the collection is one of the largest and most important of its type in the world:

> Performers represented in this collection include traditional storytell-
> ers, with stories that have been passed along in their families for many
> generations, and "professional" storytellers, with newly minted tales of
> their own families, experiences, and observations. Unlike the audiences
> of bygone days, gathered around a hearth to pass the time on a long
> winter night, audiences at Jonesborough and other such venues have
> found themselves under a tent on a bright autumn day. But the artful
> storyteller still has the power to entertain, delight, and, occasionally,
> instruct.[15]

A separate—and very different—archive held at the American Folklife Centre was created in October 2000, through an Act of Congress entitled the *Veterans' Oral History Project Act*, which enabled the creation of a col-lection of materials documenting US war veterans and those who served in support of them. The legislation reads: 'It is in the nation's best interest to collect and catalogue oral histories of America's war veterans so that future generations will have original sources of information . . . and may learn of the heroics, tediousness, horrors, and triumphs of war'.[16]

SELLING STORIES

There have always been professional storytellers: from troubadours to play-wrights, through song and orally transmitted text, to screenwriters and journalists, all have told us stories that we have paid to hear, see or read. Because stories lie so profoundly at the heart of humanity, it is part of our nature both to tell them and to absorb them. In modern life we have learned to filter them, and we enable the facility of selective attention. We may, for example, be watching a film on television or listening to a reading of a book on radio, engrossed in the story, only to find it interrupted by a series of completely different stories, in the form of advertisements or sponsors' mes-sages. We may choose to pay attention to these or not, and usually we have the skill to re-engage with the main story when it is returned to us.

Some years ago I was giving a lecture to undergraduate media students about pre-war commercial radio broadcasting in the UK. Until relatively recently this was an unfamiliar subject; officially, legal commercial/independent radio began in Britain on 8 October, 1973, when the London Broadcast-ing Company (LBC) made its first broadcast. Prior to this, a previous gen-eration remembered 'Pirate' radio stations such as Radio Caroline, Radio London, Britain Radio and others, transmitting from offshore ships on the east and north-west coasts of Britain, and others retained rich memories of

Radio Luxembourg after the Second World War. The fact that there had been nearly ten years of highly successful commercial radio beamed at Britain from the Continent before the war, radio that at the time had a major impact on listeners and the BBC, was little discussed.

Such was the thrust of my talk, and to back up my case, I interspersed it with a number of pre-war radio advertisements and sponsors' messages, period pieces which spoke eloquently of the time in which they were made: ads from the depressed years between the wars, ghostly voices speaking from the past of products long-since unavailable, invitations to send off for special offers from addresses that disappeared during the blitz on London, and so on. I was proud of this primary source material, gathered over a long period of research, and looked forward to sharing it with my students. They listened to my talk dutifully and attentively, made notes, asked questions and generally behaved impeccably. When it came to the playing out of the audio examples—the commercials and jingles from the 1930s—however, I was taken aback to see that they put their pens down and started chatting amongst themselves. It took a few minutes, and a few examples, for me to understand what was happening here; these young people were of a generation for whom the advertising break was a signal to 'switch off' mentally from the programme, perhaps make a drink or just have a conversation. They had become subconsciously conditioned to a convention enabling them to tune out of a medium when it did not concern them. Once I realised what was happening, I was able to gently point out that I was not trying to sell them biscuits, or indigestion remedies or cures for 'night starvation': these ancient jingles and mini-dramas were the key part of what I was talking about, that is to say, the beginnings in Britain of a medium that had been commonplace in the US for years previously—radio advertising.

Older generations had not been so impervious to the advertising message. During the 1930s, 1940s and 1950s, the novelty aspect of hearing advertising on radio charmed British audiences and established products and their associated audio messages in memories for a lifetime. Radio advertising during the 1930s was developed by a number of agencies, such as the giant J. Walter Thompson organisation, that had established techniques and credentials in the US from before the birth of radio and that had honed sophisticated skills of persuasion, using stories, songs, characters and dramas that complemented the products they were championing. Often—as with the night-time drink Horlicks, crossovers between print and radio were employed to familiarise audiences with characters and to create scenarios that underlined the value of the product. Such campaigns engaged the audience for their own sakes, and were listened to and absorbed willingly—and permanently—by many listeners. Interviews I conducted with people who had been young during the pre-war years show a remarkable memory for such advertisements; one elderly gentleman, almost unprompted, when discussing 1930s radio spontaneously burst into song: 'Hurrah for *Betox*, what a delightful smell . . .' When asked what this product was, he explained that it was a form of gravy browning, the smell of Sunday lunch in his childhood.

Even more memorable was a programme called *The Ovaltineys' Concert Party*, one of the most significant children's programmes ever broadcast on British radio, first transmitted from Radio Luxembourg in December 1934. Young listeners could join the *League of Ovaltineys*, and weekly messages were sent to members in code. The show ran for thirty minutes every Sunday evening from 1934 until the outbreak of war, employing a formula of songs, stories, jokes and puzzles; it returned when Radio Luxembourg reopened at the end of hostilities in much the same format, using its famous theme song, 'We are the Ovaltineys':

> We are the Ovaltineys, little girls and boys,
> Make your request, we'll not refuse you,
> We are here just to amuse you.
> Would you like a song or story,
> Will you share our joys?
> At games or sports we're more than keen,
> No merrier children can be seen,
> Because we all drink *OVALTINE*,
> We're happy girls and boys.

—[Street: 112]

This song, initially broadcast in the early 1930s, became familiar to the offspring of the children who first heard it, who, growing up in the 1950s, could sing it to their children and grandchildren well into the next century. So redolent of its time was it, that television advertising made use of it during the 1980s to create a sense of nostalgia as part of the selling story. It is fair to say that there are a number of advertisements that have a similar effect on recollection and emotion. Hearing these things—either in reality or in the imagination through memory—unlocks the past for us.

During the 1950s, one of the most memorable sponsorship messages to British listeners from Radio Luxembourg came from a man responsible for a football pools score prediction method known as Infra-Draw. His name was Horace Batchelor, and his regular fifteen-minute programmes became famous not so much for the content—few can remember that—but for his rather lugubrious vocal style, and, curiously, for the delivery of his address; the town of Keynsham, near Bristol, was the base for his campaign, and the name was always spelt slowly, letter by letter: 'K-E-Y-N . . . S-H-A-M', then repeated, 'Keynsham'. This treatment was enough for Horace Batchelor to achieve something akin to immortality to a whole generation of popular music radio listeners; sixty years after the programmes were broadcast, mentioning the town of Keynsham, Horace Batchelor or even Radio Luxembourg could produce an almost Pavlovian response in people of a certain age, who would immediately start spelling the name out loud. How successful these sponsors' messages were in selling the product is open to doubt, but there can be no questioning Horace Batchelor's place in radio memory for children of the post-war era in Britain.

As with the Infra-Draw method, a memorable advertisement does not necessarily equate with a successful selling campaign. We may become so caught up in the story that we miss the point; all of us will be able to think of advertising stories that caught our imagination and so remain lodged in our brain, whilst struggling to remember the product that was the object of the message. This can still be a problem even in the modern world of electronic media advertising. Equally, the more we are surrounded by advertising, the more we have the power to 'zone out' of sounds and messages that do not interest us. It does not mean, however, that we do not necessarily 'hear' the message—only that we do not listen. This prompted a paper commissioned in 2005 by the Radio Advertising Bureau in London. The report asked the question, how could advertisers ensure that those the industry calls 'inattentives' take something positive from the message? The answer was the use of a 'sonic or sound-mark of some kind . . . or using a voice or style in the advertising which listeners easily connect with the brand.' The paper made the point that commercials have the capacity to leave a strong emotional trace pattern even when listeners are apparently inattentive—patterns driven by mood, atmosphere, memory and feelings.[17] Robert Heath, writing in this same report, makes a strong point:

> Radio is arguably better than other media at insinuating powerful messages into the minds of the consumer, because we are unable to switch our ears off. We hear even when we are not listening.
>
> So even if we are busy doing other things we automatically process music and sound bites and link them to brands. And when we come to buy those brands, our decisions are influenced by these associations, sometimes without our ever knowing it. In this way, far from being a secondary media, radio plays a leading role in what I call 'The Hidden Power of Advertising'.[18]

For radio, the so-called 'secondary medium', (which as we shall explore later, is frequently a *primary* medium) the power of the advertisement, the interruption in the listener's chosen audio experience, needs to be explored subtly. Mark Barber, Planning Director at the Radio Advertising Bureau, identifies this subliminal aspect as one of the medium's great strengths:

> We are so often doing something else whilst listening to radio, so the advertising memory goes into the implicit memory, the listener may have little or no conscious recollection of hearing the message, but the point has been registered. This can actually be a problem when we seek to prove the power of a radio campaign; because listeners may not recall hearing the ad., the evidence for its role in the success of selling a product is not always as strong as we would like![19]

The car radio is a key example of this; driving to work, the listener is engaged in negotiating traffic and focusing on a complex series of manoeuvres, whilst absorbing subliminally stories and songs from the car's audio system. This point is fundamental to the power of sound and the mind's extrapolation of meaning from it.

In some ways, radio advertising has come a long way from the campaigns of the 1930s, but there are other examples where we may see similar techniques at play. For example, as in pre-war radio advertisements, which picked up on print stories and translated them into sound, Barber identifies modern, creative cross-over examples, where a television commercial can be successfully transmuted to radio, working on the media memory of the audience:

> A very successful TV campaign for an insurance market comparison service used puppet Meerkats, playing on the words 'Market' and 'Meerkat'. These caught the public imagination; even dolls became commercially available on the back of the campaign. Radio was able to take the mental image, knowing that the audience could visualise the characters, and continue the campaign on radio through memory recognition.[20]

THE SOUND OF SENSE

When exploring how the telling of stories defines us, we must always return to the human voice. In my book, *The Poetry of Radio: The Colour of Sound*, I explored the poetic device of onomatopoeia, the formation of a word or sequence of words through the evocation of the sound associated with its referent. [Street 2013: 15–17] It is a word music beloved of poets from the age of Homer to the present day. An example would be the famous 'Skating' sequence from William Wordsworth's long poem, *The Prelude*:

> All shod with steel,
> We hiss'd along the polish'd ice, in games
> Confederate, imitative of the chase
> And woodland pleasures,—the resounding horn,
> The pack loud chiming, and the hunted hare.
> So through the darkness and the cold we flew,
> And not a voice was idle; with the din
> Smitten, the precipices rang aloud;
> The leafless trees and every icy crag
> Tinkled like iron . . .

> [Wordsworth: 28–29]

The sound of sense was a concept identified by the American poet Robert Frost as being demonstrable through a certain feeling in the tone of speech conveying meaning, even when language is not understood. It was an idea he articulated to Edward Thomas in 1913 and which was documented by Eleanor Farjeon. [Street 2013: 17] Put simply, we can tell the mood of a person—whether they are angry or happy—by simply listening to the music of their voice. The idea that words may not always be arbitrary, that their sound can often convey some aspect of their meaning, is a major part of the storyteller's toolkit, linked to memory through sound into the imagination. Jonathan Peelle of the Department of Otolaryngology at Washington University in St. Louis has put it like this: 'One simple example is that longer words tend to refer to more abstract concepts, and shorter words to more concrete/tangible concepts. This is an example of a kind of cultural memory that is reflected in the sounds our ancestors chose to represent certain ideas.'[21] The point is significant in storytelling and relates to the idea of *concrete* words; a concrete noun links to an object or a substance and includes people and animals, things that exist physically, as opposed to an abstract noun, which relates to a concept. In the study of cognition, *concreteness* refers to the understanding that concrete nouns are processed faster and more accurately than abstract nouns. A collaborative paper between US academics, including Jonathan Peelle and Jamie Reilly of the University of Florida, explored this area of linguistics that maps sound to meaning through a non-arbitrary process using prior knowledge in the surface forms of words.[22]

There is a fundamental connection between language, sound and memory that enhances meaning through imagery. As Reilly says, ' Non-arbitrary mappings form a key part of language evolution. That is, words initially "sounded" like their referents but as pressures for lexical diversity and abstractness (e.g. faith, justice, etc.) evolved, word forms became more arbitrary.'[23] The evolution of language never ceases, but the fundamentals of direct communication remain the same; poets and storytellers remind us that sound is one of the keys to memory and that language as sound was the first link between one human memory and another. It is our responsibility to remember that fact, and then to make it transcendent. The German Alfred Wolfsohn, after hearing human suffering emitting from World War I trenches, was informed in his work as a voice coach ever after as a result. As one of his students expressed it, 'He came out of the disaster of war, the cruelty, the misery, the denial of humanity, and he made something beautiful out of the human cry.' [Pikes: 69]

In the beginning was the word.

NOTES

1. Jonnie Robinson, Lead Curator, Sociolinguistics, Department of Social Sciences, British Library, interview with the author.
2. Dmae Roberts, communication with the author.
3. Ibid.
4. Ibid.
5. Ibid.

6. D. Jones, *The Anathemata*, p. 10

7. Ibid., p. 9. Jones is here quoting from the translation of the *Prologues I and II* of the *Historia Brittonum,* in *The Works of Gildas and Nennius* by J. A. Giles, London, 1841.

8. *I Remember, He Remembered,* BBC Radio 4, 13 July, 1979, Producer Barbara Crowther.

9. Rony Robinson, interview with the author, May 2013

10. Clare Jenkins, interview with the author, April 2013.

11. In a large number of institutions and archives this is beginning to be understood, but overall the witness of pure sound and recorded speech as historical commentary is still seen as supplementary. We shall return to this in a later chapter.

12. Rob Perks, Lead Curator, Oral History, Department of History and Classics, British Library, London, interview with the author.

13. Carolyn Birdsall, 'Earwitnessing: Sound Memories of the Nazi Period', in Bijsterveld and van Dijck, 2009, p. 179.

14. British Library, *National Life Stories Review and Accounts, 2012–13*, p. 1

15. American Folklife Centre, Library of Congress: www.loc.gov/folklife/guide/storytelling.html (accessed July 2013).

16. Ibid.

17. 'Radio and Ad Avoidance: You Can't Close Your Ears.' Radio Advertising Bureau Report. December 2005. www.rab.co.uk/archived-pages/Ad-Avoidance (accessed May 2013).

18. Ibid.

19. Mark Barber, interview with the author, April 2013.

20. Ibid.

21. Jonathan Peele, Assistant Professor, Department of Otolaryngology, Washington University in St. Louis, communication with the author.

22. Jamie Reilly, Chris Westbury, Jacob Kean and Jonathan E. Peelle, 'Arbitrary Symbolism in Natural Language Revisited: When Word Forms Carry Meaning', www.plosone.org/article/info%3Adoi%2F10.1371%2Fjournal.pone.0042286 (accessed July 2013).

23. Jamie Reilly, University of Florida, communication with the author.

3 Radio
Feeding the Imagination

INTERACTIVE RADIO

In the late sixteenth century, the Jesuit Matteo Ricci was sent to China as a missionary. While there, he famously taught the Chinese the art of building a memory palace, an image structure based on a building, real or imagined, to act as a mental construct providing storage for the recollection of human knowledge. 'To everything that we wish to remember', wrote Ricci, 'we should give an image; and to every one of these images we should assign a position where it can repose peacefully until we are ready to reclaim it by an act of memory.' [Spence: 2] In teaching this method, Ricci was not creating a new concept but was passing on a technique he probably learned from a number of authors from antiquity—Pliny, Cicero and Quintilian amongst them, in turn stretching back to the story of Simonides and his fateful oration in the fifth or sixth century BC (discussed at the very start of this book), the event that is claimed as the origin of this particular art of memory.

That the memory of sound is accessed through mental imagery is fundamental to the power of radio. In the early days of British broadcasting, when the first live soccer matches were broadcast, the BBC's listings magazine *Radio Times* would print a diagram of the field of play, divided into numbered sections, and as the ball moved around the pitch, a quiet voice would murmur the number of the relevant section; it was thought the audience would be incapable of picturing the action without such a visual aid. It was quickly realised, however, that no such pictorial reference was needed, that the listener was entirely capable of visualising the game and its movement through memory of the shape and structure of a football ground. Today, we listen to sports on radio regularly—tennis, cricket, baseball and football in all its forms, bringing our own individual memory palaces to bear in our sonic interpretation of the action. What is true of sport is true of all forms of audio listening, including drama, documentaries, radio features, or simply a single voice speaking; sound is a symptom of the place in which it was created, and whether the personal image we create of that place is based on realistic knowledge or not, it remains 'true' *because* we have created it, and therefore it is of mnemonic importance to us, with the potential for recollection at great distances of time and circumstance. There is a blend between the real and the abstract, the factual and the mythic, that lies at the heart of our interaction with sound. It is our mutual imaginative involvement in the making that enables us to carry these experiences with us.

When the first representations of words were transmitted, they were not words at all, nor were they stories. They were signals; Marconi's letter 'S' was sent from Poldhu in Cornwall to Signal Hill at St. John's, Newfoundland, on 11 December 1901, and while some scientists still debate the technical detail of that experiment, there was no doubt that the principle of wireless communication had arrived on a transatlantic scale. There was, however, more wonder in the fact that it was possible than there was imaginative awe at the content. This was a utility, and would prove itself beyond argument as a vital aid to shipping and military communication. It was left to others—notably, initially, the Canadian Reginald Fessenden—to add voices, music and poetry, which Fessenden did in a transmission from a station at Brandt Rock, Massachussetts, on Christmas Eve, 1906.

Close to where Marconi listened for his signal in Newfoundland, in 2009 the Canadian features producer Chris Brookes was making a documentary about storytelling with a neighbour of his, a retired fisherman called Jack Wells. Each day, Wells would sit with friends in his twinestore (a fisherman's shed full of the paraphernalia of his work and trade), tell stories and reminisce. Jack's stories and the interplay between the men's voices might have made a programme in itself, but Brookes wove another ingredient into the sound mix in the form of the long Newfoundland tradition of telling 'Jack Tales', stories of a mythical 'Everyman' to whom everyone in the Province relates, 'centuries-old folktales passed down by word of mouth through the generations as entertaining parables of life.

> They usually begin like this: "Once there were three brothers, Tom, Bill and Jack. Now Tom and Bill, they were handy, they were actually able to do something. But Jack, well, all Jack could do was sit by the fire, and . . ." and so begins a fantastical tale starring Jack, the ne'er-do-well youngest brother.'[1]

In the traditional 'Jack Tale', this unpromising boy goes off on spectacular adventures, always in the end triumphing over evil and living happily ever after. It is a form of storytelling familiar from childhood, and still told with relish in cultures where folkloric tradition is strong, such as Newfoundland and Ireland. Brookes's programme, made for RTE Radio 1, capitalised on a common understanding of orality between the two countries. Jack Wells and his friends' stories were not myths but real memories of battles with the sea, storms and perils and hardships of fishing, blended with the shared lore of men, nets, rope and gutting fish. The result was *The Annotated Jack,* in which the real and the myth were woven together, in the process exploring the role of storytelling in life and memory. Radio in this instance became the conduit for fact and imagination, and the interaction between the two that existed in the programme was mirrored by the mental and emotional connections made with the listener, sending out new signals and pictures, which in turn opened up new areas of possibility and memory through the power of suggestion, ripples spreading outwards across a pool of aurality.

*

Just under a century after Marconi signalled across the Atlantic, on 11 September 2001, the British radio producer Andy Cartwright was working on his computer at his home in York when a newsflash broke into his consciousness. Going to the television, he witnessed the unfolding horror of the events in New York on that day. The television coverage was spectacular, transfixing, compelling, almost unbelievable. The film industry had been fictionalisng scenes such as this for years—disaster movies were, after all, a genre in their own right. At the same moment, Cartwright's partner, Rosie, was driving home from a conference, listening to the same event on the car radio. When she arrived home, there was for them, as for most of the world, only one topic of conversation, and it became clear that the radio experience had been far more potent and moving than the literal images delivered by television. 'Rosie understood the significance of it must sooner than I did. When you have someone describing what they're seeing, what's happening, one-to-one, perhaps sending the last message of their lives, a final telephone call, that is a very potent thing.'[2] A single ordinary person, perhaps just like us, caught up in an extraordinary event, is captured best by sound because it is interactive; we think about the sounds, we visualise, and it is that partnership that makes it so powerful, and which lies at the heart of the relationship between radio and memory. In the previous chapter, we discussed the importance to the human species of storytelling; in the example of 9/11, we have that relationship between teller and listener acting at the most visceral level.

On a much less dramatic level, we may encounter the subliminal power of radio every day as we travel about on our daily business. The car radio, as with the example just discussed, is one of the most powerful tools in the sound/imagination interface, because firstly, we are captive within a space as we listen, secondly, because it is entering our brain subliminally as we concentrate on other things, and thirdly, because it acts with the visuals of the places we pass through to cement sound images in memory on a geographical level. Some years ago I was driving from Bournemouth, on the south coast of England, to Oxford, a journey of about two hours. On the car sound system I was listening to work produced by postgraduate radio production students. The sounds flowed as the landscape passed: it was to all intents and purposes a radio listening experience.

At a certain point, as anyone who has driven that route will remember, the north-south A34 road passes through an interchange with the east/west M4 motorway. It is a place where the driver concentrates on the road with a particular focus; the in-car audio takes second place, becomes subliminal. As I approached the interchange, I was listening to a piece of audio that particularly caught my attention; it was a short, semi-abstract and highly imaginative programme called *Walls Have Ears* by Alan Brown, and it explored the premise that the walls of our homes, our houses, absorb the sounds of our lives, rather like a recording device.[3] As I listened, I remembered a television series from the 1970s, Nigel Kneale's *The Stone Tape*, which dealt with a similar idea in a supernatural context. Perhaps it was this connection, the power of the thoughts the audio produced in my mind, the skill of the producer or, perhaps, it was a combination of all three of these that engaged my imagination in a new way. I was no longer a tutor assessing student work, but an active and willing imaginative participant in the whole fantasy that walls absorb the sound of our emotional existence. I was totally absorbed, while part of me was also concentrating on the road. We often think of radio—audio—as a secondary activity: that is one of its strong powers. Yet there are times when things switch, and listening becomes the *primary* activity, and the other task in hand becomes secondary. Driving along a familiar route in a car may be one such example; on arrival at our destination, while being aware of the journey we have just undertaken, there are times when we have very little recollection of the journey itself, and this is particularly the case when we have been absorbed in either conversation or something we have been listening to on the car's sound system.

On the occasion in question, reaching the tricky interchange, my mind changed its focus and the audio slipped into the background of my consciousness. A minute or so later, back on the open road, I was mentally fully engaged with the unfolding imaginative exploration of walls and place-memory. I was aware that there was something that I had missed during the road manouvre, but unlike 'live' radio, I had a CD I could play again at a convenient time. This I did, as soon as I arrived in Oxford, so taken was I with this story and the idea behind it. To my surprise, I could not locate the short passage in the place I had 'missed' while negotiating the M4 interchange: I had actually absorbed everything. I remembered things I had thought I had not heard. This is of course subliminal secondary activity at work, a variation of what has been called 'the cocktail party effect', the ability to switch our consciousness, listening and attention as required.

There is a brief sequel to this story; since that first listening 'event', I have made the same journey from the south coast to Oxford on numerous occasions. Each time I pass under the M4 motorway, I 'hear' the radio feature I first heard there all those years ago. Sound and memory share a partner, and that partner is Place: just as driving through a terrain can evoke the memory of a sound encountered there, likewise that same sound—or even the recollection of the sound—can bring back the idea of the place. As a programme maker, this phenomenon affects Andy Cartwright in a similar way: 'I increasingly associate places with the making of programmes, so we can be driving around and I'll suddenly say "Oh, I once did an interview there!" That memory will bring back the interview, the circumstances, the occasion and what the recording went on to be part of. The geography takes me back to the sound.'[4]

Time and place share a mystery with music, and a common denominator is radio and, more generally, audio listening. The mystery—particularly to the non-specialist—is why there should be such a potency in this partnership at all? We imagine pictures, and sounds trigger images, but how this happens is part of the fascination. On one level, we may call up a visual message more easily than a sonic one. A pictorial memory map of an old house, lived in many years previously, may be more accessible than a recollection of the sounds that rang from its walls in times gone by. Yet if we are confronted with one of those sounds, a host of memories are evoked, some made up of other sounds (as discussed in the first chapter of this book, as well as in the appendix), some to do with smells, furnishings, layout of rooms and of course people. There is only one time, which is *now* and transient. Radio—in the traditional, old-fashioned transmitted sense, broadcast in temporal terms—encapsulates this idea of what time is and how it governs and rules us. Often without necessarily articulating the mystery, it is this strangeness that fascinates many radio producers as well as listeners, a preoccupation that prompted T. S. Eliot to write *The Four Quartets* during the years 1936–42. Time, linking sound, speech and music in a ever-vanishing dance caught in the net of the brain as it passes, is held by memory perhaps because of the very fact that it *is* passing. The human need to preserve ourselves is touched by this mystery, as the shapes go by and the images develop in the 'mind's eye', locked together in the very place where human creativity originates.

The phenomenon of the active relationship between the medium and the imagination has long been held as one of radio's greatest strengths. Additional to the power of the sound and its message to enter the mind by stealth, there is the remarkable ability of the brain to respond to this stimulus creatively, to, as it were, partner the trigger with new and complementary contributions of its own. We remember so much sound-created thought because we ourselves have played a part in its development. Often radio makers think in terms of striking a match or planting a seed; such metaphors are apposite because it is true to say that much of the memory-making qualities of audio is interactive. Early in the digital age, there were experiments in which producers used technology to self-consciously set up interaction between makers and audience; at the time there were also those who were critical of this, or at least felt such projects to be somewhat superfluous. Radio—audio—*is* and always has been interactive at a human rather than a technical level. The radio consultant and futurologist James Cridland has made a clear distinction between modes of listening that illustrates this point. Previous generations did not have to consider a distinction between 'radio' as a medium and 'radio' as the object through which this medium was experienced. Today, things are much more complex in terms of how we listen, and this in turn affects our responses:

I think there is a difference between 'radio' and 'audio' in terms of consumption here. I sometimes say that the difference between them is one of *liveness* and connection. If you are listening to a live radio signal, there is a (subconscious) knowledge that you are listening along with other people. This is a shared experience, not a solitary one. (To clarify—"live" here is the way the audio gets to you—not necessarily the broadcast being done live.) So: if you are listening to *I'm Sorry I Haven't A Clue* on Monday at 6.30pm, you know that this isn't a live programme, but you also, subconsciously, know that many other people are laughing along with you. I think that matters.[5]

Local and community radio demonstrate this extremely well at a simple yet profound level, with the 'phone-in' programme, a staple and cheap diet for editors to generate current content. Beyond this, however, radio at a local level becomes the collection point for community memory, and were small stations equipped with the facilities to store all the material they generate in their audience's response, and were that material made accessible both locally and beyond, a rich vein of living social history and experience would be available for future generations. Sadly, too often, the limits to such possibilities are financial, but the potential remains considerable. The playwright and broadcaster Rony Robinson has presented a daily morning radio programme on BBC Radio Sheffield in South Yorkshire for nearly thirty years. It is a three-hour show, not dissimilar to many such programmes on local radio stations around the world. Robinson shares the ability, the skill and the insight of the best of this type of broadcaster to tap into an empathy with his audience and provoke the imagination to debate or reminiscence. As he says:

There has always been that side—particularly of local radio—that recognizes the power of memory, that you can open up memory by asking the right question, or by playing the right music. At the very simplest level, we're asking "what does it do to you, what do you remember?" I think we should do more of it and I think we should do it better.[6]

On BBC Radio Sheffield's sister station, BBC Radio Merseyside, the veteran broadcaster Billy Butler has also used nostalgia triggers to open recognition in his listeners. It is one of the interesting aspects of British public service local radio that, while it may be broadcasting to listeners who are often past retirement age, the producers and presenters may in some cases be young enough to be the children—or grandchildren—of those for whom they make programmes. There are notable exceptions: Butler, who has been broadcasting to the same local area for more than forty years, and Robinson are examples. Given that the BBC's local radio audience is an older one, Billy Butler and his colleagues around Britain have created shortcuts that can quickly create a memory moment, a pause for reflection. Butler's approach is to plant seeds and trust the interactive nature of the medium to do the rest: 'I've always worked on the basis of creating a germ, and allowing it to grow; It works with music, with records, and with all the popular media with which our lives are surrounded.'[7] One such device is a short recorded feature called *Whatever Happened To . . .?*, a simple 90-second insert in which Butler recites a list of everyday household products, bygone activities, childhood habits and other memories prefixed by the mantra, 'Whatever happened to . . .?' over music. These symptoms of the past tend to target listeners who would associate them with their childhood or youth in the 1940s or 1950s, an ageing audience for whom recognition is the key; it only takes a few words—the reminder of a long-lost brand of toffee, or the remembrance of an everyday occurrence—to unlock a chain of other associations. 'The items I read out in *Whatever Happened To . . .* all came from listeners in the first place, so I'm just giving them back. I've been running that feature on my afternoon show for years, and it's very potent. Until the germ was tickled, you'd never remember it.'[8]

As we grow older, our world centres in a more focused way on our immediate surroundings. We notice change and our long-term memory stretches back, so we become susceptible to personal recollection; to be a part of a community that also remembers the same things is to be less isolated, and this sharing, even within a radio audience, provides a warm sense of a mutual past. It would be wrong, however, to assume that the link between radio and nostalgia only exists for the elderly; for many years, the listening audiences were perceived as polarised between the young and the old, with the most important market, particularly in the commercial sector, seen as that of youth. With the growth of commercial classical music stations and 'Gold' networks during the 1990s, this perception changed, and an older—and more affluent audience—was identified. It also became clear that memory is a lifelong thing; we live our personal lives in a largely improvised present, but everything before the current moment, whatever age we may be, belongs to our life story, our past and therefore memory. This apparently obvious fact is not always taken into account by broadcasters and programmers, as Rony Robinson says: 'Often there is a prejudice against it because there is an assumption that only old people have memories, but of course 20-year-olds have memories too.'[9]

Indeed, memory and nostalgia begins at least as early as the start of teenage years, when the sometimes difficult process of becoming an adult is made poignant by the recollection of the safe world of early childhood. What makes this difficult is the tension between past and present, particularly potent in those years because of the bewildering sense of adjustment to new values and a new world. The games we played, the programmes we watched on television, the station idents and jingles and the music that is already part of our past play a part in *giving* us that past much earlier than perhaps radio programmers consider. The radio phone-in, when practised well by a sensitive broadcaster, interspersing calls with short features and studio discussion, can be a rich and important tool in the transference of personal memory to community memory and vice versa, as Robinson points out:

> It's obviously fun, but it's more important than that because it tells us that our lives matter, and we've not lived in vain, and that seems to me to be an honourable thing that we should be celebrating. Nothing is ordinary, and the radio should practice more of the democratic art of talking, and help people to do it—it's something we can all do.[10]

*

Outside of the realm of music radio, it may seem obvious to state that much of the imaginative spark between the maker and the listener comes through words—and yet radio is a medium of sound, and so potentially the palette is sonically almost infinite. Nevertheless, it is the word that producers come back to when seeking to ignite that spark, because words are the fundamental conduit of thoughts, ideas and, above all, stories. Documentary features producers (such as the BBC's Piers Plowright), when they discuss memories of programmes, usually find themselves remembering the memories of those who have been their subjects: 'When I think about it, they all depend on people looking back—often because I've tended to interview the old rather than the young. I have a hunch that a good radio documentary needs to work vertically (looking back) and horizontally (as it happens)—or to put it another way, thought and action.'[11] This is exemplified in Plowright's 1983 BBC Radio 4 feature, *Nobody Stays in This House Long*, in effect a programme comprised of one long memory—of how a house and a family used to be, and how they are now. 'A classic moment in that, bringing together the past and the present, was when Enid Margaret Drage, the mother, stumbled through *Kinderszenen* on the battered old Bechstein with her arthritic fingers. It had to be her and not a more polished library performance, because the force of the programme depended on this conjunction of (mostly) golden memories with the more painful ('though uncomplained about) present.'[12]

Radio is essentially a poetic medium, so it is not surprising that poets have shared what are after all common denominators—memory and sound—between the written word and the sonically articulated experience. The work of the Australian poet and radio producer Michael Ladd exemplifies this:

> Near where I grew up in the Adelaide hills, a man named Hugh Magary used to play a set of whistles from old steam engines. We would hear them all over the valley every Sunday. I found Hugh and got him to fire up the boiler again. I recorded the whistles from the perspective of various childhood haunts and hiding places, then created a sound piece that used not the direct sound, but only the natural reverberation. We captured the traces of sound reflected from the valley itself, its organic, earthy memory. These sounds were quiet and

airy, somewhat ethereal and melancholic, and they had, to my mind, the sense of lost childhood.

We assembled several of these short works into a programme called *Tracks and Traces* which was first broadcast in *The Listening Room* on ABC Classic FM in 1994. The works each dealt in their own way with following trails, tracking things down, re-assembling the past from evidence left behind. The programme follows both "horizontal" trails through landscapes, and "vertical" trails through time, memory and myth.[13]

Another of Ladd's works from the same series was entitled *Seaweed*, and grew out of a chance find of a length of audio-cassette tape on a beach:

I discovered the tape had songs recorded from the radio and children's voices on it, and I produced the work by multi-tracking these stretched and backwards sounds and voices. *Seaweed* began an ongoing interest in the physical decay of audio-tape—perhaps reflecting the way sound always decays into silence, and that memory can also fade.

In later works such as *Wind and Water Weatherings* (*The Listening Room* 1999) I reversed this process by starting with pristine recordings of Steinway piano notes cut into lengths of analogue audio tape, which were suspended in a tree and in a river for one year. Every 3 months we would sample the tapes to investigate what was happening with the sound. Again, I think, the central idea in the work was to evoke a sense of time passing, to capture that emotion sonically.[14]

Thus we see that—with or without words—radio *is* sound. This is why its imaginative power is so great, and why we can summon its prompts from memory when provoked to do so by the right question or an involuntary trigger. Beyond the technical, we might see ourselves as receivers, with the capacity for tuning in to the world around us. The ears of a person with unimpaired hearing are never closed, so imaginative sound will constantly have to compete with the currency of the sound we are absorbing as 'receivers'. The Belgian sound artist Stijn Demeulenaere has written: 'When asked to remember a sound, to recreate it in our heads, we have to rely a lot more on our imagination, our cross-links between feelings, thoughts and memories to attempt to hear it again. And by using that imagination, we explore what it was that made a certain sound special to us, and why it stuck with us.'[15] Creative radio producers such as Matt Thompson of Rockethouse Productions employ sound (as opposed to speech) actively in their work to create mood and place. In 2012–13, Thompson collaborated with the academic Professor David Hendy of Sussex University and curators at the British Library's Department of Sound and Vision in the creation of a major thirty-part series, *Noise—A Human History*—for BBC Radio 4. The series, which was recorded on location around the world, also travelled through time from prehistory to the present day, using sounds from the British Library's Sound Archive collections, evoking such sound pictures as the din of trench warfare and the hubbub of modern city life. The process involved Thompson in sourcing sounds in library conditions, and reawakening their meaning in the context of place, and Hendy's script.

> For me, the more interesting sounds were ethnographic recordings of African drums, shamans and the like. I probably will associate them more with shamans than the moment I heard them in the British Library Sound Archive. That is because in making the programme I had to imagine the shamans in their tents in altered states, and in some ways that is more real to me now than the British Library.[16]

Andy Cartwright's 'sound poem', *Then—Now*, created for BBC Radio in 2005–06, explored the memory of everyday sound spread across an entire country, but focused on a single chosen minute, 6.00pm to 6.01pm on Wednesday, 9 November 2005. Amateur and professional sound recordists across the UK were invited to record the sound around them, wherever they were, whatever they were doing, and submit the audio to Cartwright, who then explored the overall themes that emerged, ordinary activities at the end of the working day such as cooking, travelling, socialising and shutting up offices. The resulting programme was a philosophical exploration of time, place and memory, and played on the fact that the present immediately becomes the past. In so doing, it asked the listener to be part of an imaginative journey through half an hour of airtime, in which a hundred or so audio memories blended and wove together to make a composite sound map of Britain at a precise moment. By the time the feature was broadcast in early 2006, 'Now' had become 'Then' while being re-experienced in a new present, thus encouraging the radio audience to interrogate the idea of time and the ever-receding succession of moments of which life comprises. In *Then—Now* Cartwright sought to 'extend time and compress activities at the same time. And time is the clue to what *Then—Now* was about— preserving moments in time *Then* and transmitting them *Now*.'[17]

WHERE SUGGESTION TAKES US

Radio is suggestive, growing out of its connection with the temporal nature of life itself; we do not know what will happen in the next moment, and 'live' radio retains its capacity to surprise in the same way. The sounds that Matt Thompson places in his programmes to evoke a mood or a sense of place through his skill have the power to stir the imagination into its own personal pictures, which in turn contain the potential to become memories for the listener, both of the programme and associated sensory 'events'. The human mind is a kind of radio producer as well as receiver in the sense that it has the capacity to interpret feelings absorbed through sound, particularly when those sounds act as reminders of past events. By partaking in this experience, we can shape fantasies and fictions, often created from disparate and various audio symptoms of life around us, in a partnership between imagination and memory. There is a famous section in *Á La Recherche du Temps Perdu* in which the central character is lying in bed on a winter's morning, hearing the voices outside, rising up from the street, beginning a chain of thought that moves through opera and sacred music, to life and love. While taste and smell are the senses usually cited as the most significant sound triggers in Proust, we shall have reason to point more than once to the significance of sound in his work: 'Our hearing, that delightful sense, brings us the company of the street, of which it traces every line for us, sketches all the figures that pass along it, showing us their colours.' [Proust 5 (1996) 124] The opening of the iron shutters of a baker's shop begins a process of associative sounds in Marcel's mind, the cries of street vendors linking his imagination with perspectives that are at once cross-cultural and temporal. A kind of music, but not song; indeed, these 'beguiling calls', coming through his ears to a mind still emerging from sleep, differed 'from song as much as the declamation—of *Boris Godunov* and *Pelléas*; but on the other hand recalled the drone of a priest intoning his office, of which these street sounds are but the good-humoured, secular, and yet half-liturgical counterpart.' [Ibid.] He hears the cry of ' "Winkles, winkles, a ha'porth worth of winkles!" ' as it is intoned, and 'it was of the barely musical declamation of Moussorgsky that the vendor reminded me.' The meditation on the associations of sound is extraordinary in the five or so pages of what we might almost called a prose poem within the great sweep of the novel's narrative: 'Dogs clipped, cats doctored, tails and ears docked', chanted in counterpoint with a woman calling to buy artichokes, or the cry and bell of a knife grinder, create in the reader's mind a sound picture of great clarity and poignancy, but it is in Proust's capacity for giant imaginative leaps that the memory of the sounds makes its most profound suggestions:

> A ritual suspension interposing a silence in the middle of a word, especially when it is repeated a second time, constantly evoked the memory of old churches. In his cart drawn by a she-ass which he stopped in front of each house before entering the courtyard, the old-clothes man, brandishing a whip, intoned: "Old clothes, any old clothes, old clo . . . thes" with the same pause between the final syllables as if he had been intoning a plainchant: "*Per omnia saecula saeculo . . . rum*" or "*requiescat in pa . . . ce . . .*"
>
> —[Ibid.]

Piers Plowright found direct parallels with this passage when reflecting on a programme made in 1996, in which he accompanied a fellow BBC producer, John Theocharis, back to his birthplace in Alexandria:

> When I listen to the tape we made together, it's the voices and music of that city, as in Proust's Paris, that provide John and us, his listeners,

with the chains of memory. He hears the voice of the great Egyptian singer Um Kalthoum, and remembers standing in the shabby doorway of an Alexandrian four-storey house, searching for the little card, among those of prostitutes and tailors, of Madame Rosa, the clairvoyante, so he can climb the stairs smelling of Lucky Strike cigarettes and cheap perfume, to her flat, and listen to what the future holds for him. He listens to the voice of a dead singer whose recorded voice at this very moment soothes tired old men in the coffee shops of Cairo and Baghdad; the singer is brought alive and she brings alive the sound of Madame Rosa's harshly inflected German/French English as she tells her young Greek client that he will travel across the sea where his work will influence "millions of people". Well, he left Egypt and travelled via Greece and Ethiopia to London where he joined the BBC. Voices within voices within voices.[18]

We 'hear' voices and stories echoing from our past prompted by radio memories all the time: the appendix of this book contains the evidence of the power of these reverberations, while we may recall very little of what we watched on television the previous evening because it has been made for us rather than with us. Pertinent to this, Plowright remembers a 1960s interview with the sculptor Henry Moore, in which the artist said, ' "I became a sculptor because I wanted to walk round what I had made", and this was worth a hundred arm-waving presenters on TV trying to tell me what sculpture was about'.[19] This statement is highly significant in terms of our understanding and interaction with radio and sound. As listeners, we can 'walk round' a sonic experience in a way that we cannot with a TV screen—even with 3-D. Memory is multi-dimensional, multi-sensual and multi-suggestible. We can walk round a memory.

There is, however, a further factor to be briefly considered. Imaginative memory, or the memory of a dream, is different to the memory of actual events. In her study of involuntary memory, *A Collection of Moments*, the writer Esther Salaman drew a distinction between the nature of a dream recollection and that of ordinary memory, pointing to the static quality of the dream, its unchanging form in the mind: 'Leaving aside the distorted reality of a dream, the phantasy, the obscurity of the message, the great difference between the memory of a real moment and the memory of a dream is that nothing is ever added to the memory of the dream.' [Salaman: 129] She goes on, 'Dreams may affect our lives as profoundly as or even more than memories: the mere fact that dreams are an indispensable part of our sleep points to that; but a dream seems to be a thing that we make like a work of art, and is not preserved in the mind in the way that memories of moments are.' [Ibid.: 130–31] The link between the dream and the creative collaboration forged by maker and listener in impressionistic radio and audio (drama, music, poetry, the feature programme, for example) is significant in the power of subliminal sound to store itself and re-emerge in an involuntary way as a response to seemingly unrelated cues. Passing under a bridge at a motorway junction may, as we have seen, unlock a form of déjà vu in us, flashing fragments of the sonic past suddenly before us, perfectly and immutably preserved. It is the unexpected touching of the two worlds that is so potent and that itself creates a memory, 'an island holding the feelings of the moment.' [Ibid.: 133]

NOTES

1. Chris Brookes, programme note, *The Annotated Jack,* Battery Radio for Radio Telefís-Eireann, Radio 1, September 2009.
2. Andy Cartwright, interview with the author.
3. The programme in question, *Walls Have Ears,* by Alan Brown, was broadcast on the Internet radio station BIRSt (Bournemouth Internet Radio Station). It can be accessed via this link: www.birst.co.uk/archive/?author=71 (accessed June 2013).
4. Ibid.
5. James Cridland, communication with the author.
6. Rony Robinson, interview with the author.
7. Billy Butler, interview with the author.
8. Ibid.
9. Rony Robinson, interview with the author.
10. Ibid.
11. Piers Plowright, communication with the author
12. Ibid.
13. Michael Ladd, communication with the author
14. Ibid.
15. http://versonatura.org/sound/soundtracks.htm (Accessed July 2013)
16. Matt Thompson, communication with the author.
17. Andy Cartwright, unpublished paper, *Sounding Out* Conference, University of Sunderland, 2006. A more detailed analysis of *Then—Now* may be found in Street 2012: 54–57.
18. Piers Plowright, *The Voice and Its Mysteries,* unpublished paper delivered to the Hunterian Society, March 2003.
19. Piers Plowright, communication with the author.

4   'Father of the Man'
Radio, Audio and Youth

RADIO WOMB AND OTHER EARLY TRANSMISSIONS

The beginnings of memory are bound up with our very being, and its origins within the development of that self may be much earlier than many have supposed. The issue would seem to be this: how are experience and memory linked in our earliest months, pre- and postnatal, and how much of the first sounds of existence do we carry forward with us as we grow? For several decades scientists have known that we begin learning prenatally by listening to the sound of our mother talking. More recently however, particularly through the research of psychologists such as Professor Christine Moon at Pacific Lutheran University, information is being gathered that shows this learning to be much more specific and earlier than had been previously supposed; we may actually learn speech sounds from within the womb before birth.[1] Moon, together with co-researchers Hugo Lagercrantz of the Karolinska Institute in Sweden and Patricia Kuhl of Washington University's Institute for Learning and Brain Sciences, tested newborn babies for recognition in both the United States and in Sweden, a total of eighty children, in the period between seven and seventy-five hours after birth. The research focused on recognition of vowel sounds because of their prominence in speech, and therefore the potential for their auditory reception within the noisy background environment of the womb. The study showed that the newborn child has the capacity to learn and remember elementary sounds of their language from the mother during the last ten weeks of pregnancy. Previous indications had shown that a foetus seemed to remember musical rhythms; here was evidence that suggested the capacity for at least a partial learning of language.

A child in its infancy is an extraordinarily sensitive receiver of sounds, images, smells and emotions, learning at an amazing rate in every conscious moment. The attention may be absorbed in an activity, or in watching a TV programme, but the sound of a door closing in the hall outside will register and cause curiosity. It is part of our survival mechanism as human beings, and we are trained to it from the start. Not only are we finely tuned and fast learners, but also our period of early intense sensory and cognitive absorption is considerably extended in comparison to other species. As the child psychologist Alison Gopnik of University College, Berkeley, has pointed out:

> That's a fundamental evolutionary fact about us, and on the surface a puzzling one. Why make babies so helpless for so long? And why do we have to invest so much time and energy, literally, just to keep them alive? Well, when you look across lots and lots of different species, birds and rodents and all sorts of critters, you see that a long period of immaturity is correlated with a high degree of flexibility, intelligence and learning. Look at crows and chickens, for example. Crows get on the cover of *Science* using tools, and chickens end up in the soup pot, right? And crows have a much longer period of immaturity, a much longer period of dependence than chickens.[2]

During this period of development, young animals from the more highly evolved species seem to be poor at paying attention. Some have suggested that this is because their short-term memory is not fully developed; a command not to do something is apparently ignored because it is quickly forgotten, and therefore has to be repeated. Another point of view might be that the reason this occurs is because the infant is actually paying *real* attention to a huge number of new stimuli at the same time, absorbing things that to an adult would be a distraction, due to the capacity for filtering as we grow. Gopnik compares a baby's consciousness as being 'like a lantern instead of being a spotlight', likening the period of infant learning to a period of time an adult might spend within an unfamiliar foreign culture:

> There are certain kinds of states that we're in as adults, like when we go to a new city for the first time, where we capture that baby information processing. When we do that we feel our consciousness has expanded. We have more vivid memories of the three days spent in Beijing [for example] than we do of all the rest of the months that we spend as walking, talking, teaching, meeting-attending zombies. So that we actually see something about what babies' consciousness is like, and that might tell us some important things about what consciousness itself is like.[3]

There are some of us however, who have memories of targeted attention—a spotlight rather than a lantern—from an extremely young age. Most of us, if we can trace our infant memory, would place it from about the age of three years, but there are those who can go further back than that. The Northumberland poet Katrina Porteous, noted for her work of historical and linguistic retrieval as well as for her poetic radio collaborations with the BBC producer Julian May, is one such:

> My earliest memory is of lying in my pram in the garden, listening to a bird singing. This was before I could talk. The memory is primarily emotional. I wanted to speak like the bird. I remember the silences between the phrases, and waiting for the next one and the next. I remember enjoying the richness of the sound and recognizing the difference from human voices.
>
> I remember having to re-remember these feelings as time went on, to remind myself of them so as not to lose them. At the same time as this re-remembering, I remember words having very vivid pictures associated with them, and an intense feeling of loss as those pictures in turn began to dissolve with time. I remember only two or three of those pictures now. The colours were very strong. They had no connection whatsoever with the meaning of the words, only with their sound or perhaps the places where I heard them. Losing the word pictures happened before my third birthday. I remember just before that birthday counting up to three on the telegraph posts as I passed them, and already feeling sad that the word pictures had mostly dissolved.[4]

To fully understand the crucial nature of learning and the capacity for memory, including sound from the earliest moments of existence, and to adjust teaching—in the broadest sense of the word—to take account of our extraordinary receptivity, especially to audio triggers, would be potentially to heighten our mental capacity and perhaps longevity in later life.

CHILDHOOD—THE BROADCAST

The early radio sound memory with which this book began is a place to return to now; it is a personal reference point, but it is also a metaphor. As a survey conducted as part of the research for this book has shown, almost all of us can achieve a similar regression through employing sound as a vector of recollection. We shall explore some of the implications drawn from contributions to this survey in the course of this chapter. The survey employed radio as the tool through which audio memory might be accessed for the purposes of the research, but there is no doubt that other sounds beyond electronic media could equally be brought into play as part of such an experiment. Prior to the advent of radio and recording, the sound world was a very different place, and the relationship between silence and noise was much more extreme. Ancient man was highly sensitive to sounds and their meanings coming to him out of the audio landscape of his world. Children today live in a changed environment, but even as they are engrossed in watching television, listening, playing games—electronic or otherwise—or reading, they remain tuned to sounds that come to them from outside their immediate understanding. Sometimes these sounds become lodged in the memory *because* they are inexplicable, without an apparent context, or because their juxtaposition with the familiar creates a tension that adopts new meanings and relevance in later life. It may also be that in today's multimedia world these skills from early life are being retained and utilised later, much more than have been in previous generations.

The radio recollections of childhood, as demonstrated in the survey, are unsurprisingly but significantly dominated by the memories of respondents born in the 1940s and 1950s, when radio was still a dominant medium. This continued as far as the 1970s, when a child born in 1965 could still be part of the continuing listening habit of older family members, while discovering the individual freedom afforded by portable transistor listening. In some cases the associative audio recollections evoked by the memory of the broadcast can be very specific, whilst in other cases the door is unlocked into a room of memories of events, rather than necessarily the actual sound itself. In many cases the exercise in which the respondents participated startled them with the strength of the emotions it produced. An Australian correspondent, remembering hearing—but not understanding—radio reports of the Vietnam war in the early 1970s on ABC as a four-year-old, found involuntary memory overwhelming her:

> I'm suddenly and totally sideswiped by missing Granny—who died over 30 years ago when I was a child. I'm sitting here crying. Funny—the grim reports of young soldiers dying is cemented in my mind, a sudden awareness of the moment that I recognised that I was listening and what I was listening to, but it's the present absence of those peripheral sounds that makes those moments most poignant.[5]

In the group aged between fifty-one and seventy at the time of writing, that is to say listeners born between 1943 and 1962, a recurring theme is listening as part of the family unit. Interestingly, although radio specifically targeted at children is mentioned, primarily the most memorable listening experiences seem to be the communal family sharing of programmes, which therefore are associated with memories of family members themselves. The earliest memories are from the age of three: 'Sitting with my mother and aunt singing along to *Rudolph the Red Nosed Reindeer*. It must have been between 1949–50', or 'listening with my father to the football results on Saturday afternoon, followed by a jazz programme—I would have been about five years old'. In some cases specific sound memories of radio voices come back; an Irish respondent in the same group remembers at the age of five 'listening to RTE Radio 1 with my mother in the kitchen—Mike Murphy in the morning and then Gay Byrne', and again these memories evoke the melancholy of nostalgia—so when asked, 'how does recalling these sounds make you feel now?' the answer is: 'small . . . young . . . vividly in the past and in the heart of people (like parents) who are now dead'.

From the period 1962 onwards, childhood radio memories become more music-based: 'Early '60s pop music—the Beatles but especially Herman's

Hermits and the smells of a hot iron on cotton. Mum ironing and at some point saying "If your dad was in he wouldn't let us listen to this", and the memory of 'a half basement with white walls. Brown chair—velvet, which I associate more with reading,' all evoking a feeling of being 'calm, rooted.' A sense of Place inevitably becomes less in younger respondents; for those born in the late 1980s and 1990s, the only communal aspects of radio listening are remembered as being in the car, often on holiday trips:

> My earliest memory of listening to the radio is when I was very young travelling to Scotland with my mum and dad. All my family were born in Scotland except me, so we used to go up from Yorkshire every Easter and Christmas in the car. My Dad also used to put on cassettes he'd recorded from vinyl of Billy Connolly or Willie McCulloch all the way up the A1 through England until we reached the capture zone for BBC Scotland and then further on Radio Clyde (or Clyde 1 as it is now). I don't really remember the programmes we heard; I just remember the satisfaction of hearing a Scottish accent on the radio after waiting in anticipation for so long.[6]

Whether radio memories recalled from childhood evoke happy or sad memories, the vividness with which they can be recalled is notable in the survey responses, as we shall explore further in the Appendix. It is also cross-generational up to a certain historical point (the early to mid 1960s), because a younger listenership prior to that point was sharing an experience largely imposed by an older generation. Notwithstanding this fact, the formative power of the recollected experience is clearly a potent one, evoking the same sense of the importance of youthful experience that the romantic poet William Wordsworth identified in 1802.

LIMBIC GHOSTS

In March of that year, Wordsworth, living at Grasmere in the English Lake District, wrote a short poem, sometimes called 'The Rainbow':

> My heart leaps up when I behold
> A rainbow in the sky:
> So was it when my life began;
> So is it now I am a man;
> So be it when I shall grow old,
> Or let me die!
> The Child is father of the Man;
> And I could wish my days to be
> Bound each to each by natural piety.

—[Wordsworth: 79]

In this brief lyric, Wordsworth celebrates not only the purity of vision as sensed by a child but also the potential for early experience to influence and overshadow us in later life, for good or ill. Our youth forms us as adults. Just as Wordsworth's image of the rainbow—and its power through beauty to burn itself into consciousness—linked his past, present and future, so do early memories of sound experience stay with us and shape our mind and behaviour as we grow. In terms of sound, it has even more potential for profound effect than a visual image because it is so often subliminal. Thus it is not just the sound that we remember, but also the circumstances in which we first heard it. In other words, sounds' powers are frequently associative.

During the summer of 1910, when Freud was vacationing with his family on the North Sea in the Netherlands, the composer Gustav Mahler, in a state of deep depression, decided to consult him. Mahler's "maddening doubt" led him to put off the meeting on three successive occasions. While it appears that the encounter between the two men had some positive effects on Mahler, its long-term impact will never be known because he died only eight months later. Many discussions, radio programmes and at least one film have developed hypotheses based on the limited information available of that meeting, mostly revolving around Mahler's sexual relationship with his wife, Alma, and his mother fixation. On one point, for Mahler at least, however, his conversation with Freud was revelatory; those familiar with his music will know that a characteristic is the occasional juxtaposition of a profound theme, often tragic, with light, banal, almost fairground-type/folk-like melodies and orchestration.

> In the course of the talk Mahler suddenly said that now he understood why his music had always been prevented from achieving the highest rank through the noblest passages, those inspired by the most profound emotions, being spoilt by the intrusion of some commonplace melody. His father, apparently a brutal person, treated his wife very badly, and when Mahler was a young boy there was a specially painful scene between them. It became quite unbearable to the boy, who rushed away from the house. At that moment, however, a hurdy-gurdy in the street was grinding out the popular Viennese air *Ach, du lieber Augustin*. In Mahler's opinion the conjunction of high tragedy and light amusement was from then on inextricably fixed in his mind, and the one mood inevitably brought the other with it.
>
> —[Jones: 88–89]

A child's response to circumstances beyond their control—in this case fear and horror engendered—if only for a moment, can become a lifelong influence, and the potency of emotion, when recalled in terms of sound, may lie in the memory below the level of consciousness for decades, while still playing a part in conscious decisions and feelings. So it was with Mahler, who once recounted another formative incident from his childhood to his friend Natalie Bauer-Lechner. Mahler's music abounds with fanfares and military march-like rhythms, and his adult account of an event from his infancy, as recorded by Bauer-Lechner, clearly identifies this familiar motif in his work as originating in childhood and amplified by memory:

> One day when I was not yet four, a funny thing happened. A military band, something I delighted in all my childhood, came marching past our house one morning. I no sooner heard it than I shot out of the living room. Wearing scarcely more than a chemise (they hadn't dressed me yet) I trailed after the soldiers with my little accordion until some time later a couple of ladies from nearby discovered me at the market-place. By that time I was feeling a bit frightened and they said they would only promise to take me home if I played them something the soldiers had been playing, on my accordion. I did so straight away, upon a fruit stall where they set me, to the utter delight of the market women, cooks and other bystanders. At that, amid shouts and laughter they bore me back to my parents, who were already in a panic over my disappearance.
>
> —[Johnson: 12–13]

Whether or not Mahler's voluntary memory of the incident is embellished or not, there is no doubt that the involuntary memory of an infanthood exposed to the sounds of military music found its way into his work as a mature composer. The way children absorb sound and the effect it has on long-term memory remains a fascinating phenomenon; likewise, there is a real ability which some adults possess to communicate with children in audio terms, a skill which is akin to regression into the childlike state oneself. In other words, it is given to some to call on the memory bank at a level not normally employed in daily adult life, directly touching the childish consciousness at the age when the young Gustav joined the marching band. It is a rare and important gift. Sound can be frightening, exciting or funny when it is unexplained, separated from the associations we place upon it through understanding, depending on the circumstances. The first experience of a significant sound or song may well be the one that provides a reference and a benchmark for all subsequent hearings of that sound. Often, for example, we may find it hard to judge a new version of a familiar song or a different interpretation of a symphony because the memory of the original is so lodged in our memory as to become the definitive model of the piece.

Gustav Mahler's childhood sound associations, both traumatic and otherwise, were put to use in his later artistic and cultural career; however, too often abuse and violence against children can create a memory trauma that has the potential to become a virus with the capacity to spread beyond the growing child, infecting others and ultimately society in general. There are many circumstances when memory and the sounds associated with it are better left untapped, or alternatively dealt with as a matter of urgency through therapy and care. The psychotherapist and campaigner for child care and rights Camila Batmanghelidjh has described memory and its effects in the cases of young adults, grown from disturbed backgrounds, as a ticking time bomb, and it brings us to a point of discussion on an area of fundamental importance in the relationship between memory and sound. In situations of fear, threat and danger, the brain releases large amounts of adrenaline; this enters the limbic system, our emotional centre, and affects the electrical and chemical activity there. In young children, sound, because it is such a potent part of our development, touches the consciousness at a visceral level, and when that sound has negative associations, whether it be threatening, unexplained or related to abuse of some kind, it becomes part of the stimulus for this adrenal overload at the same time as the young person is perhaps experiencing periods of chronic fear. Proust's memory of his father's voice, the lost staircase up which he climbed to his room, his mother and the sound of his sobs is touched on elsewhere in this book; the long-term effects of childhood sound memory is still being analysed:

> We've now got scanning ability that shows us that children who've been chronically maltreated have deficits in structure and functioning in key areas of their brain, and what the studies are showing is that our genes determine the boundaries of our development. How we develop is entirely dependent on the conditions of care we've been exposed to. If you have in your genes the capacity for aggression and the capacity for kindness, if your environment is constantly demanding of you to negotiate circumstances of violence and violation, then the aspect of your genes responsible for negotiating aggression will be up-regulated in the service of survival.[7]

On the other hand, if we have organised cognitive capacity, we have the ability to memorise sanctions so that when we come to a point in our lives where we find ourselves about to commit wrong, we may have enough control to arrest the forward move of the act and subsequently remember that sanction to affect future behaviour. Part of that 'full stop' in our action may be related to a sound association. The ability to self-regulate in this way is crucially linked to our past, our childhood and the nature of care we experienced there. All this is developed—or not—in the frontal lobe of the brain, the area concerned with empathy, exercise of personal control and regulation of emotion and energy. Interestingly, a rewiring of the frontal lobe takes place during adolescence, so these aspects of behaviour are weaker during teenage years, only to strengthen again in later life. Children who experienced poor care or abuse in infancy or early childhood are already vulnerable due to underdevelopment in the front lobe, the horror of their memories and the fear of sounds and actions stored in the mind, and their predicament is compounded by the changes in this part of the brain during teenage years, making for a potentially toxic cocktail of neurological elements. In the young child, 'the adrenal glands release "fright" hormones, these encapsulate the whole event completely, everything is memorised and delivered straight to the emotional centres of the brain.'[8] Later as they grow, children may remember these potent early experiences in spite of attempts to suppress them, often unlocked by an act or a sound that replicates in one or more ways the chemical and electrical circumstances of the earlier abuse. Thus, a four-year-old child that was continuously beaten and shouted at may as a teenager be subjected to vocal abuse in any given set of circumstances and find themselves motivated to respond in revenge on behalf of the violated child they once were. This can have a dangerous knock-on effect; if abused children go on to abuse non-abused children, the virus spreads, and further, it is now believed that the alteration in expression within the brain in the early years 'becomes base-line genetic programming for the next generation', so the infection of wrongly programmed children has the potential to unhinge society catastrophically.[9]

Empathy works both ways; just as we need to create the appropriate quality in the young through appropriate care, the other side of the same coin is that in order to understand children we need to regain in a positive sense part of the child in ourselves, and here sound is of the greatest value and importance. The earliest sounds of human communication—sounds even before words—are attainable only when we find ourselves able to remember how it was and how it felt to interact as children. This skill is given to a relatively small number of people; when the children's television producer Anne Wood, the director of Ragdoll Productions, sought adult voices for pre-school programmes, she encountered the issue first-hand. Ragdoll had a long history and much experience in the field, notably as creators of such well-known early learning programmes as *Teletubbies*, which appeared first on British TV in 1987 and ceased production in 1999 after 365 episodes. The series continues to be shown to new generations of young children in 120 countries around the world. Although the programmes are linked by a narrator, the four central characters themselves are wordless, although not soundless, and the sounds they make do not require translation for their audience. Creating those sounds carefully, however, is crucial if they are to communicate at the right level, and without condescension. This requires performers—voice-over artists—to have regress to childlike consciousness, to 'remember' accurately what it was—and is—to be a child. Sometimes this is not possible, perhaps because of a traumatic experience in childhood that effectively shuts down the desire to communicate with earliest experience. For Mahler it was an unconscious comment on his musical world, for others, particularly those working with children, it can be an inhibiting factor, as Wood experienced when auditioning voices for *Teletubbies*:

> One of the actors just couldn't do it, he couldn't get back to the required innocence. But the Chinese girl who we did eventually use was an

interesting case; she had come to Britain as a child of seven or eight years old, so English had been her main language from that time. Initially she couldn't get the right quality, until the language consultant we were working with discovered that in her early childhood she had spoken and thought in Mandarin. That was significant, because while she was thinking in English, she couldn't get back beyond the age of seven, and I was asking her to get back to three or four, and that's quite hard to do. Once she found a way to think in Mandarin again, she was OK.[10]

Often, this is an instinctive thing; some performers can attain a state of naivety quite naturally, as though part of their consciousness has retained the deep memory of childhood. Others find that worldliness can be an obstacle: 'There's a lot of cynicism in the world. Stand-up comedians find it hard to achieve this quality because there isn't a lot of innocence around.'[11] For Wood, the work of finding a way back to the right voice, the right sound, is the hardest thing she encounters in her programme-making for young children, and it is largely a question of tone. Sometimes voices can be adjusted technically to subtly help attain the innocence of expression, and occasionally a non-actor may be used to achieve a gentle unselfconsciousness that will communicate with children of three years old, sharing a naivety with a group for whom language is just coming within the grasp. Sound is extremely important, both through language and as a pure 'music', because many children are acutely sensitive to the audio experience; frequently such children prove to be extremely articulate, and by fostering sonic curiosity the programme maker is helping to develop thought and communication at a crucial stage of development.

The former staff BBC radio producer Gill Davies formed her own production company, GDP, in 2008, and has latterly specialised in producing material for the CBeebies online player. For Davies, memory is extremely important, and many of her programmes build on interaction between generations. In 2012 she made a series under the title *My Play*, in which pre-school children were introduced to the concept of history through listening to parents' and grandparents' memories.

> The older generations featured in the programmes had vivid memories of sounds as they described their childhoods. This was important to engage the pre-school audience: for instance, a grandmother remembered the sound of water bubbling in a pot hung over an open fire when she told her granddaughters that her family did not have a bathroom in the house when she was a child, and used the water to fill a tin bath.[12]

This is oral history, the communication of the memory of sound through words. Elsewhere in her work, Davies has encouraged children to listen out for and remember sounds they encounter in everyday situations. 'Recordings were made with parents and children on trips on public transport, visiting the seaside, going for a walk in the woods, and visiting swing parks, for example'.[13] Her work in multimedia production has involved the making of games, websites and applications for the BBC's children's channels, and 'within production teams, there was as much emphasis on producing high quality soundtracks as there was on producing high quality graphics. By combining image and sound to synthesize information, the experience for children is made far more effective. Sound is unquestionably as important as graphics, particularly because many computer-based games include a storytelling element.'[14]

It cannot be assumed that a child is sharing a programme experience—either through pure sound or sound and vision—with an adult family member. Indeed, Anne Wood's research shows that increasingly children are experiencing programmes alone, thus taking out of the equation the element of interaction that has often been assumed to play a part in early development in the past.[15] As the child grows to the age of seven, they increasingly become in control of the new and developing technology through which they absorb their entertainment and learning. This is a key change from previous generations, for whom adult influence was the control. Children of the twenty-first century gain control of the technology much sooner, be it computer, tablet, smart phone or games console. As the changing media gradually replaces traditional carriers such as radio and television, for programme makers such as Anne Wood and Gill Davies, content remains king. In Wood's words: 'However they consume it, it doesn't affect the way we make our programmes, because what you're looking for is a point of emotional engagement, and if the emotion is not engaged, then the memory won't work.'[16]

Davies feels strongly that shared listening experiences have the capacity to result in long-lasting sound memories. 'If children are more likely to shut themselves off from the sounds around them as they wear headphones to play computer games, perhaps they will be less likely to have memories of sounds from home or from their local environments?'[17]

It is an ironic side effect of media development that listening to radio, and now other audio devices, has travelled full circle; the first wireless receivers were machines rather than pieces of furniture, and could only be listened to via headphones. The coming of the amplifier and loudspeakers made radio a communal, family experience, shared and remembered together. Portability has reclaimed audio for the personalised, solitary world with a return to headphones, and at the same time re-appropriating the word 'wireless' in a new context. The sociological implications of such developments are potentially far reaching and may well affect cognitive relationships. If the emphasis is on audio in the broadest sense, and access is completely personalised, or perhaps a radio programme is listened to retrospectively via a computer, it may be that a generation of children and young adults growing in the first decades of the twenty-first century are the last to have traditional radio memories.

In some ways—through social networking and mobile technology—children are more connected to their peers than in previous generations, while in others they are physically less connected, often sitting in their rooms, playing computer games and separated even from the rest of the family. This phenomenon is not limited to youth; mainly governed by the mobility of the electronic communications with which we surround ourselves, we have developed a new kind of private independence. In previous times, even quite recently, family memory, particularly of social life and entertainment, came through communal experience; a common space in which the family watched television, and a single, shared family computer in a fixed place such as a home office. Thus the community of adults and children within a household had just one or two family reference points for memory. Since the beginning of the twenty-first century this structure has dramatically changed; Jacqui Taylor, Assistant Professor in the Psychology of Education in the School of Design, Engineering and Computing at Bournemouth University sees this as one of the negatives of modern technology-led life: 'The house has become more fragmented, everyone in a different room, to the extent that one parent will be working in one room, the other in a separate space and the children somewhere else on their own. It cannot be a positive thing.'[18]

Entertainment content is experienced in solitary situations, and the potency of this experience is not mitigated by sharing and conversation. Yet in 2013, the British media regulator Ofcom produced research that claimed to demonstrate a return to older-style family gatherings around living-room television sets through a small rise in communal TV viewing (91% in 2013, compared to 88% in 2002), but with the significant change that many of those watching were also attending to mobile 'phones, working on connected devices such as tablets or laptops, and being generally distracted by either related or unrelated media. Multi-tasking will be increasingly complementary in our media experiences, but at one level, while it can underpin and consolidate the content, on another it can dilute and blur the focus. It is important also to stress that the 2013 Ofcom research targeted 'adults' which the report defined as being 16 years or over. The implication is that there are in many households, important members of the family left outside this circle, whose activities are unmonitored.[19]

These findings also confirm another aspect of our changing cognitive interaction with the world around us in the form of the phenomenon known as 'Divided Attention Disorder', an issue related to constant multi-tasking that results in difficulty in focusing on one thing at a time. We are becoming conditioned by the technology with which we surround ourselves to the point where we are becoming more and more used to (for instance), operating a computer for a writing project whilst listening to music, and even simultaneously conducting a telephone conversation. Jacqui Taylor points out that teenagers are increasingly finding it difficult to attend to one thing for a concentrated period of time, clearly a problem when it comes to study. 'From an observational point of view, as a lecturer, I'm aware that I structure my lectures differently these days; I might divide a session up into smaller sections, say blocks of ten minutes, interspersed by perhaps pieces of sound or video, rather than say a full half hour of "solid learning".'[20]

The relationship between visual images absorbed through computer screens and through televisions with the use of gaming consoles, together with the intensity of sound accompanying these images, often coming at high volume through headphones, creates an artificial world, the memory of which can have an effect on how we relate to our physical environment. 'Certainly there are a lot of positives that come from video gaming skills; tactical decision-making, turning ideas into practice. On the other hand, with the music and sounds heightening emotional responses, parts of the brain, particularly in the more aggressive games, are stimulated into a "fight or flight" mode, which is really not good, because the stresses are cognitively taxing.'

> Scans have shown the make-up of the brain changing in children who have been playing a lot of video games, to the extent that it's possible to differentiate between those who play aggressive games and those who play passive games. Different parts of the brain are being stimulated. It's causing deeper memory because of the overload from the different stimuli coming in.[21]

Research is divided regarding the relationship between violence on video screens and physical violence as a resulting effect. Nevertheless, it seems clear that as a result of the intense experience of these personal activities, something can change in the brain that affects our responses to the everyday world on a subconscious level. This is a kind of memory-related event that is psyche changing:

> Playing violent video games may not lead to violent behaviour, but it does develop parts of the brain that are desensitised later on. Because of this desensitising, we may not consider some things to be as serious as we should. So it affects the perception of crime and aggression and violence. This may not be translated into real aggression, but further down the line, it could be.[22]

Understanding sound impulses in children can tell us much about the role audio plays in memory as we grow. Key to early life learning is repetition. Anne Wood has observed that when a preschool child is played a sound or an image that makes them laugh, it becomes successively more amusing each time it is viewed or heard. 'Unlike most adults; if I tell you a joke, it may be funny the first time and you may laugh, even on a second hearing you may smile, but if I keep telling the joke, soon it will lose its humour. With young children, it is the opposite: it gets funnier with successive plays, and by the sixth or seventh time, it is completely hilarious!'[23] It has to do with narrative, expectation based on previous experience and the fulfilment of that expectation. Alison Gopnik writes of episodic and cued memories in very young children, and the beginnings of personal narrative in the growing child. [Gopnik: 138–40]

Cued memories are significant in the humour of repetition described by Anne Wood; as Gopnik explains: 'In an experiment I might give you a list of words and either ask you to remember as many of them as you can or tell you one word and get you to remember the next one. For all of us, cued memory is easier than free recall, but the difference is much greater for preschoolers. They have terrific specific memories when they are cued but have a very hard time with free recall.' [Ibid: 139–140] When the cued memory is linked to an amusing story or set of images, the anticipation works with the narrative, and the child is complicit in the process.

We may perceive a similar process in the elderly, just as we may recognise an element of this in ourselves as a response to certain recorded sound-based comedy routines. While a single one-line joke told by a stand-up comedian may pall if retold repeatedly, we may enjoy sharing and passing on the humour to a third party. When the joke is expanded into a more extended narrative, that is to say, when it becomes a story, its capacity for retelling becomes more durable. During the 1950s and 1960s there was a trend for recordings of comedians and raconteurs such as Gerard Hoffnung, Shelley Berman and Bob Newhart, who would tell extended stories in front of an audience, shared with the record-buying public through the medium of long-playing vinyl. Many of these routines—based on sound and quality of voice, inflection and tone, became regular radio favourites, and request shows received many demands for them to be included. They thus became the speech equivalent of a favourite song, sometimes memorised by the listener in minute detail but still capable of eliciting an amused response. We love the idea of knowing 'what happens next', and then the gratification of the confirmation. Comedy catchphrases operate in much the same way. As we grow out of infanthood into puberty, we respond to repetition too in our popular music, and music producers understand the importance of a strong 'hook' in a song, creating recordings that capitalise on a theme, repeating it incessantly within the production, (often to the despair of older generations), burning it into the memory. In the next chapter, we will explore music memory in more detail.

NOTES

1. Moon, Lagercrantz & Kuhl. 'Language Learning Begins in Utero.' Pacific Lutheran University. December 2012. www.sciencedaily.com/releases/2013/01/130102083615.htm (accessed April, 2014).
2. Gobnik, Alison, *Amazing Babies*, http://edge.org/conversation/amazing-babies (accessed June 2013).

3. Ibid.
4. Katrina Porteous, communication with the author.
5. Respondent, online survey, *The Memory of Radio Sound,* conducted March–May 2013. See Appendix for a closer examination of some of the issues emerging from this survey.
6. Ibid.
7. Camila Batmanghelidjh, Oxford TED talk, 2012, http://tedxtalks.ted.com/video/How-to-Help-our-Most-Vulnerable Accessed April, 2014 (accessed April 2014). Batmanghelidjh's work as a psychotherapist is linked in the most practical and humane ways to her work with the children's charities she has founded in London, such as *Kid's Company* and *The Place to Be,* organisations that continue to work with young people with challenging behavioural issues that have resulted in them being labelled them as 'hard to reach'.
8. Ibid.
9. Ibid.
10. Anne Wood, interview with the author, May 2013. The Ragdoll Productions website provides useful insight into the history, development and working philosophy of the company: www.ragdoll.co.uk (accessed June 2013).
11. Ibid.
12. Gill Davies, personal communication with the author.
13. Ibid.
14. Ibid.
15. Post-war generations of UK children will have heard the BBC's preschool programme *Listen With Mother,* a fifteen-minute daily broadcast of songs, poems, activities and stories originally transmitted directly after *Woman's Hour;* both the timing and the title imply the act of sharing between adult and child. The programme ran from January 1950 to September 1982.
16. Anne Wood, interview with the author, May 2013.
17. Gill Davies, personal communication with the author,
18. Dr Jacqui Taylor, interview with the author.
19. Ofcom Report, 'The Reinvention of the 1950s Living Room', July 2013, http://stakeholders.ofcom.org.uk/market-data-research/market-data/communications-market-reports/cmr13/uk/ (accessed July 2013).
20. Dr Jacqui Taylor, interview with the author.
21. Ibid.
22. Ibid.
23. Ibid.

5 Music Memory
Music in the Moment

In March 1985, the musician and broadcaster Clive Wearing was struck by herpes encephalitis, a virus causing inflammation and subsequent damage to the brain, in particular the areas connected with memory. From having a normal, active life, with a thriving career as a musicologist, Wearing, in his mid-forties, was in a situation where his entire history, the 'back story' of his life, had been erased, as well as his ability to create new memories; events, experiences and people were wiped from his brain within seconds.

Wearing's case became famous, partly because a patient's survival from encephalitis had, up until this time, been extremely rare. The improvement of drugs to treat the condition, however, meant that he lived after a long period of unconsciousness, and his condition—dense amnesia—could therefore be observed and studied. Another reason for the fame surrounding this case was a BBC television film made by Jonathan Miller entitled *Prisoner of Consciousness*, broadcast in 1986, which brought the tragic story of Clive and his wife, Deborah, to public awareness.

So severe was Wearing's amnesia that he believed constantly that he had just emerged from unconsciousness, even months and years after coming out of the initial coma. Thus, if Deborah were out of his presence for just a moment, only to return almost immediately, he would greet her as if he had not seen her for months. One of the most poignant aspects of his condition was his awareness of it; he would write down a time, then cross it out and write down a new time minutes later and so on, all to attempt the retention of a present that might somehow become a retrievable past. Landmarks for some reason remained with him, such as the school or Cambridge college he had attended, but beyond that details had gone. The same blankness was present when confronted by images or works of famous people: the author of *Romeo and Juliet* was beyond him, as was the identity of the Queen of England when presented with a photograph.

Remarkably, there was one part of Wearing's life that seemed somehow to be well preserved, and that revolved around music. Prior to his illness he had directed a choir, and on one occasion, in an experiment created for the BBC film, he was invited to conduct these singers, the London Lassus Ensemble, once again in a performance of—appropriately—*Musica Dei*

Donum (*Music the Gift of God*). In her remarkable book, *Forever Today*, Deborah Wearing very movingly describes what happened next:

> He lifted his hands—and then he was conducting. It was second nature to him. The music's own momentum carried him from bar to bar. Inside a piece of music, Clive was in time once again. To perform music you need only the phrase you are in. While the music sounded Clive had structure, a context, safe ground. For the time he is in the music, provided it is taking his full attention, he forgets the abyss at his back. He has continuum. But when the music stops, he falls out of time all over again.
>
> —[Wearing: 243]

The explanation of this is linked to the mystery of music itself and its relationship to time, which is constantly moving through a permanent present. Clive Wearing's condition locked him consciously into this continuum, causing him enormous anguish, but because sound—and in this case music—is effectively time made audible, the experience of it is constantly current. The brain absorbs a newly heard piece of music on both a conscious and a subconscious level, and when this occurs we are very actively absorbed in learning, processing information that we then store, pending retrieval. As Oliver Sacks has said: 'When we "remember" a melody, it plays in our mind; it becomes newly alive . . . We recall one note at a time and each note entirely fills our consciousness, yet simultaneously it relates to the whole.' [Sacks: 227] Sacks goes on to quote Victor Zuckerkandl's elegant statement of this phenomenon:

> The hearing of a melody is a hearing *with* the melody . . . It is even a condition of hearing melody that the tone present at the moment should fill consciousness *entirely*, that *nothing* should be remembered, nothing except it or beside it be present in consciousness . . . Hearing a melody is hearing, having heard, and being about to hear, all at once. Every melody declares to us that the past can be there without being remembered, the future without being foreknown.
>
> —[Sacks: 228]

This statement—in particular the last sentence—is profoundly important for the understanding of how sound and music can help us when memory fails. During the 1950s, British youth was absorbed with the idea of making rather than simply listening to music, and nowhere more than in Liverpool, the city that was shortly to give birth to the greatest popular music phenomenon of the twentieth century. Among the boys swept along by this tide of sound was a young man called Phil Robinson. Phil played in a skiffle group, the Crossrocks, and the music they played came from influences such as the Chas McDevitt Group and other bands of the time.

Many years later Phil was diagnosed with Alzheimer's disease. As the condition progressed, his family explored ways of recovering aspects of the man they had known. His son Colin, now a lecturer at Liverpool John Moores University, retains a vivid recollection of the role of music in these attempts:

> During the many times I visited him in the months before his death, I started to experiment with music as a way of sparking his deepest memories. Skiffle naturally featured on the playlist with Lonnie Donegan's "Pick A Bale of Cotton" always being a useful record to help us converse, but there is one experience I'll never forget. The memory of seeing him re-emerge from his illness for just a few brief minutes when I played Chad McDevitt and Nancy Whiskey's "Freight Train" is perhaps one of the difficult experiences of my life. As the tune started up with its wonderful rhythm I heard my father sing again, his voice changed and soared, his smile was wide and for those brief few minutes as he performed, we all sang along and the father *I knew* was there. As the tune faded out his face faded too and he was gone.[1]

To some extent the present tense of music helps to explain the ability of professional musicians to play extended works without the aid of music; in the classical concert hall, it is usual for a soloist to play a long, complex work with an orchestra without the help of a score. On occasion a conductor will direct a whole orchestra from memory, although this is less common. The legendary conductor Arturo Toscanini suffered from very poor eyesight, a condition that had afflicted him from his childhood, and as a result he frequently conducted without a score, having committed the work to memory. G. R. Marek, one of Toscanini's biographers, pointed to a remarkable example of the maestro's memory just before a concert, when an oboe player in the orchestra told Toscanini that the bottom note on his instrument was not functioning. Toscanini thought for a moment and then replied, "It is alright, that note does not occur in tonight's concert." [Baddeley: 24]

As with many musical geniuses, Toscanini had been immersed in music from a very early age, and this, combined with his visual disability, was a crucial factor in his development. At the age of nine he went to Parma's Royal School of Music and gained his degree at eighteen in 1885. It is clear that his absorption of music was total and that it mirrored his speech development. The connection between speech and music is fundamental; both involve pitch, volume and frequency. Both are patterned, shaped and structured. We have invented bars and movements just as we speak in phrases and sentences. Speech IS music, and both speech and music begin their influence on us as pure sound from before birth. The process of learning language is strongest up the age of seven; in the context of our relationship with music it is important to establish how significant the link between speech and music is from the very earliest experiences of life. Schnupp, Nelken and King have shown that a useful analogy with the acquisition of language is with songbirds:

> Young birds learn their songs by listening to adults during an initial sensitive period of development . . . After this purely sensory phase of learning, the birds start to make their own highly variable vocal attempts, producing what is known as "subsong," the equivalent of babbling in babies. They then use auditory feedback during a sensorimotor phase of learning to refine their vocalizations until a stable adult song is crystallized.
>
> —[Schnupp, Nelken & King: 277]

The link between speech and song is here movingly demonstrated, and the phenomenon of musical child prodigy explained to the extent that we begin to understand how deeply rooted our sensory cognition of music is, and how important a part of our sense of self it is. Music and speech are one.

Memory is strange. There are times when it seems to touch on something else, something that is instinctual and primal. The act of composition, the 'hearing' of a melody or chord cluster, harmonies and other phenomena within the mind, retaining these and then transmuting them to the instrument or to paper, involves a short-term memory transference that the composer Jonathan Harvey has called 'reordering', a process beyond conscious thought. [Harvey: 22] Many composers have noted this in one form or another, among them Mahler, Stravinsky and Richard Strauss. In particular, Johannes Brahms is extremely lucid on the process of regaining the germ of musical inspiration:

> The idea is like the seed corn; it grows imperceptibly in secret. When I have invented or discovered the beginning of a song . . . I shut up the book and go for a walk or take up something else; I think no more of it for perhaps half a year. Nothing is lost, though. When I come back to it again, it has unconsciously taken a new shape and is ready for me to begin working at it.
>
> —[Fuller-Maitland: 69–70]

ABSORBING MUSIC MEMORY

Given that music operates at such a significant level within our being, it is hardly surprising that its presence in our consciousness forms a key part of who we are. This has been understood by music programmers on radio stations for many years, and it is the policies of skilled scheduling that exploit our sense of a past, for example within the output of 'Gold' or 'Golden

Oldie' networks. In his play *Private Lives*, Noel Coward has one of his characters say, 'Extraordinary how potent cheap music is'.[2] How we define 'cheap music' may be down to personal opinion and taste, but it is nonetheless appropriate to say that our memory is informed by music's ability to recall for us a place, a person or a time in our lives. This is particularly true of the formative teenage years, when we are experiencing life and emotions for the first time; thus, if music schedulers wish to tap into our past and through that to engage our attention, it is likely that they will programme music that touches on these experiences. It is easy to prove this oneself; someone who was thirteen in 1959 might consider the first significant popular music carried forward from that time to be, for example, that of Buddy Holly and The Crickets. That same person, reaching the age of twenty-one in 1967, in common with many of the same generation, might recall the key musical event of that year to be the release of The Beatles' *Sergeant Pepper's Lonely Hearts Club Band* album. Within the boundaries of those years and those artists lies the musical landscape of that generation's youth, and to play songs from this terrain is almost certain to trigger a response—if not direct recollection, then certainly familiarity. This is of course not to say that music from earlier or later in one's life does not have the power to stimulate responses; however, the seven or eight years of our growing up from child to adult will always remain the most potent in terms of music/memory stimulation.

This is actively taken into account by 'oldies' radio stations such as the Gold network in the UK, formed out of a merger in August, 2007 between the Capital Gold network, started in London in 1988, and the Classic Gold network, which had its origins in the same year. For some time, Gold had as its target audience people aged fifty or over. Latterly, however, there came a noticeable shift in general daytime programming, from playing classic artists such as Frank Sinatra, Elvis Presley, Nat 'King' Cole, Como, etc., in favour of more contemporary artists of the past fifteen years or so, thus capturing a generation of teenagers who had now reached their thirties. Explaining this change, the Programme Director Adrian Stewart, cites an ever-ageing target demographic:

> We are playing less 1950s tracks nowadays and quite a few more from the 1970s, and latterly we have added more songs from the 1980s too. Songs from the 1960s are still dominant in our rollout though, as this was the decade that defined so many ground breaking moments in music history; it was a decade when trends were set and new genres of music were born.[3]

Even taking this into account, music radio aiming at a particular age group clearly will be required to 'refresh' its output periodically to take into account generational changes because, self-evidently, ageing is an ongoing process. Just as the target audience for a contemporary teen music station has to keep up with its clientele, so does a company in the business of evoking memory. The radio consultant Paul Easton has put this into a chronological context:

> At the turn of the 21st century, if you were targeting, say, a 45+ audience then your listeners would have been born before 1955, while someone in their early 50s in 2000 would have been one of the post-war 'baby boomer' generation, and in their teens during "Beatlemania" and the 1967 "Summer of Love". 45 year-olds in 2010 (who would have been born in 1965) became teenagers during the rise of Punk and the 70s Disco boom, while the baby boomers were by then in their 60s. Meanwhile, the British Teddy Boys of the mid-1950s were at least in their mid-70s.[4]

It would also be over-simplistic to associate one kind of popular music—and therefore potential memory—with any particular time. Any decade is full of diverse musical styles, and not all will appeal to everyone who lived through that time. In Britain, for example, 'the 1960s started with pop from Cliff Richard, Pat Boone and Helen Shapiro. Then came The Beatles, The Rolling Stones, Tamla-Motown and Soul (from the Atlantic and Stax labels). 1967 saw "The Summer of Love" which, in turn gave us flower power and Psychedelia before eventually spawning the birth of Progressive Rock. That's quite a musical journey!'[5] Likewise, it must be kept in mind that time divisions such as years and decades are arbitrary; we use them to mark out our lives because it shapes the temporal space we live in and provides us with reference points. Cultural events happen *in* a particular period, of course, because of circumstances rather than because of a unique significance attached to a date. An era is not an accident of chronology but a coming together of disparate influences, be they political or social; the memory is from the *zeitgeist*.

> There's no defining marker between the decades. The early-60s had more in common with the late-50s and, similarly, it could be argued that the start of the 70s, musically, was actually around 1968/9. A song's appeal is also a factor. In mid-1960s Britain, both The Beatles and Ken Dodd were enjoying chart success but the kids would be more likely to be buying the former while their parents would go for the latter. If you're targeting those who were kids in the '60s then you play The Beatles.[6]

Commercial radio, dating back to its very beginnings, has always found it essential to conduct stringent audience research, given that it is required to demonstrate to its advertisers and sponsors the power of the medium. As Stewart says, breadth of appeal is crucial: 'If we were to become too obscure and niche with our playlist, audience levels would fall and we would not be commercially viable.'[7] Research involves working with regular listeners to rate potential additions to the playlist according to the engagement felt with a song from the past, with memory recall playing a major part in how high or low each song is scored. 'We ensure that we offer up a good cross section of oldies taken from the 1960s, 1970s and 1980s, together with a mix of genres, male/female/groups etc., and a variety of tempos. It's not as rigid as some people think; we are very keen nowadays to ensure that there isn't too much repetition, but we do have to maintain the quality in terms of familiarity and popularity.'[8]

From childhood and right through our lives, our personal memory archive accumulates associations that relate sound and music to situation and place. As we have seen, and as Stewart confirms, this is particularly so in our formative years and beyond:

> We believe that music plays a big part in a person's life from the age of puberty through to the late twenties; this period in someone's life is full of "first time" poignant moments such as memories of school and college or university, their first car, their first boy or girlfriend, their first kiss, falling in love, leaving home, getting married and so on.[9]

As we grow older, it becomes easier for us to identify such landmarks; later we shall examine the nature of nostalgia, and without doubt music is a major trigger for a sense of a 'golden age'—hence the Gold Network and other stations around the world that use the name. We move from a present tense to a past tense increasingly as time passes, generally becoming disengaged from current popular trends and more rooted in music as a signifier of personal history. For the radio producer Clare Jenkins, working with speech radio and in oral witness, this exercise in music memory is as potent as it would be for any listener:

> The sound of Motown music takes me to my first boyfriend's Morgan car. Those years are so vibrant, almost psychedelic when you're living them, and the music stays with you because it's associated with that, embedded in your brain, so when you press the button, the host of memories of how you were at that time, growing up, experiencing everything for the first time, it does come back very clearly.[10]

The effectiveness of this trigger is, ironically, reduced by the number of times a tune from the past re-enters our current lives. The 'gold' stations, playing the hits from the past, do our links with that past a disservice if their playlists are too limited, so a song from youth becomes associated through repeated plays with the present rather than personal history. It is the element of surprise, of being caught unexpectedly, off guard, that sends a direct message to our memory, unfiltered by intermediate associations. Levitin has written, 'As soon as we hear a song that we haven't heard since a particular time in our lives, the floodgates of memory open and we're immersed in memories. The song has acted as a unique cue, a key unlocking all the experiences associated with the memory for the song, its time and place.' [Levitin: 166]

As we have seen, radio in the car can be an extremely powerful catalyst for such an event due to the secondary nature of the listening experience. This is captured perfectly by the poet Dana Gioia in 'Cruising with the Beach Boys'. So germane is this evocative poem to our discussion that it is worth reproducing it in full here:

Cruising with the Beach Boys

> So strange to hear that song again tonight
> Travelling on business in a rented car
> Miles from anywhere I've been before.
> And now a tune I haven't heard for years,
> Probably not since it last left the charts
> Back in LA in 1969.
> I can't believe I know the words by heart
> And can't think of a girl to blame them on.
>
> Every lovesick summer has its song,
> And this one I pretended to despise,
> But if I was alone when it came on,
> I turned it up full-blast to sing along–
> A primal scream in croaky baritone,
> The notes all flat, the lyrics mostly slurred.
> No wonder I spent so much time alone
> Making the rounds in Dad's old Thunderbird.
>
> Some nights I drove down to the beach to park
> And walk along the railings of the pier.
> The water down below was cold and dark,
> The waves monotonous against the shore.
> The darkness and the mist, the midnight sea,
> The flickering lights reflected from the city–
> A perfect setting for a boy like me,
> The Cecil B. DeMille of my self-pity.
>
> I thought by now I'd left those nights behind,
> Lost like the girls that I never could get,
> Gone with the years, junked with the old T-bird.
> But one old song, a stretch of empty road,
> Can open up a door and let them fall
> Tumbling like boxes from a dusty shelf,
> Tightening my throat for no reason at all
> Bringing on tears shed only for myself.

—[Gioia: 5]

Gioia's poem eloquently captures the way music can come under our conscious *radar* and surprise our emotions. As in the poem, this can be about a state of being, restoring the way we were as people, our habits, idiosyncrasies and immaturities even more than about specific interactions; it is a connection with the emotional being we were, time exposing that person again, interrogating them in today's light through experience and by turning the past into a new present through the power of song. There is, however, another possibility already suggested, that the preponderance of 'gold' stations, playing songs from the past twenty-four hours a day, can make us impervious to a sense of the musical past; in a way all music becomes 'current' music through playlisting, to the extent that, for example, 1960s songs lose their specific place in time and memory. Additionally, music does not necessarily provide instant access to personal history for everyone, and even when it does, is that Beach Boys song reminding me of a lost time in my youth, or have I now heard it so many times on an 'oldies' station that it has finally lost its ability to shock me into memory, in the way it did for Dana Gioia? The radio futurologist and consultant James Cridland considers this to be a possibility:

> I wonder whether the abundance of music radio has destroyed our musical 'past'. I know plenty of songs from the 1960s to the present day. Very little remind me of anything. I know (because I used to have to announce these things) when songs came out; but actually, I heard most of the 1960s tracks when working for a gold station in the early 1990s. I didn't grow up to music radio, and didn't have much relationship with music in the 1970s or 1980s. To me, music has no relationship with time.[11]

MIXING IT

The answer for some to the homogenous nature of the musical past peddled through playlists has often been to personalise memory in order to share it on a one-to-one basis. Today the MP3 player provides us with the opportunity to carry our own individual music station with us wherever we go, but the desire to create the ultimate personal statement is not new. The technology may not lend itself to sharing so much now, but historically there have been times when, particularly during teen and twenty years, individuals have been fired to cohabit important songs with those they care for, highlighting either their own personality through music or sending a message, an emotional calling card. The audio cassette was notable in this respect, and its appropriation by a generation for mix tapes supplied a raft of memories, not only of songs but of times past and relationships lost. It is a poignant idea, perhaps subconsciously fuelled by the fact that music, like youth, is fleeting and evanescent. The mix tape may also have been of particular help to young males seeking to express feelings they find hard to verbalise as well as musical taste. The era of the compact cassette and the cassette recorder was a key part of the preservation and sharing of radio and music memories.

Compact cassettes were devised in 1963 by the Dutch company Philips and first manufactured on a mass-production scale from 1964; their presence was a major factor in home recording from then until the late 1980s and early 1990s amongst young people. The portability and versatility of the product, and the ease with which recordings could be made, was immediately attractive to a music-hungry teenage market, particularly so when the machines became integrated into domestic sound systems, enabling 'quality' recordings direct from other sources such as the radio and records. From this grew the youthful phenomenon of the 'mix tape', cassettes of personally selected music often given from one person to another, not only establishing an individual taste and ego, but also helping to shape—or break—a relationship. Jason Bitner, an American journalist and researcher into the significance of ephemera, explored this in a book of personal memories from individuals who were asked to recall significant mix tapes from their pasts and the person their sound evoked for them. In his introduction, Bitner states:

> Mix tapes are like personal time capsules. Not only do you get the physical tape and homemade artwork, but you've got memories attached to each of the handpicked songs . . . No matter how the relationship ended, the mix tape lasts as a physical reminder of what took place between those two people.
>
> —[Bitner: 1]

The most prolific period for mix taping lasted from the late 1970s until the 1990s, after which new technology began to impact cassette recording. Later, however, old tapes that had been intended for use as current communication began to acquire a nostalgia factor for a number of reasons: firstly, as we have seen, they were the memory of music that had been important at a key time in life, secondly, they often reflected a relationship, and thirdly, they represented a technology that linked past and present in its very form and shape. Bas Jansen has written that mix taping 'began to reappear in a number of cultural narratives in novels and essays which calibrated its meaning from an innocent pastime to a socio-cultural practice of existential significance.' [Bijsterveld & van Dijck: 43]

Notable among these was Nick Hornby's 1995 novel *High Fidelity*, later a highly successful film by Stephen Frears. In mix tapes, the music is seldom an end in itself; it is as the catalyst for the evocation of memory that the sound is most potent: 'While memories may have been mediated by the *objects* of rerecorded music, it is through *stories* about mix tapes that their memorial value became personally and culturally significant.' [Ibid.: 44] As a tape plays and the songs unfold in their carefully selected order, memories awaken and anecdotal recollections may be articulated, evoked by the structure and order of the content on the tape; each song may be a separate entity, composed and performed by an individual artiste or band, but the overall shape of the 'programme' itself is authored by the maker of the tape themselves. 'It holds together, in the closest possible proximity, some of the building blocks of what it is like to be this person and to exist in connection to music, technology, people and ideas in a certain place and time.' [Ibid.: 42]

When all else fails, a song can give us our past again; Sally Goldsmith, a poet and musician who has worked with dementia patients, points out that this can operate at a very subtle level, and the signs can easily be missed:

> If you know something about the person's history—even if they have no speech left—it's possible to communicate through music. A lady I once worked with had lost her speech, but I knew two things about her: firstly that she was Scottish, and secondly that her family had been involved in music. So I sat with her, singing every Scottish song I knew, and as I sang, I could feel her hand in mine, gripping tighter and tighter. With dementia, music is one of the last things you appreciate; there's something about the patterning of words and music together that goes into the memory.[12]

Proust explored both voluntary and involuntary memory in his novels. Circumstance may trigger a memory of a song whether we like it—wish it—or not. The phenomenon of 'Ear-worms', songs, sounds or phrases that follow us through a day, are a familiar and often annoying part of ordinary life, but neuroscientists such as Oliver Sacks and Wilder Penfield have explored extreme cases of something even beyond involuntary memory: the sense of something patients have described as akin to a radio playing music in the mind at high volume, coming between them and their sense of the outside world due to an impairment in the auditory, or temporal, lobes of the brain. Sacks has referred to this condition as 'Musical epilepsy'. [Sacks: 143–44] As an example, he cites a patient in the United States who he refers to as 'Mrs. O'C', who found herself after a stroke subject to incessant high-level Irish music, which initially disturbed her, coming as it did between her and her ability to interact with the world around her. Subsequently, however, as it began to wane, she came to gain some affection for these sounds, linking her as they did with her childhood in Ireland, taking her back away from old age in a New York care home to the very beginning of life, feeling her mother's arms around her, hearing her voice singing. Oliver Sacks, invoking the previous research of Wilder Penfield, felt that:

> Such epileptic hallucinations or dreams . . . are never fantasies: they are always memories of the most precise and vivid kind, accompanied by the emotions which accompanied the original experience. Their

extraordinary and consistent detail, which was evoked each time the cortex was stimulated, and exceeded anything which could be recalled by ordinary memory, suggested to Penfield that the brain retained an almost perfect record of every lifetime's experience, that the total stream of consciousness was preserved in the brain, and, as such, could always be called forth, whether by the ordinary needs and circumstances of life, or the extraordinary circumstances of an epileptic or electrical stimulation.

—[Ibid.: 145]

PERFORMANCE MEMORY

Music is part of our being, and our response to it is extremely personal; it is also true to say that part of its potential power for us is not only as a listening experience but also as performance. The idea of music as a positive creative force within us (as in the case of Clive Wearing) and its potential to stimulate memories of past lives is something worth reflecting on. Just as an artist sees and remembers a landscape or a form more intensely because he or she has focussed their attention on it with a view to reproducing it in a drawing, so for the musician the sound of a particular tune may evoke a memorable moment from the past in which that melody played a part through performance. The composer Stephen Deutsch, born in New York, finds himself able to evoke mentally his experience of being, as it were, the self he was when he was younger, with the engine of the time machine being music relevant to that era of his life—in many cases, a specific piece:

> The piece was Rachmaninoff's *Melodie*, op3. I can see the room in which I was playing it, the brownish wall paper which I was looking at (the upright piano was placed against this wall), and sensing the adoration of the girl-friend sitting next to me.
>
> It's true that nowadays, when I begin my practice of long buried pieces, I seem to evoke the place where I once played them, fleeting snapshots of what I saw around me as I played them before. The music itself (that is, were I to hear it in a recording) seems not to have such a direct connection to those images as when I play it myself. But as a composer, sometimes the mention of a piece sets up an 'ear worm' in my brain. When I was a motorcyclist, touring Europe, snatches of these worms used to add to the regular hum of the engine. To rid myself of the less desirable of them, I would set my mind-player to listen to Brahms' 2nd Symphony, for reasons which are now obscure to me. Nowadays, that piece occasionally seems to take me back to the saddle.[13]

Taken further, there is an intensity in the act of committing music to memory, and the retrieval at the appropriate time, when required, can draw on hidden resources in a professional performer. A dramatic example of this occurred when the concert pianist Maria João Pires was on stage and about to play a

Mozart piano concerto with the Amsterdam Concertgebouw, conducted by Riccardo Chailly, only to hear the orchestra begin playing another concerto by Mozart, not what she was expecting or had prepared for. Fortunately the duration of the orchestral introduction enabled the soloist to recover the correct music from her memory, and the performance was uninterrupted.[14] With concert performers leading a busy international life of travel, rehearsal and varied concert performances, such occurrences must be an occupational hazard. As with an actor speaking lines in a play, ideally, once the work is under way there should be a domino-like effect of logical inevitability, where the permanent present of the note-by-note journey through the music that Clive Wearing experienced carries the performer onwards. Tim van Eyken is a musician, folksinger and actor, and finds common ground in performance memory. It is not unusual for performers to find themselves unable to recall words or notes when outside the context of the performance, only to regain them, as if by magic, when the context is restored. This is what happened to Maria João Pires in her Mozart concert. An actor may speak the same lines night after night in a long run of a play, only to discover that the day after the run ends they are unable to recall a word, a phenomenon familiar to van Eyken. After finishing a six-month tour of the play *Birdsong,*

> I was struggling to recall lines when asked! Actors have so many different ways of learning lines. My preferred method is to learn thoughts rather than lines, then the lines attach themselves without me having to think about them. The only problem with this is that I sometimes have a quick panic in the wings before I go on because I can't recall my lines, but that of course is because I am trying to think about the words rather than the thoughts. The same sort of thing goes for character—I try to jettison ideas of a character I'm playing in favour of thoughts I can have as that character. This doesn't even seem like memory to me, more like finding a different way of looking at the world, which once found is just "there" for the using.[15]

It is when concentration lapses, when something takes the performer outside the box of their focus, that things break down. When this happens, even for a moment, the needle sticks in the groove and the present becomes a temporary prison, something from which to escape. The cellist Steven Isserlis remembered experiencing a mental blank during a cadenza in a live performance, and found himself deliberately playing the same phrase over and over in an attempt to seek the progression forward. 'I remember seeing expressions of bewilderment and concern on the faces of the first rows in the audience. Fortunately, just in time, the memory returned and we continued.'[16] Stephen Deutsch has reflected on the issue of memory linked to the creation of sound without the aid of musical notation:

> It is a curious phenomenon. There is a combination of kinetic, aural and pattern memory which all comes into play. Of course, of the three the

kinetic is the least reliable under tension. My teacher, a pupil of Walter Gieseking used to tell me to memorise pieces *before* I played them, by visualising the keys going down as I played. This worked for him, and for Gieseking. I had less spectacular results, but it did save time in learning music.[17]

Performance of music from memory takes us into a world where the creation of the melody may become almost instinctual, moving us beyond recollection and into interpretation. In the realm of folksong, as Tim van Eyken explains, there is sometimes a curious shared memory, collective and personal, that perhaps moves beyond music itself:

> It is very common for people who haven't previously heard a folk song to say they feel as if they have always known it. I can remember as a child having exactly that sense. Now in my own case my Mother is a folk singer, so perhaps I could remember it from my earliest awareness before I was even born. But I'm inclined to believe that folk songs tap in to an innate human experience which people identify with, regardless of their experience or exposure.[18]

It is communication at a deeply emotional, even spiritual, level, and a number of composers, such as Olivier Messiaen and Jonathan Harvey, have explored this through parallels with birdsong. Once we begin to examine the relationship between music and the natural world, we become preoccupied with genetic memory, generational learning and imitation drawn from external and inherited influences. For the RTE Radio 1 programme *Sound Stories*, the wildlife sound recordist Chris Watson recalled recording the song of a starling in the ruins of an abandoned farm croft on an island in the Outer Hebrides. The building was a ruin, with no roof and only bare stone walls still standing, and the bird had made a nest in what had been the dwelling's main living room. 'I heard straight away that this wasn't the usual rambling starling song. These birds are great mimics, and the sounds were familiar, although they certainly weren't part of the normal song of a bird.'[19] As Watson recorded the starling's song, he looked around more closely at the environment in which he found himself. He noticed the remnants of an old tractor, disused for twenty or thirty years on the abandoned farm, and an aged, rusted pump, half hidden in the overgrown garden. It struck him that the bird was singing the song of this machinery. How could this be? Clearly this was not the same bird that had heard these sounds in their original form, yet somehow a song had been recalled from its ancestors, passed on through this particular avian family that was strongly rooted to one place, learned, mimicked and copied and handed down as a kind of avian oral history of the place.

> The strange thing was that I was sitting recording this in what had been somebody's living room, and the people had passed into history, but the

birds had claimed back this space, and were not just singing their own song, but ironically singing the songs of the things that were around when the people were there.[20]

The purity of music memory as performance—whether such a performance may be classed as memory or as evidence of a form of Darwinian evolutionary voice—is a moving link with the human motivation for music making, perhaps similar to the handing down of folk song from one generation of singers to another.

NOTES

1. Colin Robinson, communication with the author.
2. Coward, N., *Private Lives*, Act 1, 1930.
3. Adrian Stewart, Programme Director, Gold Network, UK, interview with the author.
4. Paul Easton, communication with the author.
5. Ibid.
6. Ibid.
7. Adrian Stewart, Programme Director, Gold Network, UK, interview with the author.
8. Ibid.
9. Ibid.
10. Clare Jenkins, interview with the author.
11. James Cridland, communication with the author.
12. Sally Goldsmith, interview with the author, 2013.
13. Stephen Deutsch, personal communication with the author.
14. *The Daily Telegraph*, 26 October 2013.
15. Ibid.
16. Stephen Isserlis, interview with the author.
17. Stephen Deutsch, communication with the author.
18. Tim van Eyken, communication with the author.
19. Chris Watson, in conversation with Luke Clancy on *Sound Stories*, Series 2, Episode 1—"Endangered Sounds" Broadcast 8pm Tuesday, 1 August 2006 on RTÉ Radio 1. Producer: Kevin Brew.
20. Ibid.

6   Ourselves as History
An Encyclopaedia of Sounds

HOME RECORDED VOICES

We are all archivists; it is part of human instinct to collect the material evidence of existence, be it books, records and CDs, photographs or letters. It may be that this instinct is a subconscious attempt to hold on to the invisible force of time or to preserve something material that confirms the journey thus far; as we rummage back through the library of memory, a physical aide-memoire offers us clues, stimulates forgotten situations in the mind and recalls circumstance. The instinct to collect is in all of us, some more so than others. Later we shall consider the role of public archives as part of collective memory, yet it is collective only insofar as it is gathered to one place; each book, artefact, disc or sound file had its origins in the personal, in the hands and mind of an individual. Walter Benjamin was correct when he wrote that 'the phenomenon of collecting loses its meaning when it loses its personal owner. Even though public collections may be less objectionable socially and more useful academically than private collections, the objects get their due only in the latter'. [Benjamin: 67][1] For the private collector, the personal archivist, the moment of acquisition is a major part of the object's history and relationship with its owner. It is the origin of souvenir-hunting, be it a book of local history, a phial of coloured sand or a pilgrim badge. In his essay, Benjamin was considering book collecting, but he ranges wider and deeper than a single instance when he tells us that 'everything remembered and thought, everything conscious, becomes the pedestal, the frame, the base, and the lock of . . . ownership—for a true collector the background of an item adds up to a magic encyclopaedia whose quintessence is the fate of his object'. [Ibid.: 60]

Objective collecting is one thing: the preservation of artefacts associated with our own lives and intimate memories is quite another. It can be a melancholy pleasure to browse through personal history, and it is perhaps because of this that we tend not to question loved ones as much as we should about shared pasts and memories. Memory is too poignant, recollection is too often not only the remembrance of things past, but also the recalling of things lost. This is particularly true of the human voice—poignant too, because unlike the objects with which we surround ourselves, it is invisible.

In December 2008, the radio producer Andy Cartwright of Soundscape Productions and I made a programme for BBC Radio 4 with the title *Home Recorded Voices*. In it, we sought to explore the phenomenon of domestic taping that developed in the 1950s with the appearance of home recording devices such as inexpensive reel-to-reel tape machines and, later, the audio cassette. The development of tape—even in professional circles—was remarkably slow in countries other than Germany prior to the Second World War. The coming of portable technology that liberated the work of BBC producers such as Charles Parker in the late 1950s was a key factor in the development of location-based recordings and the unlocking of memory through field recording; nevertheless a large number of studio managers in broadcasting institutions remember playing recorded material into programmes from disc even up to the early 1960s. Given that, it is interesting to note that the Dutch company Philips introduced a domestic tape machine to the market as early as 1953, with a battery model available from the following year. Philips led the way in the domestic market, issuing a stereo model in 1958. As we have seen, in 1963, at a time of popular music expansion and ultra portable technology in radio receivers made possible by the use of transistors, the compact cassette was introduced, creating an explosion in home recording, although principally for music rather than for speech and 'found' sound. Even prior to the cassette, however, home taping enabled the development of the audio letter, and companies marketed small reels of tape ready-packaged for postage, seeking to attract families who had been separated through post-war emigration, overseas military service and so on.

It was this period, in which the novelty of the tape recorder seemed to provide an audio equivalent of the exchange of family photographs, that *Home Recorded Voices* sought to explore. The programme had as its centrepiece an extraordinary collection of tapes collected over many years by Richard Harrison, a lecturer at Norwich College in Eastern England. Harrison had gathered the material through online and traditional auctions, car boot sales and word of mouth. In addition to the Harrison collection, the production company making the programme invited listeners to submit material of their own; the result was an eclectic and often moving mixture of material that told us a great deal about the varied motivations behind home recording. The coming of domestic recording facilities tapped into an appetite among many people—particularly males—who had been wireless operators and technical assistants during the Second World War; in this, it mirrored a similar tide of interest amongst military communications professionals in the First World War, something that undoubtedly fuelled the early development of radio in Britain.

The recordings included impromptu performances, recitations, children's games and audio letters. What was notable amongst many of the taped letters was the degree of ease and informality amongst the speakers; given that a number of these recordings dated from the 1950s and 1960s, at a relatively early stage of home recording, the ability of speakers to overcome 'microphone-shyness' came as a surprise. Also remarkable was the sense of detail; perhaps because of the idea of a preserved record, speakers were frequently very particular about setting the scene in audio terms: such phrases as 'it's March 9th, it's 4.30pm, and I've just made a cup of tea' were typical openings.[2] Examples of audio material included travelogues—there was a moving and highly professional recording of the Last Post at the Menin Gate in Ypres, Belgium—and family stories and memories, caught in interviews with often elderly relatives. In both these cases there communicated a poignant sense that the sound was more potent and more lastingly important than even a photograph.

Sometimes there were accidental finds; tape recorders of the time were capable of recording several tracks, and on occasion there would be the bonus of a long-gone radio show on the reverse of one of the home recordings. The appeal was clearly manifold. The novelty of hearing one's own— or another's—voice was seductive, and the seeming magic of instant replay made for an added wonder. Above all, the overriding sense was of preserving memory, of holding the moment against the tide of time. One sound recordist had almost obsessively recorded all the most significant incidents in his life, including the moment of his engagement and the birth of his daughter. The man's wife had died in the intervening years, and listening to this recording with him for the programme, decades after he had made it, was a powerful experience, really too personal for an outsider to hear without discomfort, but deeply emotional for the tape's owner as we witnessed in sound his late wife's cries and then the birth itself. It was something more than memory: it was the event itself.

The programme delved back to the very beginnings of home recording, taking us to a home in Salisbury, Wiltshire, where a local family, using an Edison home recording cylinder kit, sang Christmas songs, laughed and played the piano in December 1917. The sounds were anonymous, no name was on the recording, but here were children and their mother, hoping father would return from the front soon, caught informally in the way that a posed photograph could never achieve. The eloquence of sound as memory was powerfully demonstrated and was directly linked to the home-made podcasts of today, created and uploaded from private locations and shared globally, all part of a dual desire to communicate and preserve ourselves.

*

Sound recordists and radio producers possess an advantage over others in domestic chronicling through the form of sophisticated means to capture intimate sounds, and the skills to shape them into something poetic, meaningful and significant to a broader world beyond the personal. The poet and radio producer Michael Ladd, working for ABC in Australia, based a poetic feature on recordings he made for the first five years of his daughter's life. The sounds were captured every six months from birth. The resultant programme was *One Voice Through Time*, a piece Ladd refers to as a radio poem:

> You could call them sound-works or sound poems but I always conceived of them as radio poems because I always intended for them to be received via broadcast. I was trying to track down the point at which her sounds turned into words but it happened suddenly so it became something else: a record of one voice through time. It used sounds and vocalisations, and fragments of childish speech, plus imitations and responses from a trumpet, picking up on melodies, intonations and rhythms in the speech. It was short, (less than six minutes), emotional, and worked through evocation, not exposition.[3]

In early 2013, the sound recordist Mathieu Ruhlmann issued a CD entitled *This Star Teaches Bending*, exploring the last illness of his mother through sound recorded at the time. The title was taken from a work by the artist Paul Klee, and references Klee's last illness[4] from 1935 until his death in 1940, and his philosophy under the shadow of that illness to bend to the blows of fate. Ruhlmann's sound piece is in five movements, the title of each being taken from paintings Klee completed in the last year of his life: *Captive, this World/Next World*; *Eidola: Erstwhile Cannibal Man-Eater*; *Stilleben*; *The Hour Before One Night* and *Whence? Where? Whither?* Taken together, the work is an unflinching attempt to capture the moment, and is cumulatively a moving commentary on mortality through the impersonal sounds of machines and everyday environments that become significant in memory through their place as witnesses to human suffering. As Ruhlmann explained, circumstance changes the meaning of sound:

> In May 2012, my mother was given a 6 month life expectancy after being diagnosed with a rare lung condition. She was informed there was no available cure. The recordings . . . explore the medical equipment used to help treat her disease, as well as the surroundings and environments pertaining to the terminal illness that my mother acquired, recorded over a 6 month period.[5]

The sounds of such inanimate objects as a compressed air pump, an electronic heart rate monitor, a respirator and even a rubber glove being picked up and put on, the unemotional music of everyday hospital life, become a commentary on the struggle for survival, as they acquired new meaning in Ruhlmann's memory. Through the process of listening, they also enter the memory of the listener by suggestion; these are environments and sounds that may well be familiar—or may yet become so to us. Even the sounds of Place on a broader level, a raccoon or the hospital car park, become part of the narrative; when the enormity of a situation touches us through an understood context, it is often the everyday in its prosaic detail that registers in our minds. This is a drama, understated and apparently unemotional, seeming to exclude the human element completely; in fact, on the contrary, the power of the recordings lies in the implicit presence of the central character. The dying woman is always there, although just 'out of shot'. *This Star Teaches Bending* is the product of a machine recording machines, one might almost suggest, a dialogue between non-human agencies. This would of course be to miss the point, because in both the transmission of the sound and its capture, as well as the editing process, the human is the unseen protagonist. Ruhlmann is using his recording device to 'interview' the inanimate. The process is curated; it is an extension of the human desire to preserve the personal moment, an impulse we usually associate with recording the voice. Yet even when we do that, we are recording also the place and the time, the room acoustic, peripheral sounds and the accidental small occurrences around us. We live—and sounds occur—in a world where other lives and events go on, regardless.

In 2012 the radio producer and oral historian Clare Jenkins made a thirty-minute documentary feature for BBC Radio 4 called *Dad's Last Tape*. The genesis of the programme had been Jenkins' discovery of a series of recorded interviews she had made some years before with her father. The programme was about remembering, and in particular it was about the sound of a voice. Importantly, it was also—for the most part—built on recorded conversations between two people who knew one another intimately, and the recalling of one personality—now no longer present—by another through sound. These conversations were a hybrid of formal interview and relaxed familiarity, and the subtle structure that the act of recording brought to the table enabled them to fulfil an editorial function in the programme-making process, while existing at another, highly personal level for Jenkins and her family.

Often, our memory of loved ones is defined by the end of their lives, when they are, inevitably, too frequently untypical of themselves and unable to do justice to the force of their personality when in health and the full vigour of life. Family recordings offer us the person we knew, they are the sonic equivalent of a street photograph of a known and loved place, special for the very reason that they provide us with a memory of a day and a place when life was normal, even ordinary, and thus they are deeply touching in recollection for that very reason. The asides, the heard smile that reveals the person, even the stumbles and unedited hesitations—all these give us our loved ones back to us in a way to which written stories and recollections themselves can only contribute. The latter is the documentary, the former is the human.

The power of the voice to recall a personality is so strong that, while we may cherish our recordings of loved ones, we may find it difficult to confront their sound: it is a preserved part of the physical person in a way that goes beyond the visual remembrance of a snapshot in a family album. A photograph is a moment in time, a split second of existence. The sense of the place or the person immediately before or after its taking is lost to us. It can be an aide-memoire, but it can seldom compare to the experience of listening to sound for a sense of the living human. This is because a recording is temporal; it *has* to be experienced in terms of time. As we passed through time when we made it, so we pass through time again as we listen. Because the recording of the voice we are listening to, even if it is the voice of dead person, moves along on this temporal journey, for the time it plays we have a feeling that that person lives again, and we regain their presence. This came home strongly to Clare Jenkins when reviewing material for the programme: 'I'd forgotten until I heard his voice on the tape, how strong my Father's Scottish accent was. I knew he was Scottish of course, but I'd forgotten how Scottish he sounded.'[6] The process she underwent, from the commissioning of the idea by the network to the completion of the project, placed her as a professional broadcaster in an unusual position: radio producers are used to dealing with material objectively, yet it is hard to be objective with such startling reminders. This shock of forgotten familiarity, of the grain of sound that gave us the person in life, is something that touches a profound need in us, sometimes hard to deal with because sound is temporal and fleeting in a way that a visual image is not. The programme that resulted from the process begun by Clare Jenkins out of a personal reflection tactfully explored the nuances of grieving and memory in others:

> We know that people will keep answering machine messages, to hold on to the voice. It's part of the person, like a lock of hair. In the programme, a lady with terminal cancer who had made recordings of herself for her grandchildren, said that she'd not wanted to record 'because that isn't my voice anymore. But then I thought, " well, it's the best it's going to be now".' People get very sad when they tell you, "I can't remember his voice". It is an essential part of somebody.[7]

Yet through an act of concentration, sometimes we *can* find that sound again. It is a curious fact that the sound of a voice can exist silently in memory. I can 'hear' my father's voice, recorded there in my mind, but I cannot reproduce that sound as a physical tape or memory card could; I cannot share it, except perhaps in some kind of genetic way, in which I may deliver unconsciously in my own speech sounds and patterns echoes of ancestral voices. The human voice is often handed down from generation to generation, and in so doing, as part of our familial fabric, it is also part of our genetic memory. The playwright and broadcaster Rony Robinson can hear his brother's voice in his, and their father's voice in both of them: 'It's like looking at those old brown photographs of dead relatives; you can see the resemblance, you know they're family because you can see it. So if facial characteristics can be handed down, why not vocal characteristics too?'[8] Clearly the voice changes through age, while retaining an essence.

We can recognise the voice of someone we have not seen for years after a few words on the telephone, without visual clues. Likewise, occasionally a strange thing can happen when interviewing the elderly: as the past is recalled and relived, an old voice can actually grow younger in the telling. A kind of vocal regression occurs, giving back to people themselves in sound as well as their recollection.

The ability of memory to regain ourselves and our past through the combination of dramatisation and documentary gathering was demonstrated to Rony Robinson when he started working with oral history as a dramatist at Stratford East in London, interviewing people in extreme age, sometimes with dementia, about their youth. These interviews formed the basis of the material for a play, but performed by actors in their twenties and thirties: 'For the audience to see themselves young again was amazing; in a funny way they *became* young again. There was something in the chemistry of the process that made them young again, especially the act of giving them a young body with a young voice to tell the stories that had come out of them.'[9]

THE USES OF NOSTALGIA

The word 'nostalgia' comes from two Greek roots, *nostos*—return home, and *algia*—longing. The word was coined in 1688 by a Swiss doctor, Johannes Hofer, who perceived it as a medical condition afflicting people displaced from their native home, such as immigrants and soldiers. According to Albert von Haller, 'one of the earliest symptoms is the sensation of hearing the voice of a person that one loves in the voice of another with whom one is conversing, or to see one's family again in dreams'. [Boym: 1]

Sometimes it is perceived as a negative quality, something relating to a 'golden age' which is largely illusory. This perception is unhelpful in two ways: firstly, as we have seen, personal memory is just that—personal. It is therefore not only acceptable but also probable that we have fallible recollections of our past, shaped and retained according to our wishes and often simply the activities of time. Secondly, nostalgia is a fundamental part of what makes us want to remember and is linked to the desire to retain and tell our stories. There are, as Svetlana Boym has written, at least two different kinds of nostalgia, one of which being what she calls 'restorative nostalgia', a condition (if one might call it that) evoking national pasts and futures, whilst the other, 'reflective nostalgia', is to 'be aware of the gap between identity and resemblance; the home is in ruins, or, on the contrary, has just been renovated and gentrified beyond recognition'. [Ibid.: 50] The two forms can overlap at times, but the same triggers of symbols and memory can apply to both, whilst different types of story emerge from those triggers. Reflective nostalgia in Boym's view feeds off the distancing of people from the event or place, actually strengthening the imaginative bond by longing and fond recollection, distance blurring the reality or selecting truths from the original event, and generating a new energy from that mythologising; hence the power of folk song, folklore and story to shape a sense of belonging.

> This defamiliarization and sense of distance drives them to tell their story, to narrate the relationship between past, present and future. Through such longing these nostalgics discover that the past is not merely that which doesn't exist anymore more, but, to quote Henry Bergson, [Deleuze: 59–60] the past "might act and will act by inserting itself into a present situation from which it borrows the vitality".
>
> —[Boym: 51]

This would seem to relate directly to the experience of the partnership between the elderly storytellers and their young interpreters at Stratford East cited by Rony Robinson. A longing for home may be seen as a metaphor; home is a past for which there is a known story, be it good or bad. It has a safety about it because we have memory of it and therefore it is evidence of our life. In the improvised present, anything can happen, but in the past, things are fixed: the past made us what we are. We have explored the power of music to evoke memory in every generation, demonstrating that the memory of the past evoked in a sound or a song is potent. Music we may understand in its broadest sense as strongly evocative sound, either organised, spontaneous or natural. The song of a particular bird or the sound of water gently lapping on a shoreline at morning can have the same effect, and often strikes home with the most emotional power in the shadow of change or uncertainty.

A sound can also have the power to confirm a memory that was in some cases expressed through the written word or a photograph. This was demonstrated powerfully by the novelist Elizabeth Darrell in a personal piece of recollection she was kind enough to share for this book. In 1993, Darrell's father and husband both died, the effect being that she found herself grieving for herself whilst seeking to comfort her own bereaved mother. The family had been a military one, and Darrell's childhood had been spent in Hong Kong, where her father had been stationed. She had few recollections of this time, but had grown up with family memories and photographs which evoked it strongly in her imagination. In the year 2000 she revisited Hong Kong, now much-changed after many years and a lifetime of writing.

> My first visit was to the famous Peninsula Hotel, where my parents had met army friends for tiffin, and where the annual regimental ball had been held. I used a convenient side entrance, and was instantly disappointed to see just the same designer shops found in every prestige hotel. Then a faint sound of music drew me along a corridor. I turned a corner, and found myself in another era. Amid potted palms, white-coated

waiters were serving the most elegant English afternoon teas, while on a small minstrels' gallery, a palm court orchestra played those melodies so beloved of my parents. I was immediately overwhelmed by the strength of their presence there. It held me motionless, and brought the tears I'd been unable to shed for them until that moment.[10]

Since that time, Elizabeth Darrell has returned to Hong Kong on a number of occasions, always recreating exactly the same process of entering the hotel and rediscovering the experience, following the traces of the music and entering the room where the sound remains a common link between her and her parents' present. In her words, 'they are always there'. Memory is active, nostalgia is a creation built from memory and sound is a key building block. As the American sociologist Fred Davis wrote:

> Generational nostalgic sentiment . . . creates as it conserves. It creates because the past is never something simply there just waiting to be discovered. Rather, the remembered past like all other products of human consciousness is something that must constantly be filtered, selected, arranged, constructed, and reconstructed from collective experience . . . The nostalgic creation is . . . a special kind of creation, one powerfully permeated in feeling and thought by a conviction of the essential superiority of what was over what is or appears destined to be.
>
> —[Olick, Vinitzky-Seroussi & Levy: 450]

There is, Davis suggests, a positive, even necessary and desirable aspect to nostalgia: 'learn from your mistakes', 'heed the lessons of history', as the sayings go. We live increasingly in a kind of permanent present, pushed by technology and societal peer pressure into a future towards which we are propelled headlong with little time for consideration. The memory of how things were, initiated by a sound that brings with it its own nostalgia, causes a hiatus, a pause in this headlong rush, 'perhaps enough of a brake to cause some individuals and peoples to look before they knowingly leap'. [Ibid.: 451]

*

Before there was a multimedia world of artefacts and devices in which the word 'wireless' came to denote Wi-Fi, the identity of the carrier itself was almost as important as the signal it communicated. In an era of vinyl records, the sleeve and its artwork provided information and a visual context for what was to be found within. The LP record, more so than the CD that replaced it, was a physical incarnation of—and appendix to—the particular sound culture it represented, be it jazz, classical or pop; it was a statement of and context for its owner and subsequently became an object of some veneration to a society that had grown used to the invisibility of music. A record collection, like a library of books, tells oneself and one's friends and acquaintances a lot about character, taste and personal history. The restoring of past time through the fixed record of a moment mediates nostalgia and seemingly defies mortality through such mediation. As Michael Bull has written, 'the history of mechanical reproduction is . . . a history of the increased ability of people to create patterns of instant recall in which they conjure up real or imagined memories of home, place and identity'. [Bijsterveld & van Dijck: 85]

Likewise with radio. From the start, because the medium was invisible, the receiver was important. Initially a machine (because its origins lay in military and utilitarian use rather than domestic and entertainment), as the purpose changed it was adopted into the home and turned into a piece of furniture. The 'wireless' received wireless signals. Subsequently the military term 'radio' became the norm, but the same identification of the object with the medium persisted; radio was listened to on a radio set. With the coming of television, the radio, far from being subsumed and replaced by the new medium, became ubiquitous within the home; in many houses there was a radio set in almost every room, and the object came to be identified with the part of the house in which it was situated. Again, with the passage of time, these objects became things to which people became personally attached, in a way that never happened with television sets and computers. Many would find it hard to part with an old transistor radio, while not thinking twice about replacing more recent technology. This is curious, but the reasons are perhaps to be found in the nature of the thing itself, the direct through-relationship between medium, object and audience. For many, the radio set has been a companion, just as the voice from within it has been a friend.

From the 1920s, when the medium first gained mass interest, manufacturers identified this fact. Companies such as Marconi, Pye, RCA, Kolster Brands and others designed receivers that were intended to blend with home furnishings, initially with the same longevity as sofas, sideboards, drinks cabinets and so on. The object complemented the lifestyle and became a familiar part of daily surroundings, belonging to the fabric of the private home. This quality of companionship continued into the portable age; with the coming of battery-powered transistor radios and later digital receivers, imaginative manufacturers built characteristics of retro style into their designs, incorporating wood and leather to provide the object with a feeling of timelessness and stability. The sound may be invisible and ephemeral, but its physical representation at least should preserve the security of permanence and continuity in its appearance.

The nostalgia of objects has been much exploited by retail manufacturers over generations. Because we surround ourselves with things as part of our physical lives, these become part of memory; this applies particularly to objects related to sound, be it a radio or an old record player. José van Dijck has named this 'Technostalgia', a phenomena through which our attachment to an object grows through the ageing of the object itself and its physical link with a past that is ever receding. Such an object is a gramophone record, be it much-treasured vinyl or a fragile 78 rpm disc. As we have seen, the very word 'record' is a clue to its temporal significance in that the term originates as a reference to a *record* of an event. Thus the event is the memory, and the object is the tangible mnemonic proof that it occurred. As van Dijck has said, 'media technologies and objects are often deployed as metaphors, expressing a cultural desire for personal memory to function *like* an archive or *like* a storeage facility for lived experience'. [Ibid.: 111]

During research into pre-war UK radio and listings magazines, Dr. Julia Taylor of Bournemouth University became immersed in the idea of the relationship between the object as carrier of sound memory and its symbol of that memory, to the extent that she established a retail outlet (since closed) selling authentic and retro radios near her home in Dorset. *Hamworthy Radios* was created from the start to be in appearance less of a shop and more of a combined time capsule and museum: 'It was set up like a 1930s domestic lounge, with a fireplace, some armchairs, and pictures on the wall. In other words, it was like a stage set, into which people walked, and found themselves suddenly transported to another time.'[11] The emotional effect of this could be quite profound, as visitors were subjected to memory cues from the items around them that evoked an era appropriate for the age of the radios in the shop. It was the jolt of involuntary memory, a moment of recollection that took a person by surprise and subverted their emotional defences. 'Because visitors believed they were just walking into a radio shop, they were not emotionally prepared for the experience they were opened up to. So sometimes they were happy memories, and sometimes there was regret at the loss of the object—as a metaphor for a lost time of life. People DID get emotional, and we found ourselves acting as listeners as a whole stream of consciousness opened, and poured out memories of parents, and life beyond the radio itself, but evoked by its reappearance in their life.'[12] Radios can be much more than simply an appliance, and listeners from a certain era will often have memories of major events—the outbreak or end of war, or famous international happenings—associated or directly linked with the receiver through which the news came.

Given the nature of the object, there is of course a fracture in perception between the visual and the aural. However evocative the image of the radio may be, a working model will betray itself as soon as it speaks or sings; it comes as a palpable shock to hear a vintage 1936 receiver fill a room with a contemporary music station. We find it hard to believe, somehow, that a radio signal is not the same thing as the radio that gives us access to it. 'One lady brought a 1940s Ekco set into the shop, and when I asked her if it stilled worked she said, "Oh yes, it can still get the Light Programme." When we checked the dial, it was indeed tuned to the old BBC Light Programme symbol, but that was certainly not what we were hearing!'[13]

Thus radios for several generations have carried sound that transferred to memory while becoming a part of memory themselves, and in so doing have become absorbed into our own histories. Audio nostalgia originates through this conduit in our consciousness, and can unlock evidence and witness that is at once personal and at the same time part of a broader community history. It is now clear that here is a valuable although transient resource that modern archival technology can capture and hold as part of societal memory.

PARTNERSHIPS IN PRESERVATION

While an awareness of a generational legacy through the spoken word has always been stronger in certain cultures than others, since the latter half of the twentieth century—partly fuelled by the increasingly sophisticated development in portable recording technology—there have been a number of initiatives in the Western world that highlight a growing democracy in oral history and interest in evolving language.

Ironically, however, one of the earliest examples of a comparative study of English as it is spoken came not from a country where the language is native, but from Germany.

The Berliner Lautarchiv British & Commonwealth Recordings held at the British Library are part of an audio archive made between 1915 and 1938 by German sound pioneer Wilhelm Doegen, who, with a number of academics, sought to capture the voices of famous people, languages, music and songs from all over the world, much as Edison had done in the late nineteenth century. Doegen's work, however, is significant in that it was supported by academic intent; it was a real attempt, using new technology of the time, to capture language in sound rather than transcription. The collection acquired by the British Library in 2008 comprises 821 digital copies of shellac discs held at the Berliner Lautarchiv at Humboldt University. It includes recordings of British prisoners of war and colonial troops held in captivity on German soil between 1915 and 1918 and later recordings made by Doegen in Berlin and on field trips to Ireland and elsewhere. The recordings often utilise texts from books read aloud, as well as word lists, speeches and recitals of songs and folk tales in a variety of languages and dialects. It is a unique resource, unlocking the memory of voices from the time of the Great War, and, like the Christmas cylinder recording of the Salisbury family in 1917 described earlier, provides us with a moving and powerful set of mental images into a distant time, insights that are somehow more potent than photographs or even film. The motivation for the exploration of our selves and our sense of belonging within a chronology and a place has expanded, accelerated and focused since the start of the twenty-first century, perhaps shaped by an underlying awareness of the importance of a sense of community in a fragmenting and fast-changing world, and framed by a number of significant initiatives in some ways not dissimilar to these early experiments. The Doegen recordings are an early example of the quest for preservation.

*

During 1998 and 1999, forty BBC local radio stations across the UK recorded personal oral histories from a broad cross-section of the population for a series entitled *The Century Speaks*. The result was a series of half-hour radio documentaries broadcast in the final weeks of the millennium, an initiative that went on to form the basis for one of the largest single oral history collections in Europe, the *Millennium Memory Bank (MMB)*, with extracts made available online through the British Library website. Contributors to this vast project were either recruited from established groups within the community or chosen from responses to broadcast appeals. The range of contributors was extremely wide: 56% of the interviewees were male and 44% female, with ages from 5 to 107 years old and drawn from a diversity of ethnic and socio-economic backgrounds. From the start, the aim of the project was to focus on local, everyday experiences; to this end, interviewees were encouraged to reflect on events and change within their local community rather than on the wider world stage.

Alongside the *MMB*, researchers using the British Library website can also access the *Survey of English Dialects (SED)*, a much older initiative dating from 1950–1961. The developments in mobile recording technology that were freeing radio producers and broadcasters such as Charles Parker from the confines of the studio were likewise contributory in enabling this nationwide survey of vernacular speech across England, which was undertaken by researchers based at the University of Leeds under the direction of Harold Orton. During these years a team of fieldworkers collected data in a network of 313 localities around the country, initially in the form of transcribed responses to a questionnaire containing over 1,300 items. Latterly, with access to portable equipment, locations and speakers were revisited, or contributors with similar social backgrounds identified. These unscripted conversations, recorded on location, are exercises in memory, focusing as they do on the extent of recollection into childhood, work, family and community life. The recordings themselves are mostly of rural male farm labourers. It had been intended to extend the project to urban areas; however, due to economic issues this was never accomplished. Nonetheless, the *Survey of English Dialects* remains a highly important witness to both personal and community memory carrying us back to the latter part of the nineteenth century, and it has been an exemplar for many related projects since it was created.

The two projects serve distinct purposes: the *SED* was a linguistic survey and the speakers were chosen specifically to reveal rural dialects, often in remote parts of the country, whereas the contributors to the *MMB* were participants in an oral history project; in the latter, therefore, the social range of speakers is far wider. Nevertheless, although the primary objective was to record thoughts and attitudes rather than speech patterns by the very nature of the *MMB* project, the English spoken has an extremely strong community and place-based resonance; thus for the student of language memory as well as social memory, these two projects provide a fascinating and valuable snapshot of a country and its people, using the emotional catalyst of the millennium end as a focus. Given the contrasting intentions, scopes and scales of the two collections on the BL website, the recordings are not strictly comparable, partly because the *MMB* is far more representative of the urban population. Nevertheless, for the web-based material there was an intention to select extracts only from interviews with speakers who had spent most of their life in a particular place, thus making the material representative of a particular speech community, in a selection process that gave precedence to contributions demonstrating significant linguistic features.[14]

Related to this and available through the same site is *BBC Voices*, an audio archive of 303 group conversations recorded by the BBC as part of a nationwide linguistic survey conducted between May 2004 and July 2005 by 46 local and national radio stations within BBC Nations and Regions and the independent Manx Radio. 'The intention on the part of the BBC was 'to take a "snapshot" of everyday speech and speech-attitudes of its United Kingdom audience at the start of the twenty-first century. It was seen as informing popular understanding of English and other languages, generating programmes for national and local radio and television, and material for the BBC website and publications.' [Upton & Davies: xii] Some of these were broadcast on BBC Local Radio throughout August 2005 and formed the basis of *Word 4 Word*, a six-part BBC Radio 4 series exploring language use across the country. In order to ensure the recordings were comparable with each other, every conversation followed the same loose structure and used the same set of prompts. Before a recording session, each interviewee was sent an identical set of thirty-nine common words and asked to think about the words and phrases they might use. This methodology, developed by researchers at the University of Leeds, encouraged contributors to supply responses as naturally as possible and to reflect on their words, their accent, their styles of talk and their attitudes to language. Each recording was accompanied by a PDF document containing a detailed linguistic description created during the British Library's *Voices of the UK* project, with a list of responses given by the contributors to each of the thirty-nine words.

Between November 2010 and April 2011, the Library used a number of these resources as part of the exhibition *Evolving English: One Language, Many Voices*, which explored the English language across national and international boundaries, placing artefacts and paper texts such as manuscripts of *Beowulf*, Shakespeare quartos and Caxton's printing of Chaucer's

Canterbury Tales alongside recordings of speeches by Pankhurst, Churchill, Gandhi and Thatcher, together with advertisements, examples of dialect and music from around the world.

*

In 2003, the United States producer David Isay created a project in which ordinary people, as opposed to broadcasters or producers, could preserve family stories and history in audio terms by recording conversations between them. He called the scheme *StoryCorps*, and it grew out of Isay's work for National Public Radio (NPR) during the 1990s, a series of documentary features that explored the concept of a broader form of radio journalism. Just as Denis Mitchell and Charles Parker had worked to democratise the medium of UK radio and television during the 1940s, 1950s and 1960s with the aid of the new tape technology of their time, I saw a way forward in the idea of effectively handing the medium of audio to the subjects themselves, creating at once a personal and national oral history archive. The immediate *StoryCorps* project came from of Isay's *Sound Portraits Productions* in 2003, located in the Fort Greene Neighbourhood of Brooklyn, New York. Historically, the model came from the Works Progress Administration (WPA), in which oral history written interviews were conducted across the United States from 1936–1940, part of a relief programme instigated by President Franklin D. Roosevelt. The Library of Congress collection for this project includes 2,900 documents representing the work of over 300 writers from 24 states. Typically 2,000–15,000 words in length, the documents consist of drafts and revisions, varying in form from narrative, to dialogue, to reportage, to case history. The histories describe the informant's family education, income, occupation, political views, religion, medical needs, diet and various other miscellaneous observations.

Another inspiration for *StoryCorps* was the work of the author, historian, actor, broadcaster and oral historian Studs Terkel, who cut the ribbon on the first *StoryCorps* recording booth at Grand Central Station, New York. During the 1930s Terkel had joined the Works Progress Administration's Federal Writers' Project, working in radio in a variety of capacities. His famous radio show, *The Studs Terkel Programme*, was broadcast on WFMT Chicago between 1952 and 1997 each weekday during those forty-five years. On this programme he interviewed guests as diverse as Bob Dylan, Leonard Bernstein, Alexander Frey and Jean Shepherd. Yet it was Terkel's conversations with 'ordinary' Americans that marked him out as one of radio's greatest interviewers and oral historians. In his obituary, *The Guardian* identified this aspect of his work:

> Terkel's obsessive interest in the propulsion of people's lives was at its most curious and passionate—and his subjects at their most brilliantly articulate—when he was dealing with everyday people, from whatever

background: carpenters, judges, hub-cap fitters, priests, admirals, sharecroppers, models, signalmen, tennis players, war veterans and cooks.[15]

Since the creation of *StoryCorps*, its mobile booths have travelled the United States, augmenting the permanent sites, now in Foley Square, New York, the Contemporary Jewish Museum in San Francisco and at Atlanta's public radio station, WABE. There is also a home-recording 'do-it-yourself' kit that can be shipped to participants to enable recording in a domestic environment. Through this method, as of November 2013, *StoryCorps* held 51,585 interviews in its collection, of which over 500 had been edited into broadcast pieces and made available on the website.[16]

The concept is straightforward: a person is interviewed, not by a radio journalist, but by a friend or relative, overseen by a *StoryCorps* facilitator. Each session lasts forty minutes, at the end of which participants receive an audio copy of the conversation, while a second copy is deposited with the American Folklife Centre at the Library of Congress. Edited versions of selected interviews are broadcast on NPR, and some may also be heard as downloads or via the *StoryCorps* website.

The placement of the *StoryCorps* collection is appropriate; the American Folklife Centre's Archive was originally founded as the Archive of American Folk Song at the Library in 1928. To date the archive includes over three million photographs, manuscripts, audio recordings and moving images. It consists of documentation relating to traditional culture from all around the world, including the earliest field recordings made in the 1890s on wax cylinder, through to recordings made using digital technology. The relationship between the AFC and *StoryCorps* is an interactive one; interviews are usually accompanied by colour photographs of the participants taken at the time of interview as well as supporting documentation, scanned by *Story-Corps* staff and stored as part of the collection. While some of the material as we have seen is available online from *StoryCorps,* it is only at the AFC premises that the entire collection is available for research access. In the meantime work is in progress within *StoryCorps*, through the work of Virginia Millington, Recording and Archive Manager, and her staff, to broaden the profile of usage:

> We are working towards making our enormous archive more accessible to the public, and are eager to grant more access to our collection. In the meantime, we actively encourage the use of our archive by researchers and journalists. We've had a great deal of interest in our special initiatives: two researchers are looking at Historias material (one focusing on ageing in the Latino community and one on the experiences of Colombians living in New York) and one is writing a doctoral dissertation using interviews from the National Teachers Initiative that investigates the way that teachers talk about teaching.[17]

In the next chapter, we shall explore the power of location sound and narrative to respond to—and to evoke—memory. In this field, *StoryCorps'* archives are already proving valuable as source material, as in the work of Krissy Clark, who has created *StoryCorps: Hear and There*:

> This is a "sound ramble" through Lower Manhattan using clips of *Story-Corps* interviews about Chinatown, the East Village, and the Lower East Side. We've presented the sound walk at two consecutive *Ideas City* festivals at the New Museum. *StoryCorps: Hear and There* was also assigned on a syllabus for New School classes on sound art called "Urban Soundscapes."[18]

*

In 2012, a BBC Radio 4 commissioning editor, Tony Phillips, adapted the *StoryCorps* model for UK development, under the title *The Listening Project*. For Phillips, it was a deeply personal enterprise; trained as a professional actor before joining the BBC, he had spent time as a young man searching for authentic voices, 'voices I could really identify with. One day I was in a bookshop, and I picked up a book called *To Be a Slave* by Julius Lester'.[19] Lester's book, written for a teenage readership, was a series of first-hand accounts by ex-slaves, and Phillips' attention was at once caught by a note in the front, the words of a man who had been a slave in Tennessee: 'If you want Negro history, you will have to get it from somebody who wore the shoe . . .' [Lester: 12] In the process of compiling the witnesses from slaves, Lester used two main sources, narratives dictated to white abolitonists in the nineteenth century and the twentieth-century Federal Writers' Project, part of the Federal Workers' Project stored in the Archive of Folksong (now the American Folklife Centre Archive) at the Library of Congress in Washington, DC. The two sets of narratives both held the true accounts of ex-slaves, but they differed in one important way: the earlier records had been 'doctored' for language, grammar and syntax by abolitionists anxious to conform to literary standards, and to create, in their view, the best possible impression of their subjects. On the other hand, in Lester's words, 'the Federal Writers' Project was as interested in preserving the speech patterns and language of ex-slaves as it was in gathering information about slavery'. [Ibid.: 13]

In other words, this was the sort of truth that a microphone could capture so well. In a tradition that had grown from work such as Charles Parker's and Ewan MacColl's *Radio Ballads*, through oral history, the development of recording technologies and now the coming of *StoryCorps*, Tony Phillips could see a number of strands—personal and professional—coming together in a project for which the infrastructure of the BBC seemed to be ready made. From the start, it was clear that the Corporation, with its national networks, its regional centres and its web of local radio stations, would lend itself perfectly to an enterprise of this sort. In practice, there are close similarities between *The Listening Project* and *StoryCorps*: a forty-minute interview, where selected, is broadcast in an edited form on a local station to its community, and in some cases to a national audience via Radio 4, with all content being subsequently processed by the British Library. From the start it was a concept that required meticulous initial planning:

> The first thing was to make use of our existing infrastructure, to con-nect the local stations and regions to Radio 4 under the banner of *The Listening Project*. We identified specific regional and local producers, selected stations that could act as hubs for areas with satellite com-munities, and, with the help of *StoryCorps*, who advised us, set about enabling people to have the sorts of conversations they wanted to have, rather than what we would LIKE them to have as broadcasters. As a national network, Radio 4 cherry-picks from the resulting contents for transmitting on air and via its website.[20]

The British Library's part in the process also followed the *StoryCorps* original closely. The full forty-minute interview is placed on a hard drive as a WAV file, and every three months the material gathered during this time is deposited at the British Library's sound archive. JPEG photographs of participants and Excel spreadsheets containing speaker and recording meta-data are also included, as well as biographical profiles of each participant and content summaries consistent with other British Library oral history collections.[21]

With a project as young as *The Listening Project* at the time of writing, it is difficult to assess its long-term value within the context of such areas as oral history and sociolinguistics. In an earlier chapter we discussed the for-mal process of recording oral history and the sometimes exhaustive nature of that process. At one extreme there are the fifteen-hour interviews conducted by such institutions as the British Library; at the other extreme we might classify two or three-minute 'sound-bites' as the simplest form of recording memory. Some would not regard *The Listening Project* as oral history at all, citing the intensive immersion in memory that the fuller process involves as more useful through its completeness, while others would point to the inti-macy of the concept inherent within *StoryCorps*, *The Listening Project* and other mass media–based projects as being a unique aspect of this form of witness. While the British Library is the repository for these conversations, it may well be that their ultimate value will lie in an area allied to but sepa-rate from the structured interviews conducted by the Oral History gatherers as described in Chapter Two, and explained by Rob Perks, lead curator of Oral History at the British Library:

> What we're looking for is something much more detailed and defini-tive about a life, and it's not typical of all oral historians or academics,

who may be seeking to obtain information about things they'll use for other—perhaps specific—purposes. My view has always been that as the lifestory unfolds, so the trust relationship builds during the interview, and people will tell you things they perhaps wouldn't in a shorter interview. That's the unique and different thing you get from the long life story.[22]

The material deposited by the BBC will need to grow into a substantial collection before it can be properly judged in this context. Specifically in the area of sociolinguistics, many of the conversations recorded as part of the *Millennium Memory Bank* contain some reflections on speech; although dialect/accent were not themes in themselves, observations on language occur quite frequently due to the focus on local, domestic and community issues. Only time and quantity can measure through consistency the overall value in this area. On the other hand, *The Listening Project* highlights some unique aspects of language in close relationships, something Jonnie Robinson, lead curator of Sociolinguistics and Education at the British Library is considering:

They are conversations between 'equals' rather than interviewer-led so we expect they might be linguistically quite different—very relaxed, extremely personal in terms of tone, and also they might prove to be structurally unique. Lots of language surveys and oral histories are characterised by a lack of interrogatives, for instance, the informant will respond to questions but seldom ask any him/herself. For this reason I wonder if they might possibly prove useful to linguists interested in grammatical/discourse features rather than, say, language variation or change. One thing we hope might be possible (and very different from other oral history collections), for instance, is the fact that the recordings are united by a focus above all on relationships. Once there are sufficient recordings it will, for instance, be possible to compare sets of mother-daughter conversations with mother-son conversations (or other combinations) to investigate whether or not there are characteristic features that distinguish such conversations.[23]

*

There is an African proverb that says, 'When an old man dies, a library burns to the ground'.[24] The words are profound; they go beyond knowledge, fact and even tradition, encompassing everything human that goes to connect one generation with another, and the link in the chain on an individual basis is the human voice. The vocal coach and writer Noah Pikes, a student of Roy Hart[25] and founder of Roy Hart Theatre, which in turn grew out of the teaching of the German singing coach Alfred Wolfson, continues the work of these two men in seeking to reconnect voice—as vocal sound—back to its sources in body and soul. As we saw earlier, the origins of Wolfson's teaching come themselves from his visceral memory of the cries of dying soldiers during the First World War, something he later integrated into his idea of singing as an expression of the whole human being rather than the categorisation of voice into straightforward vocal ranges.

Pikes has identified strong connections between sound and the very word *person*: 'It is our capacity to make sound, sound out, resound, that makes us individual. We recognise others by sound.' Yet human sound moves beyond the personal towards the universal, particularly at times of passion; we recognise emotion in others because we remember it in ourselves. Pikes identifies this quality of 'non personal sound and vocal qualities' as something 'Hart once referred to as "the Objective Voice" sounds that in some cases are linked to the voices of emotions, others to the emotions of animals, birds, whales and so on, others to the elements. In other words archetypal sounds or voices'.[26] We are animal in nature and find our way through a map of sound memory deeply embedded in instinct and evolution. We are both transmitters and receivers, possessing the essential ability to send, receive and—importantly—understand signals. This takes us beyond the ears, just as it takes us beyond the larynx. We hear with our whole body through vibration in the upper, middle and lower zones, just as in Pikes's words, 'the voice is not just what happens in the larynx but what happens to the sound originating there but finding a huge pallet of timbres from throughout the head and trunk in particular.' Our memory of a familiar voice is made up of interpretation based on individual shape and form both infinite and extraordinary; even in the case of profound deafness, it is crucial to the cartography of the human spirit as it encounters and negotiates the world around us.

NOTES

1. This essay by Benjamin is entitled 'Unpacking My Library: A Talk About Book Collecting.' It was first published in *Literarische Welt* in 1931.
2. *Home Recorded Voices*, Soundscape Productions for BBC Radio 4, Produced by Andy Cartwright, written and presented by Seán Street, 20 December 2008.
3. Michael Ladd, communication with the author.
4. Paul Klee suffered from the wasting disease *Scleroderma* towards the end of his life.
5. Mathieu Ruhlmann, *This Star Teaches Bending*, CD insert note, 2013.
6. Clare Jenkins, interview with the author, 2013.
7. Ibid.
8. Rony Robinson, interview with the author, 2013.
9. Ibid.
10. Elizabeth Darrell, personal communication with the author.
11. Julia Taylor, *Hamworthy Radios*, interview with the author.
12. Ibid.
13. Ibid.

14. The British Library's *Sounds* site is the starting point for exploring the initiatives described here: http://sounds.bl.uk/ (accessed September 2013)
15. www.guardian.co.uk/world/2008/nov/01/studs-terkel-usa. More can be learnt of Terkel's life and work via this link: www.studsterkel.org/bio.php (accessed October 2013).
16. Figures supplied by Virginia Millington, Recording and Archive Manager, StoryCorps.
17. Virginia Millington, communication with the author.
18. Ibid. Access to *StoryCorps: Hear and There* can be gained via this link: http://storycorps.org/new-museum/ (accessed November 2013).
19. Tony Phillips, Commissioning Editor, BBC Radio 4, interview with the author.
20. Ibid.
21. The British Library's Sound and Moving Image Catalogue can be accessed via this link: http://cadensa.bl.uk/cgi-bin/webcat (accessed July 2013).
22. Rob Perks, Lead Curator, Oral History, British Library, interview with the author.
23. Jonnie Robinson, Lead Curator, Sociolinguistics and Education, British Library, interview with the author.
24. The origins of the quotation are uncertain, and it has appeared in a number of similar variations. Whatever its source, it remains useful as a mantra linking oral and written traditions and a reminder of the importance of the preservation of personal witness.
25. Hart (1926–75) was a South African actor, singer and teacher, for whom Peter Maxwell Davies wrote his monodrama *Eight Voices for a Mad King*, which premiered in 1969, utilising Hart's extraordinary six-octave vocal range. Hart's ability led him to also work with composers such as Karlheinz Stockhausen and Hans Werner Henze.
26. Noah Pikes, communication with the author. To understand more of the work of Wolfson, Hart and Pikes, those interested in this avenue of research are recommended to read Pikes' book, *Dark Voices—the Genesis of Roy Hart Theatre* (New Orleans, Spring Journal Books, 2004).

7 Walls Have Voices

HAUNTED PLACES

The association of a place with a sound and that sound's retention in the memory as a result is not unusual. We have already discussed the hugely important role of music in our lives; a song that becomes meaningful to us may well spark memories of the place and circumstance when it was first experienced or when it became particularly significant. The recollection of the room or hall that was the location of the event may be strongly focused, heightened by the very architecture of the place.

In the case of live performance, we may be aware of peripheral sound, the audience around us, the sight and smells of the auditorium—all things which, at the time of writing, a studio recording cannot replicate. The Romanian conductor Sergiu Celibidache, famed for his work with the Munich and Berlin Philharmonic Orchestras up to his death in 1996, believed the only way to gain a transcendental experience from music was in a concert hall. Accordingly he was greatly opposed to the recording and release of his performances on record. Those recordings of his work that exist today tend to be from live concerts, often taken from transmissions by radio or TV stations. Anyone who was present at a Celibidache concert will remember the event and the place as being a major part of the musical experience.

There are places in which the location and the sound are deliberately and consciously linked to create and underpin a common message; Wagner's Bayreuth is a clear example of this. The motivation may be political, cultural, idealogical or sacred. In the latter, it is true to say that a recording of music or speech in a church goes further than almost any other internal location recording towards replicating the live experience within the place, due to the transmission of the location itself through its acoustic, something that becomes an actual part of the audio experience and therefore capturable by microphones.

In their remarkable book *Sound and Space in Renaissance Venice*, Deborah Howard and Laura Moretti examined the relationship between the intention of Italian Renaissance architects Sansovino and Palladio and the development of polyphonic choral music in split-choir formation (*coro spezzato*), pioneered in St Mark's, Venice, by the Flemish composer Adrian Willaert. Polyphonic liturgical music spread across Europe as the great churches were created, moving the sound of religion from Plainchant to something that consciously evoked the voices of angels. The various parts of a piece such as Thomas Tallis's great forty-part motet, *Spem in Alium*, itself strongly influenced by the work of the Italian composer Allesandro Striggio (in particular his *Ecce Beatam Lucem*), overlap and interweave in a way that conceals skillfully the intake of breath on the part of the singers. Angels are not mortal and therefore have no need of breath.

Listening to this music, even in a recording, the mind is transported to the great spaces for which it was conceived. During 2007, Howard and Moretti took this further, exploring the relationship between music and architecture through practical *in situ* choral experiments and acoustic measurements in churches across Venice, demonstrating through this work a vibrant partnership in sonic awareness, the cause and effect of sound in sacred spaces between patrons and liturgical leaders in the Renaissance period and, more, the scientific and artistic makers of the religious experience—the architects and musicians. Johann Wolfgang von Goethe once wrote, 'I call architecture "petrified music"'. [Howard & Moretti: 8] Certainly in our great churches and temples, music heard or recorded within the space pulls echoes and ambiences out of the stone that become part of the musical experience itself. A recording of, say, the Monteverdi *Vespers* performed in a dry studio acoustic would lose the very essence of the sound, because it was written to have a relationship with soaring vaults and marble floors.

Howard and Moretti were able to demonstrate powerfully through their experiments in San Marco, Venice, that the relationship between the architect Sansovino and the composer Willaert was a practical working one, and that it resulted in modifications to the design of the church in order to enhance the performance and acoustic reception of the liturgy.

> His [Sansovino's] alterations to the chancel of San Marco, initiated in the time of Doge Gritti, responded—at least to some degree—to the needs of musical performance. Our detailed exploration of the acoustics of San Marco demonstrated unambiguously that the clearest acoustics for psalms in *cora spezzato* in every listener position were achieved with the singers in Sansovino's two *pergoli* (or singing galleries) on either side of the chancel. The placing of the two groups together in the *bigonzo* or large octagonal pulpit gave a more blended sound, but the clarity remained good for listeners in the position of the doge and his entourage in the chancel.
>
> —[Howard & Moretti: 202]

Thus we may suggest that great churches such as San Marco were designed not only with an intention to awe the senses visually, but also with the same care and attention to acoustic detail as an audio studio architect or the creator of a modern concert hall would seek to build into a dedicated recording or performance space. Further, these spaces were invested with a unique *voice* distinct from other acoustic stages, so it therefore follows that the attentive and sensitive ear, tuned to the various sound qualities of musical environments, should be able to identify the location of a recording of a performance of, for example, the Striggio mass *Ecce Beatam Lucem* from a memory of the acoustics of the place in which it was performed. If we are able to remember the identity of a human voice, there is no reason why we cannot hold the memory of the voice of a building in our mind. Almost every tourist who enters San Marco in Venice will take a photograph of the spectacular interior of the famous church as a souvenir; those same tourists, were they to record that memory in sound, (and in particular within the Chancel, where the most radical stereo experiments were undertaken) might discover on playback the audio record to be equally if not more redolent of the spirit of the place than the visual record is.

ICE, EARTH, WATER

On 17 January 1912, a British exploration team led by Captain Robert Falcon Scott reached the geographic South Pole, only to find that a Norwegian party led by Roald Amundsen had preceded them by five weeks. Scott wrote in his diary: 'All the day dreams must go . . . Great God, this is an awful place'. [Scott: 376] A photograph was taken to record the arrival. Of the five men in the British group—Scott, Edward Wilson, Henry Bowers, Lawrence Oates and Edgar Evans—none were to survive the eight-hundred-mile trek on foot back to their base camp. With hindsight, we may look at this famous photograph as a symbol of tragic heroism. The pain of failure and exhaustion is etched into the mens' faces, and the very stance and body language seems to us to predict the greater disaster before them.

In 2011 a major television series, *Frozen Planet,* was screened on British television. It was a co-production by the BBC Television, the Discovery Channel and the Open University, and focused on life and the environment in the Arctic and Antarctic. One member of the production team was the well-known natural history sound recordist Chris Watson. While recording in Antarctica, Watson kept an audio diary. As part of this, he recorded the sound around him at the geographic South Pole, close to the spot where Scott and his men had stood for their photograph almost a century before. It is an eerie, empty sound, full of the sheer bleakness of the place: it is the sound that the 1912 team would have heard around them, an audio memory of the experience of dead men. Placed as a soundtrack behind a projection of the last photograph of the team, the sound gains an almost unbearable poignancy; it is an example of how pure sound can elevate an image into a life that actually gains a new dimension of emotion.[1] It is not silence—far from it; it is undeniably the ambience of 'the Place', and it picks up on the theme of a great film by Herbert Ponting, shot at the time of Scott's expedition, which entered the public consciousness under the title *The Great White Silence*. Ponting's film was of course shot in silence, but to today's sound recordists, the word 'silence' becomes ironic, because there is virtually nowhere that is truly without sound. This idea has taken on a historico-political meaning in the work of Jay-Dea López, whose 2013 CD, *The Great Silence,* challenges the notion that a pre-1788, uncolonised Australia was silent and therefore—to the foreign British ear—inferior and unworthy. Indeed, as he says in his introduction to the audio, 'the refusal to acknowledge the sounds of the landscape was so strong that a new term entered the cultural lexicon—The Great Australian Silence'. This claim—that the whole continent was silent, and by definition, void of life—demonstrated crucial and convenient imperialistic values.

> In part it illustrated the mistaken belief that the country lacked a significant civilisation prior to colonisation. This belief justified a brutal expansion of the colonial territory into traditional Aboriginal land. Almost half of the 250 Aboriginal language groups that existed prior to 1788 were systematically silenced through frontier warfare. Vital indigenous knowledge was lost, as was an ancient way of listening to the Australian environment.[2]

Ironic indeed that incomers who heard a cultural silence should add to it by destroying the sounds and ideas of an indigenous people or peoples. In López's recording, the memory is restored, or, rather, the witness of the landscape is heard and disseminated. This, he claims, is what those first colonists would have heard, the sounds that were considered of so little significance as to amount to silence, 'The Great Australian Silence'. The use of nocturnal field recordings taken from Australia's subtropical forests in López's composition (for that is what it is, natural sounds singing through the mediation of modern audio facilities), in his words 'imagines our way into the past'. In so doing, the work leads us into a night that is anything but quiet. 'Crickets and cicadas sing from the trees, frogs keep steady rhythms in the creeks below, fruit bats call through the darkness. It is an environment filled with a boisterous vitality.' In preserving the memory of a continent, López sets out to touch the conscience of colonial history from an unexpected and potent source and direction. In order to do this he is tapping into not only animal life but also beyond what Stuart Gage and Bernie Krause have termed the *geophony* of the place: the non-biological entities such as earth movement, wind, rain, the sound of moving water and so on. Of this, Krause has written:

> The sounds of the geophony were the first sounds on earth—and this element of the soundscape is the context in which animal voices, and even important aspects of human sonic culture, evolved. Every acoustically

sensitive organism had to accomodate the geophony; each had to establish a bandwidth in which its clicks, breaths, hisses, roars, songs or calls
could stand out in relation to nonbiological natural sounds. Humans,
like others in the animal world, were drawn to geophonic voices because
they contained fundamental messages: those of food, a sense of place,
and spiritual connection.

—[Krause: 39]

López and other field recordists working in this area are right when
they point their microphones towards the geophony; to do so is to hear
voices *beyond* walls, the fundamentals upon which the first building
blocks were placed, and therefore a memory of an uncluttered sound
purity that, once focused upon, releases a whole new layer of complex
and beautiful music.

The 3Leaves label, the company that issued *The Great Silence* on CD, was
founded in 2009 by the Hungarian sound recordist Ákos Garai. Garai was
born in 1974, and sound works created by him are distinguished by both
their subtle editing and their manipulation of time. In his words, 'micro-
moving-structures are often the starting points' for the work. Given this, it is
not hard to see how work such as that of Jay-Dea López would fit comfort-
ably into such a philosophy. Equally, 3Leaves was established, as Garai says,
to support 'artists with a certain sensitivity towards their environment, who
research into its deeper relationship, and who seek to present permanent or
even momentary connections in field recording based sound works'.[3]

The label's policy in relation to its customers, that is to say, the listener, is
one which supports *active listening* and is against prevalent trends, present-
ing its artists and products as physical releases rather than downloads or
online apps; careful attention is paid to presentation of the artefact, usually
in limited editions.

One such work was Annea Lockwood's *Sound Map of the Housatonic
River*, issued in 2012 by 3Leaves. Born in New Zealand, Lockwood is well
known for her sound explorations of the natural world, with material ranging
from sound art and installations to concert music, and her pieces have been
heard internationally in Europe and the United States. Her *Sound Map of
the Housatonic River* was her third river study, following her *Sound Map
of the Danube* (2005) and *A Sound Map of the Hudson River* (1982). Both
of these works have been presented widely in national parks and galleries as
installations, but with the completion of the trilogy all are now available
on fixed media and as download.The reason for this preoccupation can
be found in Lockwood's fascination with the multilayered complexity of
sounds created by fast-flowing rivers. As she says, 'an aural scan is a different experience from a visual scan—more intimate, I find. The energy flow of
a river can be sensed very directly through the sounds created by the friction
between current and riverbanks, current and riverbed'.[4] It is also a part of
the deepest history of earth. Within the geophony, as Krause says, it is 'likely

that water would have been the first natural sound any sentient organism interacted with'. [Krause: 39]

The Housatonic River flows 224 km from its sources in the Berkshire mountains of western Massachusetts to the river's mouth at Milford, Long Island Sound, in Connecticut. During the nineteenth and twentieth centuries the river was heavily industrialised and extensively polluted, but since the 1970s things have changed through local action and a crucial Wetlands Protection Act (1972) in Massachusetts; latterly, as a result, water quality and the riverine environment have been greatly improved. Lockwood recorded along the length of the river from source to estuary, both from the surface and underwater using hydrophones. Her above-water recordings were made not from boats, but from the river bank itself at numerous sites, 'thus mirroring the changing river-created environment'.[5] Originally a quadrophonic installation accompanied by a large wall map, the work was linked to a time display allowing visitors to track the locations. These have been included with the CD, and the listener to the full seventy-five-minute soundscape gains, as a result, a genuine sense of the journey, thus making this a memory not only of place—or places—and of the river itself, but of time, a capturing of the curated sound of the interaction of traveller and bystander at a precise moment.

This precision within time raises a dichotomy in the mind. Sound is physically experienced in a permanent present. Just as López's 'memory' of pre-1788 Australia can only be, as stated, an 'imaginative' or emotional trigger rather than an actual memory, so Lockwood's sound journey freezes the river at the time of recording. The next second after the recording stopped would have produced a different sound. We have the Housatonic River in its relatively healthy state, as heard during the period of recording—in this case between June 2008 and July 2009, the time frame within which the recordings were made. How would the same heavily polluted river have sounded, say, in 1971, before the Massachusetts Wetlands Protections Act began the gradual process of environmental and riverine improvement? This is not to negate either of these fascinating projects, but merely to repeat the identification of a fundamental fact in all sound—including music—which is to say that in terms of our reception of it, sound is always 'live' and temporal: it is always 'the present'. As Karl Wörner has quoted within another context, in his book on the German Karlheinz Stockhausen, the composer's own dictum: 'What happens consists only of what the world is broadcasting *now* . . . Everything is simultaneously the *whole*. The notion of time is swallowed into the mind's past.' [Wörner: 69]

The temporal nature of sound is demonstrable through recordings of flowing water, as we have seen, each wave a ripple subtly different from the last. It has provided poets and composers with a powerful metaphor, and extended playback of seas, rivers and rainfall have been used as meditation and relaxation aids. The uses of these recordings are therefore varied. On one level they may been seen as background ambient sound, on another, as sound effect; yet most powerfully, the strength of location recordings is that they provide us with a sonic window into a moment in time in a place.

Every recording—every studio sound, live or recorded—is a *record* in the documentary sense of not only the sound but also the space in which it was created, and the sound recordist's presence in it and interrogation of it. If we listen to the faint voice of Florence Nightingale speaking to survivors of the Crimean Balaclava campaign on 30 July 1890 at her home, 10 South Street, Park Lane, London, we are hearing not only the moment she spoke and the timbre of her then ageing voice, but also the room in which she spoke those words and the time—year, month, day, hour and second—she uttered them, prompted by her living thought process. Listening, we may faintly hear her say: 'When I am no longer even a memory, just a name, I hope my voice may perpetuate the great work of my life.'[6] As we hear the faint crackling voice, we remember that she was in a room with a technician, probably Colonel George Gouraud, Edison's British representative. There were walls, windows, all familiar to her, there was London light (although Gouraud may have blanketed this out in the interests of the recording), and, by implication, the peripheral sounds of the world going on around her that the microphone was not sensitive enough to absorb. She had entered the room and she would leave it. This recording is a memory of that moment in time and her life as it happened, a piece of Victorian existence preserved.

The issue becomes a philosophical, even an existential one; field sound poems such as Lockwood's and Lopez's, stepping outside the walls of human space, go beyond documentation because of the motive and the intent in the sound artists' minds; Lockwood's river recordings are about 'the special state of mind and body which the sounds of moving water create when one listens intently to the complex mesh of rhythms and pitches'.[7]

There is something profound that recording in the field releases in us. Listening through headphones to the voice of landscapes is an intense experience, either as recordist or listener. Focused listening is akin to meditation; indeed it can engender a deeply concentrated state when pursued for a period of time, and water, the flow of it, the life of rivers and tides, contain for human beings a strong metaphor. In 2011 Cheryl Tipp, Curator of Natural History Sound at the British Library, produced a commercial CD under the title, *Waves: The Sounds of Britain's Shores*. The disc contains audio taken from beaches, bays and coves around the UK and makes an excellent effects disc, providing would-be sound artists and dubbing staff with enough information to place the right sound with the right picture or mood: 'Medium Seawash on Shingle', recorded on Denge Beach, Kent, in October 1996 by Phil Riddett, 'Heavy Sea on Rocks', from Bamburgh, Northumberland, in October 1997, caught by Simon Elliott, 'Mull Gully Waves', recorded by Simon Elliott on the Isle of Mull in Scotland in April 1992, 'Calm Sea' on Wells Beach, Norfolk, in February 1993 by Richard Margoschis and so on.

Yet this CD, cumulatively, is about much more than sound effects; taken as a whole, these recordings are nothing less than the voice and moods of Britain's various coastlines at a given moment. Wells beach might have sounded very different during a storm perhaps the next day, Denge Beach might have had calmer days, although it is hard to imagine anything but 'Heavy Sea on Rocks' at Bamburgh, on the north-eastern coast of England. What makes these recordings interesting, even moving, is their presence in the moment they were made and the present moment that became a memory caught for us by the microphone. That is not just 'Heavy Sea on Rocks' you are listening to; that *is* Bamburgh, the place, being itself at that time. We may never go there, but we 'see' through the sounds to the place whilst staying surrounded by the familiar environment in which we are hearing the sounds. So while we are conscious of being in one place, the sound is speaking of another. The sense of memory provided by sound is shaped by both ends of the process, by the recording and by the auditory experience later. All takes place within time, and so I may ever afterwards remember the sound of the sea on Bamburgh rocks, accompanied by either an image conjured by the sound itself or a picture of the busy street I was looking out onto when I first put the CD in the machine. Indeed, my longterm memory of that initial playing might be a combination of both images. Sound triggers the imagination in many ways, but sound requires a consciousness to hear it; while it exists beyond the living human mind, it is through a sense that it exists for us.

We may absorb the natural world through sound for its own sake—a recording of seawash or gentle rain can soothe us to sleep when sleep will not come—or, as in the case of the recordings discussed here, it can become a focus for intense concentrated listening, and in such a state the attention can be caught by a minute sound amongst many, a detail in the sonic painting which in turn sets up a chain of lateral images and ideas, emotions and memories. It is hardly surprising that musicians and composers have sought to interact with natural sound; Olivier Messiaen interpreted birdsong in his work, and Jonathan Harvey, in a late piece—*Bird Concerto with Piano Song*—used real birdsong, metamorphosed it into electronic sound and created a human counterpoint in the piano's human interaction. Composition and the sounds of the natural landscape have been linked for centuries, (Vivaldi's *The Four Seasons* and Beethoven's *Symphony no. 6, 'The Pastoral,'* come immediately to mind.) More recently the American Bernie Krause and the Englishman Simon Scott have independently worked in their own areas to directly connect the sounds of the natural world to their composing, and in Scott's case, with his *Below Sea Level* project, Scott created an intensely personal piece that links memory and place in a statement drawing us into an intimate sound world in which the heightened sense of our presence in the landscape draws attention to the responsibility we hold for conservation. It is through the memory of what *was* that we understand the impact of change.

Simon Scott was born and brought up in Cambridge, in the eastern part of England on the edge of the Fen country, a landscape of water, flat landscapes and above all enormous skies. Family outings into this strange *other* world, so different from the busy university city, had a major effect on the growing boy, and when he eventually moved away to London, he found himself haunted by the memory of the vast open spaces and the sounds that came out of them. Our memories of childhood are often inflated: buildings and places grow in our recollection, and revisiting them can sometimes show us a reality that is somehow lesser, smaller than we remember. Not so for Scott when he finally returned to his homeland: 'The huge *three quarter skies* of the Fens were just as huge and gloriously full of life as I remembered them as a boy.'[8] The *Below Sea Level* project grew out of this return and a wish to explore sonically—using natural sounds interacting with his own musical composition—the landscape of the Fens, creating a work which sought to capture the inate musicality of the place itself. The recording process took two years, with Scott using hydrophones and self-built recording equipment to explore in intimate detail a land that is cartographically below mean sea level, and in so doing to interrogate the devastating history of environmental damage caused by the drainage of the land. This is *composed* work, with Man and Environment as duetting performers; *Below Sea Level* takes us— wherever we may be listening—*into* the place, sometimes moving through grasses, hearing birdsong, sometimes underwater, with a strange cacophony of sub-aqua sounds interacting with the music. In so doing, Scott explores the æsthetics of active listening, interweaving soundscapes that blend the recognisable with—at first listen—unidentifiable sounds, confusing the senses with an evocative mix of what is natural and what is synthetic. Of the process of making, he has written:

> Over the two years I visited the Fens to record, my childhood memories were reawakened and realised as I explored a landscape that was personal to me, but contained unfamiliar and hidden acoustic details. What I have composed is an illusory musical reconstruction of the landscape that intentionally draws the ear into the music, thus promoting active listening. However, *Below Sea Level* intentionally disengages any realistic representation of the Fens. This is to reflect the historical dislocation of this landscape when it was drained of its lifeblood. Listening is engaged hearing; it lies at the very heart of sound ecology—and by establishing a dialogue between the Fenland environment and an autonomous musical exploration, I have produced a subjective representation of the Fens.
>
> —[Scott: 22]

It was never Scott's intention to create a documentary of the landscape, something which given the sheer subtlety of many of the sounds would be impossible anyway; the aim of *Below Sea Level* was to take site-specific sounds, mediate these sounds through musical intervention and offer the complete experience to a listener for absorption at a remote distance from the place of origin, outside the Fenland environment, and therefore encourage through the blend of real and abstract a deepened sense-perceptual awareness of the sonic world.

For the project, Scott spent considerable periods of time integrating himself into the landscape to become part of the environment and not a spectator. He would then begin to digitally record the sites and sounds of particular vernacular items, such as wire fences, bridge supports, canal footpaths and various water surfaces, using an Edirol R-09 recorder to capture sonic material with various microphones and a hydrophone for underwater sound sources, and also sometimes a smart phone. 'As I recorded each location I knew that the sound I'd recorded was an abstraction, and that I should not try to represent this environment as a "real-life" sound document. It was a snap shot in time, a sonic postcard I'd created with myself inside the present, to be explored in post-production.'[9] Using music software to delve into the microscopic sound worlds and improvising with small sound loops taken from long sections of recordings, he began to create new musical forms, all the time seeking to remain true to the essence and spirit of a particular site and retaining his personal connection to the location, either as a new discovery or as a place once visited in childhood. To these were added organic sound recordings, such as an acoustic guitar or music box within one of the designated areas; there was next a process of responding to mixes played back out into that landscape and rerecording it so that the distinction between what had been previously composed and what was being subsequently altered by the present took the songs into new areas of sound timbre.

The process involved regularly returning to an area and recording each season and differing times of day to capture the varying weather conditions. 'An example of this was recording Wicken Fen covered in ice by putting a contact microphone into the ice sheets but also capturing the summer, and recording the dry grasses swaying.'[10] Using the hydrophone to record under and on the surface of the water, Scott, in a sense, was able to physically touch the sound as he moved the microphone around. 'Sound caught on the surface is very different to the fast movement of sub-aqua sound (sound travels five times faster through water than air) and I felt I could be creative by using both sound worlds in one recording session to compose with those sounds.'

It is worth exploring Scott's thinking in more detail because *Below Sea Level* is a good example of personal and place memory singing together; this may sound fanciful, but there is a sense in the capturing of a moment in a landscape through sound that is much more than a visual image, a moment, but also because of perspective something bigger.

> I wanted to be in the moment completely, in the present being mindful of the fleeting ontological passing of time and slowing down to harness the sonorous information. This is easier said than done but after two years

I became good at switching my ego off to just be able to appreciate the sonic landscape as it revealed itself to me. Children live and perceive in the moment, unlike adults who tend to rush ahead to the future, and I began to re-experience the sense of wonder that I had when I was seven years old. Hearing sounds and all of the complex auditory information, perceiving reality as it ontologically occurs, was essential to *Below Sea Level*.

Someone said that children are always listening and it saddens me that as we grow older we increasingly discriminate what we hear and we miss the splendour of what is going on around us. It is another reason I love listening with headphones, as our brains aren't allowed to block out sounds that we've over time perceived as unwanted. Living in the moment, with your microphone attached to your headphones just listening, you realise that you miss so much sonic information and it takes you back to a time when you were a child, discovering the world through each of your senses. We become visually dominated, as we grow older, so our wonder diminishes because we aren't in tune with all of our senses and we gradually stop listening.

By actively listening I began to perceive myself as just another living organism, just another being contributing to the sound of the landscape in such a busy natural environment. I'd remember the historical context of The Fens when on site recording. Of how every living organism you are surrounded by has been affected by the events of the past there. This devastated landscape is now being man managed for arable purposes and it has been manicured by various organisations to attract tourists. This awareness only comes from gaining knowledge of its history through research. The land drops considerably below the roads and paths you travel along and the canals are so straight, as they were when I was a child, but I now understand why.[11]

In the end, it remains a human memory—a remembrance of the moment when we share witness with a place, and also the imaginative memory of what the place has been in the past and how it has been changed.

As we perceive something it becomes a memory instantaneously because the present is so brief. I think I was honoured to be in the English countryside and witness these incredible moments over the course of two years of recording in The Fens. Now they are memories but shared as distortions of reality. I guess they become audio documents that are tributes to these treasured moments (sonic postcards) and there is connection to one's childhood and re-experiencing a landscape that you went to as a child and reconnecting to that specific place.[12]

*

In April 2012 Chris Watson was also working in East Anglia, commencing recording for a piece evoking the sounds the composer Benjamin Britten would have heard in the landscape around him near his home in Suffolk. As with Simon Scott's work, this too would come to fruition as a piece which blended the sounds of the natural world with composed music. In an interview with Pascal Wyse for *The Guardian*, Watson recalled the process:

> Every day at 1pm, after a morning spent playing the piano and taking notes, Britten would put on a jacket and tie and have lunch. Afterwards, he would take off his jacket and tie—and go for a walk through the countryside around his house in Aldeburgh. During these strolls, he would consider his morning's work, then come back and refashion it. In his writings, Britten made several references to his "composing walks". He used to say: "I work as I'm walking."[13]

Watson's idea was to hear the sounds that Britten heard on those walks from his home as far as possible. In his research for the recordings, he discovered that Britten was a keen bird watcher, with a particular love for the nightingale, so early one spring morning Watson set up his microphones around the Red House, as Britten's house is now known, and waited. 'I first got a night chorus with roe deer, foxes and tawny owls. Then, just after 3am, the first bird called: a nightingale. It was magical, standing there in the gardens of Britten's house.'[14]

Unsurprisingly, Britten was a sensitive and careful listener. During the 1960s the sound of jets landing at nearby RAF Bentwaters drove him from the Red House to a cottage in the village of Horham, half an hour's drive away. A sound memory of Britten's ideal walking tours would not include aircraft. Memory however, can be selective, and Watson made an imaginative connection between that pre-dawn male nightingale, singing to call his mate down out of the skies, and the human music that had grown out of the Aldeburgh landscape. How to exploit the connection to demonstrate this link? In the autumn of 2012, the BBC had celebrated the ninetieth anniversary of the first transmissions in 1922. As part of this, Watson had been commissioned to revisit a famous moment in broadcasting history in 1924, when the cellist Beatrice Harrison had played a a duet with a nightingale in her Surrey garden. The broadcast caused a sensation and was later recreated in a commercial recording. Influenced by this, he made a mental link between Britten's nightingale and the cello, in the ebb and flow of the phrasing.

> I thought it would be interesting to incorporate some of his music into my final pieces which, created from the recordings I made, [were] performed at Aldeburgh . . . as part of the Britten centenary celebrations. So cellist Oliver Coates [played] some of the composer's solo cello work live during the performance—at the dawn chorus section, when we hear the nightingale.[15]

PLACE MEMORY

In 1995 BBC Radio 4 broadcast a series of programmes in which I visited the sites of villages that had for one reason or another been abandoned during the twentieth century. These ranged from such places as Tyneham in Dorset, on the south coast of England, which had been evacuated at the time of the Second World War for use as an army training ground, to St Kilda, a remote archepaelago off the western coast of Scotland, depopulated in the 1930s as life in such a place became unviable, to Derwent, in Derbyshire, a once picturesque place that lay in a valley, the fate of which was to become the Ladybower Reservoir, providing water for nearby cities such as Sheffeld. In 1943, Derwent church held its last service, and by 1944 the waters were rising over the deserted gardens and village lanes.

Returning to the place for the radio programme fifty years later, I was joined by Ernest Madeley, a man who had spent his childhood in Derwent. Our plan had been to record an interview on the banks of the reservoir, looking down on the waters concealing the remains of his home. In the event, upon arrival we were confronted by a very different scene to the one we had been expecting; the local water authority had for various reasons drained the valley and thus revealed the remains of Derwent, drowned and concealed from view for so many years. Together we were able to walk the lanes of his home again, and as we did so he would occasionally pause and remark on something that confronted him from his childhood: 'My father built that wall . . .' he said. 'This was our garden, there was an apple tree here . . . and there were wonderful apples that grew here . . .' By being *in* the place, the promptings of a forgotten time came back in a way that an interview recorded in a studio—or even on the valley side—would not have exposed. Likewise, because it was radio—audio—there was only a microphone listening, no intrusive cameras and crew that TV would have imposed on the moment. It was intimate, personal and very moving.

The importance of location to an interviewer is crucial; not only is the sound of the place emotive in itself, but also a physical presence in familiar surroundings, or with objects from another time, can evoke extraordinarily vivid memories. It is almost as though the places and the objects gain a voice through the recollection of the interviewee. The oral historian Rob Perks has noted the value of tactile memory, taking an interviewee to the subject of the conversation for the British Library:

> The one I remember vividly was a man who had worked on Harrier Jump Jets. We had done a 15-hour interview with him, and then we decided to take him to a Harrier, and there was something about the way he engaged with the aircraft that was incredibly resonant of his work, and his engagement with it. We obtained material from him because of this engagement with the actual object that we couldn't have got from

an interview without being in the presence of the aircraft itself. There is something about the object that is quite telling; something happens.[16]

Memory can be a partnership between place or thing and the mind, and its cause and effect is important because it moves us from the literal experience through the emotion that experience evinces into the realm of the imaginative, the creative and the spiritual. Alfred Braun (1888–1978) was a German actor, screen writer and film director. He was also a pioneer of German radio, who from an early stage in his career—even before the arrival of sound film—explored the idea of transferring cinematic techniques such as cuts, dissolves and montage to radio, making what he and some of his contemporaries called acoustical films. [Alter & Koepnick: 126]. Braun created sound pictures of German cities in which 'images both flowed dreamily and flitted by in quickest succession, abbreviated images, super-imposed images, alternating and blending close-ups and distant shots. Each of the short images was positioned in a particular acoustical place, surrounded by a particular acoustical set: 1 minute with the loud music of Leipzig Square; 1 minute protest march; 1 minute stock market on the day of the crash; 1 minute factory with its machine symphony; 1 minute soccer stadium; 1 minute train station; 1 minute train underway, etc'. [Breton: 24]

Braun's work is to some extent representative of the radical sound experiments explored by the Weimar radio avant-gardists that included Hans Bodenstedt, Hans Flesch, Eduard Reinacker and Walter Ruttman. In his radio plays, 'Braun incorporates cinematic techniques, not to remake radio as a cinema of the blind, but to free sound from serving predefined images or from simply being substituted for missing visual props. Like a rag picker, Braun sifts through the acoustical landscapes of modern life, aspiring to gather unique sonic materials and assemble them within a new kind of post-autonimous artwork'. [Alter & Koepnick: 126]

What Braun and his colleagues would have made of twenty-first-century technology such as GPS can only be imagined. Certainly the idea of places becoming characters within a sonic dialogue, with the listener actively participating in the creation of meaning rather than remaining simply a consumer, was something the surrealists encouraged and was also a concept that Bertold Brecht advocated. Some of our most imaginative producers and audio makers are today picking up a number of these ideas and developing place memory as a dialogue in which we can follow the history of an environment from within, creating a sense which acts on at least two levels: the absorption of location history as one passes through it, and the overall recollection of the three-dimensional experience itself.

The work of Tim Wright, Hildegard Westercamp, Janet Cardiff and Francesca Panetta and others seeks to link us emotionally with landscape and environment, often by engaging with it visually whilst absorbing complementary-created audio narratives informing the experience through history or human witness. In 2012 the *Hackney Hear* GPS-led project, conceived by Francesca Panetta, won the innovation category for Audio and Technology at the Prix Europa Awards in Berlin. The London Borough of Hackney, close to the 2012 Olympic Games site, is a rich, diverse and changing area of London. It also has an equally complex history, and the *Hackney Hear* project, absorbed on location by listeners through a Smartphone app, relates relevant sound to the environment through which the listener is passing. Thus place memory is a partnership between a three-dimensional sense experience informed by an audio narrative that is variable at the participants' discretion; the route, and therefore the order of the stories, can be changed at will. Here, it seems, the walls really *do* have voices. More recently, the *Hackney Hear* team have introduced other apps such as *Soho Stories*, which engages residents and visitors in another unique and culturally diverse area of central London through sound. In these initiatives, it is as though the place is sharing its memories with us. These are devices that enable telling stories in a place, reflecting on what used to be there and what exists now, but curated: at the heart of these experiences it remains, as Panetta says, 'one person's version, interpretation of and response to a place at a particular time.'[17]

When we curate our own sonic lives—as we have the means to do through the diversity of personal technologies we carry with us every day—we tap into the potential for unique and intimate forms of sound memory preservation, more powerful than pictures can ever be; with visual images we become observers, whilst the strength of a binaural stereo audio recording, for example, can be completely immersive. In Panetta's words, 'If we had a sonic recording of, say, our family at Sunday lunch twenty years ago, and we listened to that on headphones, there would be a strong sense of being there, in a way that a film would not convey, because once moving pictures are introduced we are outside the experience. With a sound recording you are reconstructing yourself in the moment you are remembering—sound can do that better than pictures, where you're just so removed'.[18]

Similarly, the work of Janet Cardiff, a Canadian now living and working in Europe with her collaborator/partner George Bures Miller, has gained a growing reputation internationally through innovative and imaginative site-specific sound walk projects, including *Words Drawn in Water* at the Smithsonian Institute, Washington, DC, in 2005, *Ghost Machine* at the Hebbel Theatre in Berlin, also in 2005, and *Conspiracy Theory/ Théorie du complot* at the Musée d'Art Contemporain in Montreal. Through her company Artangel, she has also created installations such as *Pandemonium* at the Eastern State Penitentiary in Philadelphia in 2005 and *The Murder of Crows* for Berlin's Museum für Gegenwart in 2008.

As early as 1999—before GPS technology became available—Cardiff was experimenting with the idea of walks linked to imaginative audio narratives, as in *The Missing Voice: Case Study B,* which started at the now defunct Whitechapel Library, moved through Spitalfields towards the City of London and resolved near Commercial Street. Unlike *Hackney Hear,* which was to evolve much later, *The Missing Voice* followed a prescribed route, providing participants with an experience via a Discman portable device, which combined fact and fantasy, posing psychological questions with a narrative that eventually led to a resolution, linking the genres of audio guide and detective fiction. Since then her work has expanded technically, geographically and imaginatively, including a number of collaborations with poets and composers such as Lavinia Greenlaw, Laurie Anderson, Brian Eno and Gavin Briars.

In 2006 Cardiff created the *Jena Walk (Memorial Field).* In this project participants move through a pastoral landscape to which belong emotive place memories of history and possibility. Jena is a city in central Germany on the River Saale. It has a rich past, and it is this that the walk explores through layers of time and sound; the sound of Russian tanks that used to exercise across the landscape is blended with diary entries by Louise Seidler, the artist who painted Goethe and came from Jena, and who therefore—perhaps—walked through this space, and the battle sounds of Prussian and French armies fighting on the very same land two hundred years before is heard as the listener walks there. It is an exercise in the physicality of memory through layered narrative, and as visitors experience the interweaving sounds, they become aware of their own presence in the place, contributing to the growing and evolving history and memory of a specific location at a moment in time.[19]

We can practice our own interactive geophysical experience simply by walking through an environment, tuned to the sound as well as to the visual around us. Active listening is a skill to be consciously acquired because we are used to filtering layers of sound within a hierarchy of necessity; as humans we need to be selective in the information our senses gather. This is why for many people, as for Simon Scott, listening to landscapes on headphones can be so revelatory: it is the conscious act of listening that is invoked, but it can be achieved without any technology at all, just an awareness that the experience is something that can be documented either mentally or physically. The poet and song writer Sally Goldsmith, a keen lover of birdsong, applied this to her daily walks in a Sheffield park, absorbing the place in all its changes and reflecting on those changes as they became memory in her writing:

> I'm listening as I walk, and I walk slowly to take in the sounds and the landscape. I have been on walks where I consciously try to write. I kept a blog of a park I used to go to regularly, with the idea that whenever I went into the park, it was like going to witness a new play every day; there would be different lighting, different sounds and different stories going on, if you paid attention to them. So I used to walk around the park, just paying attention.[20]

SOUND IN THE CITY

The radio presenter Billy Butler has been a familiar voice in his native Liverpool for more than forty years, broadcasting on local radio stations BBC Radio Merseyside and Radio City. In his early years he worked in the city's docks, and remembers a very different place from the Liverpool of the twenty-first century. In many cases our urban environments have become homogenised in terms of sound; at first hearing, one city sounds very much the same as another. It was not always so. Butler remembers the street cries of market stall holders and horses along the dock road, the sirens of great ships on the River Mersey: 'It's a lot quieter now', he recalls, 'and that reflects the way we live our lives, even down to our places of work. When I started at Radio Merseyside, offices were noisy places, because there was the sound of typewriters, and everyone had to raise their voices above the sound to make themselves heard. Today, offices are largely silent places'.[21]

When city dwellers remember their environment from a perspective of memory, individual sounds come into focus: dockyard work sirens, the one o'clock gun, the grinding sound of a tram's wheels turning a corner. Some sounds are common to many urban environments, a shared soundscape, while others are particular to certain places. Either way, they enter into the memory of those who grew up in a specific environment, even if they remain unarticulated for long periods. Soundscapes attempt to preserve the sonic 'view' of a place at a particular time, in a similar way to a folklorist capturing stories and thereby an essence of a culture caught in time. The means of such preservation is, of course, a relatively recent phenomenon. The American sound designer David Sonnenschein has written of time's effect on cityscapes, and their change and effect on how we live with sound:

> In the Paris of the 17th century, reports of noise included shouting, carts, horses, bells, artisans at work, etc. All these sounds came from specific directions and were very impulsive, rather than long constant tones, with few low frequencies.
>
> —[Sonnenchein: 96]

With the coming of the internal combustion engine, city sounds changed; a lower, more continuous sound encompassed the soundscape, surrounding and obscuring other individual sounds, with the result that 'we lose the sense of humanness'.

> In a postmodern environment, the sound may also be omnidirectional, but higher pitched, more electronic rather than mechanical. There is a certain sterility and predictability to the background hum of a computer, but humans have given character to their ever-shrinking, attention demanding machines—like musically ringing cell phones, for example.
>
> —[Ibid.: 97]

However we attempt to live in an ever-present world, the past, be it a piece of technology, a sound or a place—or something containing the essence of all three—is always sinking into memory, becoming a kind of sepia with a patina of life experience that may bring with it wisdom, but may equally come to touch us with nostalgia and even regret. The memory of Place, its sound, smell and visual impressions, exists in the mind in a form of the present in which they were last encountered. We may return to a set of walls long remembered and find them changed and even destroyed; yet until such a moment disillusions us, they continue to exist within our imagination as if we had returned to the time in which we knew them. Marcel Proust wistfully evoked this idea in the first volume of *In Search of Lost Time*:

> The places we have known do not belong solely to the world of space in which we situate them for our greater convenience. They were only a thin slice among contiguous impressions that formed our life at that time; the memory of a certain image is only regret for a certain moment; and houses, roads, avenues are as fleeting, alas, as the years.
>
> —[Proust 1 (2003): 430]

Sound can help us here in a way that it was not available to Proust, even if the place itself has changed out of all recognition. Go to a place—or even to somewhere a building once was—equipped with some knowledge and the right sounds, and the memory of the long-lost walls can speak again.

NOTES

1. Watson demonstrated this complementary relationship between sound and image at the School of Sound International Symposium on 6 April 2013 at the South Bank Centre, London.
2. Jay-Dea López, CD insert note, *The Great Silence*.
3. Ákos Garai, communication with the author.
4. Annea Lockwood, interview on the *Landscape Stories* site, www.landscape stories.net/interviews/65-2013-annea-lockwood?lang=en (accessed June 2013).
5. Annea Lockwood, *A Sound Map of the Housatonic River*, 3Leaves 3L018, 2013.
6. Extract from cylinder recording of Florence Nightingale's voice, one of three she made, preserved by the British Library Sound Archive's conservation centre, digitised in 2004 in association with the Wellcome Trust Library. It may be listened to by following this link: www.bl.uk/onlinegallery/onlineex/voicesh ist/flonight/ (accessed May 2013).
7. Lockwood, CD insert note.
8. Simon Scott, interview with the author.
9. Ibid.
10. Ibid.
11. Ibid.
12. Ibid.

13. Chris Watson, *The Guardian*, 30 January 2013.
14. Ibid.
15. Ibid.
16. Rob Perks, Lead Curator, Oral History, Department of History and Classics, British Library, interview with the author.
17. Francesca Panetta, interview with the author.
18. Ibid.
19. More can be learned about Artangel projects in general and Janet Cardiff's work in particular here: www.artangel.org.uk/home (accessed June 2013).
20. Sally Goldsmith, interview with the author.
21. Billy Butler, interview with the author.

8 Saving the Sound, Spreading the Word

SOUND RETRIEVED FROM AIR

Shortly before his death in 1999, the broadcaster, author and former BBC executive Dr Desmond Hawkins reflected on his earliest memories of radio, and the personal significance for him of those broadcasts. Hawkins had a distinguished career within the BBC as controller of the West Region, becoming a moving force in the creation of the famous Natural History Unit in Bristol. He also led a full and colourful literary life, and knew such poets as Ezra Pound and Dylan Thomas. The remembered early transmissions from childhood, listened to by a young boy from a middle-class background in East Sheen, Surrey, during the 1920s, were culturally vital to his subsequent life and represented a sea change in how his generation as a whole would engage intellectually and emotionally with the world. 'I first experienced a Shakespeare play through radio . . . and Beethoven—I heard my first string quartet not in a concert hall, but in my living room. My parents were not the types to take me to such events *in situ* so to speak, but fortunately I was part of the first generation for whom sound broadcasting provided access to the cultural world beyond the family walls.'[1]

For the young Desmond Hawkins, radio's democratising power was a key to his first response to the medium, and it was a lesson he never forgot: the principle informed the rest of his professional and personal life. For subsequent generations, prior to the full development of television, the same was true not solely in terms of high art but also importantly in the fields of entertainment, popular music and news. The power of sound to create pictures in the mind, to fuel the imagination or to simply tell stories has remained constant through the years, incorporating on the journey developments in new media. One of the beneficiaries of the exploding world of downloads, audio on demand and citizen-created sound projects has shown itself to be speech-based radio (the term itself becomes problematic in the face of such proliferation). The technology that enables listeners to be their own makers and to store content from a multitude of sources on MP3 players also permits them to create and understand the value of their own personal archives. We are coming to a point where sound archives and their value as artefacts can claim parity with what were once seen as more traditional paper and object-based historical repositories and access facilities. Things are changing, although, as we shall see, even in an increasingly 'virtual' world there is some distance to go in order to establish such parity in the fullest terms.

Sound archives may preserve the transience in the medium itself, but they must also create opportunities to analyse, reference and disseminate the voices and sounds of the past in order to be truly 'living'; it is in the relationship between the witness of history and the cultural and societal life in our present that recorded sound—a relatively new-found thing after all—offers its greatest gifts. Innovation in audio must be taken into account as it develops, and strategies must be adjusted to allow for preservation and access issues. When in 1958 Charles Parker, Ewan MacColl and Peggy Seeger made *The Ballad of John Axon*, the first of the now legendary *Radio Ballads* for the BBC, a new form of radio feature was created, blending actuality, location-recorded speech and music as narrative, using the then new technology of the portable tape recorder. In themselves, the *Radio Ballads* were about memory recorded in the field, speakers engaging with their world rather than attempting to recall it in a sterile studio. It is likely that Parker and his colleagues understood that here they were programme makers developing radio into fresh fields of creativity and production. The fact that more than fifty years later their work would be discussed and celebrated in academic conferences, archived and issued commercially to generations not even born when the original programmes were made, may not have occurred to them. Nevertheless, the fact is that there has emerged in recent years a new academic discipline in the form of 'Radio Studies', now a global network across hundreds of institutions, while at the same time the media industries, by virtue of their identities that are so much a part of the present, are becoming increasingly aware of their past. Radio approaches its centenary, and from all sides useful work is being developed in the exploration of how—and why—radio and other forms of audio interact in such a potent way with audiences. In this climate, sound archives provide the vital memory bank for the rediscovery of broadcasting and social history.

The pace of change is bewildering, and as it propels us forward there is sometimes a sense of living in a permanent present; this makes the preservation of memory in terms of public sources, communal elements of memory held on behalf of society, all the more important. Within something over one hundred years, we have moved to a point only dreamed of by historians of previous eras. The poet and novelist Thomas Hardy, in his book of memoirs, underlined the fact that within a family we are only two or three lives away from a seemingly distant time:

> My mother says that my [paternal] grandmother told her she was ironing her best muslin gown (then worn by young women at any season) when news came that the Queen of France was beheaded. She put down her iron, and stood still, the event so greatly affecting her mind. She

remembered the pattern of the gown so well that she would recognize it in a moment.

—[Hardy: 224]

This is oral history that today would be informed by the sound of the voice telling the story. More, we would have the means of bringing the news directly into the Hardy household, live and immediate, rather than the days or weeks it took at the time. Thomas Hardy was born in 1840, and so he was within the reach of memory dating back to the eighteenth century, and part of a rural community in the west of England that had not changed in many of its essentials for centuries, yet he lived to experience the motor car, flight and radio (although sadly for us, he did not broadcast or record his work or voice). Likewise, a man or a woman born in, say, 1910, would grow into a world where mass media would provide a commentary on their life, with the potential to preserve the witness of their time for posterity. Imagine reading Pliny the Younger and *hearing* the voice of the Emperor Trajan, or from a later time being able to play news reports and field recordings from the French Revolution, the shadow of which flickered over the Hardy family's peaceful Dorset cottage one autumn day in 1793. Above all, sound, the human voice, concentrates the mind on the *spoken* text. A transcript may provide the sense and the meaning, but a recording demonstrates the nuances of speech, the hesitations, the inflections, the thought process and the emotion.

We must reconcile ourselves to the fact that much of the early years of broadcast history is lost to us due to the lack of recording/playback facilities at the time. Although commercial disc recording existed at the birth of radio, it was costly and time consuming, and it was not until 1930 that a London musician called Cecil Watts developed direct disc recording, a principle whereby an aluminium-based, cellulose-nitrate, lacquer-coated disc could be cut from a 'live' performance and played back instantly. Watts explained that the impetus came not from broadcast requirements but practical issues of rehearsal: 'The disc recording system came about because I became a musician and had various bands, and I longed for a play-back recording machine that would give an immediate play-back to rehearsing musicians.'[2] In other words, Watts needed a platform to hold memory. It was a device such as this, in its American form of the *Presto Disc*, that had the portability and instant recording ability that enabled Herb Morrison to make his Hindenburg recording and thus encouraged NBC to embrace the possibilities of location recording.

As with all developing technologies, in the early years of broadcast there were a number of competing answers to the same question. In 1931, Dr J. A. Miller of Flushing, New York, developed a system of recording using film as a sound-only medium. The invention was picked up by the Philips company of Eindhoven in Holland, and for a number of years was successfully adopted by a number of broadcasters under the title of the Philips-Miller Recording Process. The quality of recording was very high, but the film could not be reused, was very costly and was not portable. This competed for a time with the Marconi-Stille System, developed from a process for recording on steel by Louis Blattner, a German living in the UK. While it was less suitable that the Philips-Miller process for music recording due to issues of quality, a full thirty minutes of recording was possible on a single reel of steel tape. In 1932, when the BBC was moving into its new Broadcasting House building in Portland Place, London, they installed their first Blattner-phone. Within days—on 23 May of that year—it was to prove its worth when Amelia Earhart, fresh from her famous transatlantic flight, arrived at the BBC for an interview, and at extremely short notice there was a request that she be recorded. The newly installed Blattnerphone, untested and not fully set up, was pressed into service, and the resultant success of the event went a long way towards proving recording as a valuable adjunct to the technology of broadcasting.[3]

The flurry of interest in recording for transmission came at the start of the 1930s due to increasing preoccupation amongst broadcasters in international services, and so the reality of 'bottled' programmes became an essential part of media production. With the inauguration of the BBC's Empire Service in December 1932, there was a requirement to record material for repeated broadcasts across different time zones. In spite of the fact that the new machines were subject to the technical problems besetting most new inventions and that the editing of steel-tape involved a laborious process of welding or soldering, it is possible to see how the use of recording began to change the way programmes were constructed. On 13 January 1933, *Pieces of Tape*, a composite programme made up of items recorded during the year, was created and broadcast, and demonstrated what could be achieved. Leslie Baily, at the time the radio correspondent for *The Sunday Referee*, wrote enthusiastically of the programme:

> We shall hear a great deal more of the Blattnerphone. It has obvious possibilities as a means of introducing realistic sound-effects into radio plays, and the historical value of being able to store speeches, and music, and the sounds of events in this way must have been in the mind of every listener. I am told by a BBC engineer that nobody can tell how long it will be possible to preserve the Blattnerphone tapes, thirty miles of which are already stored at Broadcasting House. Friday's programme was a selection from this library, and consisted of over 200 pieces of steel tape cut from the original reels and soldered together.[4]

Once networks began recording programmes, they were faced with new issues of storing, indexing and cross-referencing material, as well as decisions related to selection: what to keep, and what not to keep for posterity and future use? In 1937, a young Oxford graduate, Marie Slocombe, joined the BBC as a holiday temp and was assigned to the Recorded Programmes Department. In a programme made for BBC Radio 4's *Archive on 4* strand in 2007 I explored her story, and how her decision to keep and organise those early recordings laid the foundations for the BBC's sound archive, now one of the most significant broadcast collections in the world.[5] While the producer Julian May and I were working on the programme we were greatly helped by a recording of Slocombe herself, interviewed in retirement for the BBC Sound Archive's own departmental history, in which she recalled that day:

> One day, the boss came in and there were some discs on the floor, and he said "Oh, clear out all these old discs, and have a tidy up", so [we] got down to work–and this is quite literally true, and I know my memory is not playing me false—there was a pile of discs, getting worn and dusty, and we began to look at them; there was a talk by Bernard Shaw, a talk by H. G. Wells, a talk by Asquith, Churchill, Lloyd George, Chesterton. We looked at one another and we said, "No way can these be destroyed! Something's got to be done.[6]

Archiving sound memories involves a twofold mindset. The initial process is akin to rescue archaeology, involving acquisition followed by assessment and, where necessary, remedial technical issues. Deterioration of the original may need to be addressed, or obsolete formats have to be taken into account. In 2007 the British Library Sound Archive opened a new conservation centre over three floors, with ten audio studios, a lab for rescuing sounds in all formats—some on the verge of extinction—and every known kind of play-back facility. The dream of preserving the memory, not only of words but also of music, has preoccupied us for as long as communication; imagine hearing Beethoven playing one of his sonatas, or hearing Buddy Bolden play, active until 1907 and seen by many as the father of jazz. Bolden suffered schizophrenia in his later years, dying in an asylum in 1931. He left no recordings.[7] Eighteenth and nineteenth-century music boxes, barrel organs, pianolas and other automata gave us a fixed version of a performance, either human or otherwise, but these forms were beset with the same curse that has afflicted all recording technologies down to the present day, that is to say the potential obsolescence of the original reproduction platform. Thus, the conservator must first wrestle with making the artefact audible again before seeking to ensure its compatibility with modern systems.

Once preserved, transferred to what is hoped (given the unpredictability of emerging formats) to be a stable medium, the second aspect of the project takes over: that of making the work available for current and coming generations. We might, in rediscovering sounds from history, with the privilege of giving them new life, occasionally pause and reflect on the remarkable background to their very survival, and consider how fortunate we are that they exist at all and that their importance is beginning to be recognised. Yet at the same time we should not be complacent about preserving the voices of our present, the sounds that, taken together, will become the societal memory of the future. Just as every personal thought and emotion contributes to human memory, so every image and sound caught by an increasingly bewildering array of portable devices such as smart phones turns each of us into archivists and chroniclers of our time. What will happen to this universal babble of sometimes inconsequential—sometimes vital—commentaries? Can they—should they—be gathered into a central memory bank before they themselves become obscured by the next layer of time? We shall return to this subject in a later chapter. In the meantime, our national libraries and archive centres are working to conserve and digitise a wealth of fragile audio acquired in a relatively short span of time. It is interesting—although perhaps not surprising on reflection, given that over the past century the 'new' technology of recording has undergone a constant process of refinement which continues today—that obsolescence remains a major concern. As Richard Ranft, director of the Sound Archive at the British Library says, the investment in conservation and digitisation, supported by the creation of associated metadata currently being undertaken by institutions such as his own, recognises that audio artefacts are as important as any other documents from history:

> The British Library has 3,000 year-old oracle bones representing the birth of writing, so in the context of that, sound recordings are very new. But we've had sound recordings for over a century now, and people are looking back and realising that a lot of information about that century is contained in sound and moving image.[8]

This documentary evidence is becoming accepted as an important part of academic research, although there remains some way to go to fully integrate audio into the mindset of all scholars and research institutions. Nevertheless, the sound recording, with its ability to capture a place and an event in time, can hold things the written word cannot, largely in the realm of expression, emotion and circumstance. Situations in which key historical events took place gain a context when the microphone holds the acoustic, the ambient and the peripheral sounds of a location, even before the voice, with all its grades and subtleties of human music begins speaking. The memory of sound can at the very least complement other materials such as maps, manuscripts, journals, books or historical speeches. A moving example lies in the recovered recording of Nelson Mandela's speech at the so-called *Rivonia* trial of 1963–1964, in which he declared himself willing to die for his ideals, as Ranft explains:

> The restoration of Dictabelt recordings made of the speech at the time, just before he was sentenced, brought an obscure sound format back

from the brink of extinction to give us the passion in the *sound* of the words. Although the text was known, what comes across is the sound of the sheer integrity and bravery of this remarkable man, about to be imprisoned for 27 years.[9]

This recording, brought back from the brink of extinction and saved for posterity, has gone on to attain international fame, not least through the 2013 film *Mandela*, in which the actor playing the central character was able to simulate every nuance of the original in his performance—a creative memory, passed on and preserved in another medium.

*

In 2005, the UK media regulator OFCOM began a programme of periodic licensing of community broadcasters across the British Isles. This new layer of media, in particular radio stations servicing very specific areas, either of geography or of interest, provided platforms on which society could hold a dialogue with itself, catching a moment in time at local or ethnic level, a snapshot of existence. Globally the community radio initiative, linked to Internet and download technology such as the podcast, provides perhaps the ultimate example of Desmond Hawkins' idea of the democratising potential of radio.

What would Parker, MacColl and Seeger have made of such material, had it been available to them in the 1950s and 1960s? More importantly, where does—and where will—all the material generated by such stations on a daily basis go? Some stations may keep local archives, but community broadcasting is by its very nature often predominantly volunteer based, chronically short of finances and resources and born into a world where the pace of reflecting *today* through media at every level moves us too quickly beyond *yesterday*. There is a unique, once-only opportunity, which is also an immense challenge, for academic institutions, local, regional and national archival centres and other library-based facilities to preserve audio memory at a micro-local level in an ongoing attempt, in the first decades of a new millennium, to preserve for future generations a sense of what the word 'community' means and how it changes through time. In Birmingham, UK, a library-based initiative entitled *Connecting Histories* has demonstrated how past and present can hold a crucial dialogue together to the benefit of a wide diversity of communities within the city.

The development, range and scale of public archives have grown at an impressive rate in the twenty-first century, fuelled by new technologies of digital preservation and dissemination. To take one example in 2012 alone, the American Folklife Centre Archive at the Library of Congress either created or acquired 77,927 digital objects, of which over 33,976 were manuscripts, 24,297 were still images, 2,164 were moving images and 17,490 were audio recordings. Bertram Lyons, the Digital Assets Manager, points out that given the size and ongoing process of acquisition, accountability is key:

> At the heart of our concerns, being an organisation that holds collections in the public trust, is that we can be able to turn around in 10 or 100 years from now and say here, here's this particular resource that we acquired, and it has or hasn't changed over the years, and if it has changed, here's how and why.[10]

Within the American Folklife Centre is the *Centre for Applied Linguistics Collection,* which contains 118 hours of recordings documenting North American English dialects. The recordings include speech samples, linguistic interviews, oral histories, conversations and excerpts from public speeches, drawn from various archives and from the private archives of collectors such as linguists, dialectologists and folklorists. It is a resource that grew from a project entitled 'A Survey and Collection of American English Dialect Recordings,' funded by the Centre with further resources supplied by the US National Endowment for the Humanities, and it contains documentation relating to the social aspects of English language usage in different regions of the United States. 'The oral history interviews are a valuable resource on many topics, such as storytelling and family histories; descriptions of holiday celebrations, traditional farming, schools, education, health care, and the uses of traditional medicines as well as discussions of race relations, politics, and natural disasters such as floods.'[11] Voices and memories from forty-three states gathered between 1941 and 1984 are represented, as well as from the District of Columbia, Puerto Rico and parts of Canada.

Public archives have a vital role to play not only in saving the evidence of gradually evolving language, but also in saving the witness of sudden cataclysmic events, where a society or a way of life and thinking is overturned in a moment. When a community or a place is eradicated in an instant through an act of nature or war, the memory of the past, so vital in rebuilding the future, can only be held through human memory. In Chapter 6, 'Ourselves as History', we discussed the partnership between such organisations as the British Library Sound Archive, The American Folklife Centre Archive, *Story-Corps* and the BBC *Listening Project*, working actively with the public to create living history through the sound and emotion of spoken memory. This aspect of archives—the human witness—is inseparable from the sense of the individual and the personal in a way that is akin to a handwritten document; there is a sense of human presence that is all the more moving and potent when the events they describe are on an inhuman scale.

There are two such collections in the American Folklife Centre Archive. *After the Day of Infamy: "Man-on-the-Street" Interviews Following the Attack on Pearl Harbor* contains approximately twelve hours of recordings made in the days and months following the bombing of Pearl Harbour from more than two hundred individuals in cities and towns across the

United States. On 8 December 1941 (the day after the Japanese attack on Pearl Harbour), Alan Lomax, then "assistant in charge" of the Archive of American Folk Song (now the Archive of Folk Culture, American Folklife Centre), sent a telegram to fieldworkers in ten different localities across the United States, asking them to collect "man-on-the-street" reactions of ordinary Americans to the event and the subsequent declaration of war by the United States. A second series of interviews, called 'Dear Mr. President,' was recorded in January and February 1942. These interviews feature a wide diversity of opinion concerning the war and other social and political issues of the day, such as racial prejudice and labour disputes. The result is much more than a response to a disaster; in these recordings we are offered a human 'snapshot' of a moment in a society on the brink of profound change: a portrait of everyday life in America as the United States entered World War II.[12]

Almost exactly sixty years later, America was subjected to another such moment. The *September 11, 2001, Documentary Project* captures reactions, eyewitness accounts and diverse opinions of Americans and others in the months that followed the terrorist attacks on the World Trade Centre, the Pentagon and United Airlines Flight 93. The day after the attacks, the American Folklife Centre called on folklorists and ethnographers across the United States to collect, record and document America's reaction. Material collected through this effort was used to create a record in which patriotism and unity, mixed with sadness, anger and insecurity, are common themes expressed, with a sample used in an online resource, containing almost two hundred audio and video interviews, forty-five graphic items and twenty-one written narratives. As with the Pearl Harbour sound collection by Lomax, it serves as an historical and cultural resource of considerable emotional power and importance for future generations.[13] In situations like these, archivists and collectors need to think and act quickly in the face of extreme communal shock and confusion; it is at such moments when we become graphically aware of the future looking back on our time, reliant on the living memory being preserved. It is comparable with the hundreds of living, spoken memories we do *not* possess, such as human witness to the destruction of Pompeii or Krakatoa. Ann Hoog, a reference specialist at the American Folklife Centre who has worked extensively on both these collections, has noted how over subsequent years their emotional meaning subtly changes retrospectively: 'At the time these recordings were made, it was less about memory and more about reaction to current events, however they now serve as a memory of those times and capture the raw emotions and reactions immediately after the events.'[14]

In some cases the recordings acquired by national and regional archives bridge the gap between memory and conscience. Cheryl Tipp, Curator of Natural Sounds at the British Library Sound Archive, is aware that everything that is collected is a memory; a recording is a memory of a place, and it is the individual memory of the person who curated the recording. By making such an artefact available publicly, it has the capacity to become a new memory, and the word is passed on. A place may change, a bird may become extinct, but the recording continues to exist, which is where memory and conscience come together:

> We have recordings in the collection of places that no longer exist in the form they once did; what may have been a woodland or a reed bed fifty years ago, might now be a car park or a supermarket. If we have the sound of the place as it was, the signature sound, we have a witness for the future, which can be radically different to its past. If you fell trees, you change habitats, so the birds and other wildlife leave. A disturbance in landscape changes the sound of landscape, so that recording becomes a memory of a lost landscape.[15]

While we document our present with an eye on the future, the acquisition of existing, historically vital human sounds never ends, and it is of course impossible to know what may yet be found; new audio witnesses from the past are still being identified in private collections and small forgotten archives, some of which had themselves been considered extinct. Valuable as they are, such discoveries sometimes throw up anomalies and questions of provenance that require further investigation. Some years ago, the producer Julian May and I made a documentary for BBC Radio about the renowned German natural history sound recordist Ludwig Koch. Koch was a Jewish refugee from the Nazis who made his home in Britain and donated his vast collection of recordings to the BBC, including an Indian Shama bird, the first known recording of a bird in history, made when he was a boy in 1896 on a home recording kit. The young Ludwig had set about recording almost everything he could, includng visitors and guests to his well-connected household. Among these, as he later recalled on tape, was his own recording of the great Otto von Bismarck, the 'Iron Chancellor' and the power behind German unification, the man whose policies were famously wrought out of 'blood and iron'. The reputation of the man and the available photographs and paintings speak of a large, rather aggressive figure who, one would assume, would have a voice to match. Yet Koch's memory was of a man with an almost falsetto voice. When asked to speak a few words for the machine, Bismarck laughed and said, in Koch's recollection, 'My son, beware my life, and don't drink as much as me!' in what Koch recalled as a high-pitched squeak. Koch spoke with regret that the Nazis had taken this along with many of his other recordings and destroyed it when persecution began, meaning it was lost forever.

Latterly however, a recording purporting to be Bismarck *has* come to light, although from a different source. In 2012, a wax cylinder recording made in 1889 of the German statesman was discovered, the first time that his voice, rather than the memory of it, had been heard for more than one hundred years. It was made by the Edison Company, and digital technology at the Thomas Edison National Historical Park museum has restored and preserved it. The Foundation had believed the recording to be lost, together with sixteen others found in 1957 in an unlabelled box at Edison's laboratory in the state of New Jersey. Bismarck is barely audible on the recordings but can be heard reciting extracts of poetry and songs. Surprisingly, the voice is not as high pitched as Koch recalled; it is perhaps somewhat lighter than the physical image might suggest, but it could hardly be described as falsetto. The issue therefore would seem to be this: was a *record* made of Bismarck's words made as with Gladstone, described in an earlier chapter, as a 'memory' of the utterance rather than as a factual preservation of actual sound—or was Koch's memory at the end of his long life playing him false?

Whatever the truth, the fact remains that such finds only reinforce the idea that the line between acquisition and permanent loss is a very fine one. Dietrich Schüller, former director of the Vienna Phonogrammarchiv, believes that perhaps eighty per cent of the audio relating to the world's cultural heritage remains in private hands, and that, given mortality, and the fragility and increasing vulnerability of changing formats, within ten to fifteen years much could be lost forever.[16] Yet such preservation is only a part of the story, as we have seen. The ultimate trajectory of content in archives must be dissemination; preserved sounds serve little purpose if they languish in academic institutions, regional or national repositories, available for the use of a limited few. Likewise, particularly in the case of ethnic recordings that reflect world cultures, access should be user-friendly for the communities to whom these memories ultimately belong: the groups and societies of which they are a record.

The proactive relationship between an archive and individual memory has been highlighted in work by Dr Emma Brinkhurst of Goldsmith's College, University of London, through her research into Somali communities in central London. Somali history and culture are for the most part carried in the memories of individuals, and the concept of physical storage of the past is largely alien. What made Brinkhurst's study of unique interest was that the community chosen for her research has grown up in and around King's Cross, London, coincidentally close to the home of the British Library, with its wealth of documentary material. As Brinkhurst states, 'as neighbours, the Somali community and the BL are geographically close but ideologically distant.'[17] Nevertheless, forging a relationship between the two and enabling engagement between the group and the archive, with its existing recordings from Somalian history 'has demonstrated the potential for proactive archiving to contribute to ethnomusicological research and methodology, to elucidate and impact upon diasporic and collective memory processes, and to benefit diasporic communities'.[18]

Brinkhurst's interest in the relationship between personal and institutional archives has been key to her exploration through listening and recording sessions both at the British Library and in various Somali community locations, during which she encouraged group members to engage with recordings of Somali song and poetry that are archived at the British Library, seeking to break down institutional and ideological barriers.

The sessions stimulated reminiscence, discussion and physical reactions, and during some sessions participants were inspired to record their own musical memories, adding to the archive and stimulating the memories of other listeners in a diachronic cycle of transmission. As such I believe that different types of archive (personal, institutional, online . . .) have the potential to stimulate and animate one another.[19]

The value of this process is highlighted in Brinkhurst's example of Xudeydi, an elderly Somali Oud player, singer and composer living in South West London. Known as 'the King of the Oud', his songs and reminiscence capture and reflect different periods and moments from his past, which are likewise the history of his country and culture.

As an artist Xudeydi was socially and politically influential in Somalia before the civil war. In the diaspora his repertoire (which is largely remembered rather than recorded) sounds out Xudeydi's identity and retains his status in a situation that for many Somali men is one of disempowerment and marginalisation. Oral texts that once influenced the political and social life of Somalia are now being used to enhance his personal position in a new context, serving as evidence to support a particular identity. In this way Xudeydi's songs combine fixity of form and preservation of memory with changing purpose, place and meaning.[20]

As we saw in Chapter 6, there is a vital link between the personal and the preserved, be it a manuscript, a spoken memory or a song. Were we able to discuss the writings of the Venerable Bede with its author, we would be infinitely wiser and more knowledgeable about his times than we can ever be by study of what he has left us, however rich and valuable that is. The former CBC radio producer and folk singer Stephanie Conn has explored 'the dynamic role of memory and social interaction in the transmission and performance of Gaelic song in Cape Breton, through which a relationship between past and present is cultivated'.[21] Songs handed down through generations hold meaning not just because of their story but because of their changing character through time, and 'because of the treasury of memory which they unlock; singers explain that they "got it from so-and-so" or "so-and-so sang it that night at our home," and this leads to a host of related personal experiences, both private and social'.[22] This is not to denigrate the functions and services of a formal archive, particularly where indexing and cross-referencing provide the researcher with valuable background information; but by very virtue of the institution in which they are stored, the songs become 'divorced from their original context, and so in perusing them one must work hard to find related letters, newspapers and other documents to connect the melodies and words with all that once surrounded them'.[23] One could propose a counterargument: that the institution might also provide sophisticated search facilities that could aid the researcher to regain the context that Conn is seeking. It is nevertheless true that the documentation a library or archive offers may often be beyond the reach, either culturally or physically—or both—of the creators of song and story coming from a predominantly oral tradition, for whom the transmission of such material is exclusively through sound alone.

A graphic illustration of this may be found in the recent history of Uganda. One day, in the late 1940s, the legendary Adungu harp virtuoso Timotei Muktha played and sang for the Ugandan king in the Kabaka's Palace with the court musicians. The song was a traditional piece of Uganda's cultural history. In 1966, the king of Uganda was exiled, and many of the Royal Palace's musicians were killed. The court music tradition more or less died out, and the music itself was banned. The country went through a dark time. Then, in 1987, the king was allowed to return, and as he did so, the surviving court musicians gathered to celebrate his return, marking a revival of a tradition that had been silent for nearly twenty years. Yet the schism in the history of the country had left a cultural gap. Because many musical traditions around the world are orally transmitted, they are not written down, and there is no paper document to put on a shelf like a book and archive for posterity.

Fortunately, as Timotei Muktha played and sang on that distant day in the middle of the twentieth century, an electronic witness recorded his performance. It was made by Klauss Wachsmann, one of the pioneering scholars of African music, then curator of the Uganda Museum in Kampala. In total, Wachsmann made approximately 1,500 recordings of indigenous music in Uganda, both in the museum and in the field. These recordings are now part of the collections in the British Library's World and Traditional Music department, and as such, when the monarchy was restored, they were made available to a country relearning its traditions and court music heritage. The importance of such documents is hard to over-estimate; without exaggeration, a crucial part of a culture's memory was being restored through the recollection of the recording device.

If it is true that memory makes us what we are, then this applies to peoples and cultures as well as to the person. Janet Topp-Farjeon, Lead Curator of World and Traditional Music at the British Library, has seen these recordings form a link and a regenerative impulse connecting the past to the present, and enabling a forward movement, taking contemporary influences and re-establishing an organic connection in a fractured culture:

> The recording IS the document, and once it exists, is archived and preserved, then it needs to be accessed. In recent years, we have made access copies of these recordings, taken them back to Uganda, and I know that students of ethnomusicology at Makerere University in Kampala are now using this material, firstly in their research, and also taking the sounds back around the Ugandan countryside to the original communities from where the music originally came, in the process, learning how it has changed, and reintroducing the tradition into these communities.

If we hadn't been able to preserve the recordings in the way we have, none of this activity could have taken place today.[24]

The significance of the relationship between sound archives and auditory memory has been seen as a developing area for academic study. Digitisation is an ongoing process of saving sounds, yet time has told us that previous attempts of preservation have revealed deficiencies in formats that have sometimes been disastrous. How are we to know that we are truly saving sounds forever? Indeed, is there actually *more* security in an analogue form that slowly decays, and is therefore restorable in due course, than in an audio file that may, through whatever circumstance, suddenly and without warning become completely unreadable? We can only do our best as archivists and conservators, save our sounds in as many formats and in as many places as possible, and while preserving as much as possible understand that we can never preserve everything, just as we have never been able to save every artefact and paper witness from the past. New techniques and formats will come; in the meantime, sound archives, such a young discipline, have the advantage as well as the disadvantage of being just that—still developing— but in the process seeking material that, unlike the great paper documents from history, exists at the edges of human memory.

What makes this task so important is that an oral history archive is the sum of a multitude of human parts, a library comprised of individual phonemes shaped by a vast murmuring chorus of participants who in most cases will never have known one another. 'The mind in the world is full of the accents of both its personal past and its culture's past, and the inflections of its voice play a confused music of memory and names.' [Piette: 252] Sometimes we may be confronted with anachronisms and contradictions between spoken witnesses, but the archivist is dealing with not only fact but also the history of human vocal interaction, the preservation of auditory imagination that provides evidence of that imagination's capacity to return 'to the oldest of roots in primitive culture and childhood language-play'. [Piette: 175] An archive preserves ourselves as a culture and as individuals; it is precious because it assumes the responsibility for the memory of what we are and were, beyond our mortality.

NOTES

1. Dr Desmond Hawkins, interview with the author.
2. Cecil Watts, interview, British Library Sound Archive *Developments in Recorded Sound*, Oral History Collection, rec. January 1961, ref. LP26453
3. For a fuller description of the development of sound recording technologies at this time, see Street 2006: 115–134.
4. Leslie Baily, 'The Blattnerphone', *The Sunday Referee and Entertainment Supplement*, 15 January 1933, p. 12.
5. 'Marie Slocombe and the BBC Sound Archive', in *Archive on 4*, BBC Radio 4, 1 September 2007. This programme is available to listen to online via the

following link: www.bbc.co.uk/archive/archive_pioneers/6502.shtml (accessed August 2013).

6. Interview with Marie Slocombe for BBC Radio Archives, recorded 1986. Available through this link: www.bbc.co.uk/archive/archive_pioneers/6501. shtml (accessed August 2013).

7. It is a particular frustration for music lovers that composers such as Gustav Mahler, a legendary conductor of his own and others' work, who lived until 1911, *could* have been recorded. In fact, the only glimpse of his work is through the Welte-Mignon system, perfected in Germany in 1903 and used by Mahler in November 1905. The process was secret, but it would appear that a master was made with ink markings that were then punched as two sets of holes—one for each note and the other for its volume. It was this that gave the recordings a sense of real performance. 'Reproduction is achieved not through a player piano, but with a so-called "vorsetzer" unit, which actually plays a concert grand using felt-tipped "fingers" activated by varying degrees of pneumatic pressure triggered by the sets of holes. The result is uncannily realistic and far superior to the limited range of the acoustic disc in conveying the "touch" of an artist.' [Peter Gutmann: www.classicalnotes.net/reviews/mahler.html (accessed July 2013)].

8. Richard Ranft, Director of Sound and Vision, British Library Sound Archive, interview with the author.

9. Ibid.

10. Bertram Lyons, Digital Assets Manager, American Folklife Centre Archive, Library of Congress, presentation and communication with the author.

11. The Centre for Applied Linguistics, Library of Congress: http://memory.loc.gov/ammem/collections/linguistics/ (accessed June 2013).

12. *After the Day of Infamy: "Man-on-the-Street" Interviews Following the Attack on Pearl Harbor:* http://memory.loc.gov/ammem/afcphhtml/afcphhome.html (accessed June 2013).

13. *The September 11, 2001, Documentary Project* http://memory.loc.gov/ammem/collections/911_archive/ (accessed June 2013).

14. Ann Hoog, Reference Specialist, American Folklife Center, Library of Congress, personal communication with the author.

15. Cheryl Tipp, interview with the author.

16. Schuller, quoted in Landau and Topp Farjeon, 'We're All Archivists Now: Towards a More Equitable Ethnolmusicaology', in *Ethnomusicology Forum* vol. 21, no. 2, August 2012, p. 130.

17. Brinkhurst, E., 'Archives and Access: Reaching Out to the Somali Community of London's King's Cross', in *Ethnomusicology Forum* vol. 21, no. 2, August 2012, pp. 243–258.

18. Ibid.

19. Emma Brinkhurst, communication with the author.

20. Ibid

21. Conn, S., 'Fitting between Present and Past: Memory and Social Interaction in Cape Breton Singing', in *Ethnomusicology Forum* vol. 21, no. 3, December 2012, pp. 354–373.

22. Ibid., p. 363.

23. Ibid.

24. Dr Janet Topp Farjeon, Lead Curator, World and Traditional Music, British Library, interview with the author.

9 Holding on to Sounds

RADIO ANGELS

In 1999, Angel Radio, a community-run local initiative based in the town of Havant on the south coast of England, made its first broadcast using a Restricted Service Licence (RSL). Two years later, the station was selected with fourteen others to be part of a year-long experimental pilot project by the Radio Authority on the value, technical feasibility and viability of community radio in Britain through a new form of radio licencing. In 2005, following the successful experiment, 192 applications were received to launch stations of all kinds, broadcasting to various communities, both of geography and of interest, and Angel was again selected. In February 2006, the UK government's Department of Culture, Media and Sport (DCMS) announced its intention to conduct in-depth research into the impact of community radio, using three of the initial fifteen stations, one of which being Angel Radio. Since that time, Angel Radio has continued to broadcast via a traditional FM frequency, through Digital Audio Broadcasting (DAB), live online, Wi-fi radios and smart phones. The station is, therefore, local, regional and global at one and the same time.

None of this is unusual; what makes Angel Radio different is that its programmes, twenty-four hours a day, seven days a week, are made by—and for—people aged sixty and over. The station's mission statement is to provide:

> Uplifting nostalgic entertainment in the form of music, humour and memories from the years 1900 to 1959, together with current information regarding health, diet, pensions etc, and stimulation in the form of reminiscence therapy for mental health, and dance and exercise for physical health, helping to accentuate the positive aspects of old age.[1]

In so doing, the station's policy is to 'create a sense of value and self-worth for staff and audience' and to give a voice to a section of the community that is often segregated, undervalued and underserved by the media. Judging by listening figures, Angel Radio demonstrates the success of both its premise and its policies eloquently, with a regular audience on FM and DAB of 60,000 listeners locally and regionally in Havant and West Sussex, more than three quarters of a million visitors to its website and an impressive Internet audience, as shown in the station's research during the twelve months from March 2010 to March 2011.[2] It continues to report to Ofcom (the UK's successor to the Radio Authority, with a widened remit to take account of the development of new media in the twenty-first century), which praised its policy of employing some eighty volunteers drawn from its target community, as well as developing partnerships with appropriate local and national organisations.[3]

This chapter explores ways in which sound and radio can help to address some of the issues related to an ageing society, and in particular the matter of memory. In doing so, it is important to understand that there are practical issues to be addressed in any discussion of the value of sound in memory when considering the needs of elderly listeners. As well as broadcasting information about various hearing impairments, and the promotion of medical care centres offering dedicated help and information, Angel has explored technically ways in which its audience can access its output more effectively; as the treble end of the audio spectrum is the first to fail in old age, the station's audio signal is boosted slightly in its higher frequencies, compared to conventional output. Clarity of speech is a requirement for its presenters, but additionally, the station broadcasts a weekly magazine programme using precise pronunciation, specifically for the hard of hearing.

The connection between decline in hearing and cognition is significant; age-related hearing loss typically begins to show after the age of sixty, although other conditions such as Meniere's Disease can exacerbate deafness at any time. It has shown itself in broadcasters themselves, typically through listening to studio sound at high levels through headphones, and with a frequent symptom of tinnitus that almost invariably accompanies high-tone receptor deterioration. As hearing declines, we may find ourselves almost literally relying on the memory of sound, as Beethoven did when summoning the musical version of a thunderstorm in his Symphony No. 6, *The Pastoral*). Sound can exist silently inside our minds through memory; in such a case one of the only ways to reproduce and share it is to notate what our imagination tells us. Whenever composition and deafness are discussed together, almost inevitably the case of Beethoven springs to mind.

In 2010, however, the contemporary British composer Michael Berkeley came face to face with a similar problem when a respiratory infection led overnight to an issue more terrifying to a musician than even silence: extreme discomfort and noise combined:

> Sudden pain was accompanied by frenetic gurgling, bubbling and popping that never seemed to give that final gratifying lurch into free, equalised air. Next morning, I could hear nothing on [the right] side. This would have been merely an inconvenience were it not for the fact

that I already have severe hearing loss in my left ear, thanks to a mastoid operation in childhood, compounded by exposure to ridiculously loud rock music as a young keyboard player.[4]

In spite of the torture of the condition and its consequent overwhelming distortion of external sound, changing familiar sounds into ugly caricatures of themselves, Berkeley found he was able to compose, although, being unable to sample his work on a physical instrument, the experience was an internal one:

> The loss of proper, external musical sensation does heighten my sense of what Beethoven arrived at in those late String Quartets, living entirely for an inner world and creating within it an edifice in which you tend to wrestle away the superficial and the unnecessary. Ideas are stripped down to their essence and the intensity of your involvement becomes ever more personal and passionate. The drama is turned inward, almost alarmingly so.[5]

The internal world that one is forced into by situations such as this can have long-term consequences if it persists, with the potential for a breakdown in the relationship between the self and the outside world. It may be easier to live inside than to venture beyond ourselves in some environments. At the same time, when striving to absorb signals from this wider world, the brain is using up mental energy on the basic utility of understanding, energy that should be directed to interpretation. If one part of a machine starts to malfunction, it naturally puts a strain on other components. So it is in the relationship between hearing and cognition. Jonathan Peelle of Washington University in St Louis is developing ongoing research into the correlation between hearing ability and both brain activity and grey matter volume. In the coming years it is likely that more direct connections will be made between the two. Peelle's early work in this area has involved having people with various levels of hearing loss listen to short stories and then recall them. Short radio programmes will also feature in this work. 'We predict that listeners with poorer hearing will be able to remember less from the stories, because they will have needed to use more cognitive resources to understand the acoustic signal, leaving less over for narrative processing, integration and memory encoding.'[6] The work of Peelle and others demonstrates that hearing sensitivity has an important part to play in the support of neural processes that are key to cognition. The implication is that we should take more action, sooner, to prevent hearing loss; it may be a gradual decline, something all too easy to deny, but 'preserving your hearing doesn't only protect your ears, but also helps your brain perform at its best.'[7] Many people might resist the use of a hearing aid, where they would not hesitate to employ glasses to correct failing eyesight. Yet the work of Jonathan Peelle among others shows us that untreated hearing loss causes the brain to expend too much energy attempting to hear important information relating to our lives, leaving fewer resources to comprehend, remember and process information.

There is a real sense of 'use it or lose it' here, just as so-called reminiscence therapy plays a large part in the exercise of cognitive powers; radio stations that are closely in touch with their audience are well placed to act in partnership both with the listener and with the relevant medical knowledge bases to enhance and develop positive well-being at various levels, not least memory, entirely through the use of sound. Angel Radio's programme policy, both through its music output—it boasts a huge record library of material made in the first half of the twentieth century, playing nothing more recent than 1960 in its playlists—and its speech archive of local people recalling their lives and social conditions in the locale over the years, may be an exemplar for practice in this respect. Interviewers use tact and subtlety in their techniques, and invite interviewees to reach back into their memories, encouraging them to seek out early recollections of sometimes small details that take the mind to a deeper level of personal history. When such interviews are broadcast, the speech is laced with appropriate music from the era under discussion, thus working as entertainment, but more significantly helping to create a form of time capsule, stimulating related memories in the listening audience. Such oral history projects stretch beyond the immediate listening demographic and can be used in schools and colleges, and as the soundtrack to exhibitions and displays of historical artefacts and illustrations. The educational value of generational memory in social history has extremely strong potential and is a resource too often underused.

The relationship between radio and its audience, and the understanding of that relationship on the part of the broadcaster, is always crucial to successful output, but nowhere more so than on a station whose audience may rely on the content at a fundamental level. Angel Radio's research has shown that the station's listenership is divided in the ratio of 45% male and 55% female. Of a sample of 304 listeners conducted in 2004, 28% were between 60–65, 20% were in the range of 66–70, 28% were between 71–75, 14% aged 76–80 and 8% were over the age of 80. This represents an audience that is largely ignored by most mainstream broadcasters and is certainly very seldom targeted. Research further showed that of this sample 90% were retired, 41% were single, divorced or widowed, and 97% did not have a relative living at home.[8] Such figures graphically demonstrate the potential for radio to play an active role in stimulating well-being and providing companionship in all sorts of ways, a major aspect being the enhancement of memory through interaction. Music is clearly a vital component, but the presence of a presenter fulfils a role that simply playing songs continuously can never match, and when the presenter comes from the same peer group as the audience, that relationship deepens in intimacy and response. For people who may feel isolated from society or lacking in purpose, and for whom everyday human contact is often lacking, the 'muscle' of memory withers through lack of exercise. Radio, because it works directly on the imagination, creates personal pictures, the making of which the listener is complicit in creating. Thus there is an emotional and intellectual dialogue in which memory and sound are inextricably linked.

The most significant aspect of this partnership is in active involvement; while there is no doubt that listening to music stimulates memory and active participation, creation and performance enhance the experience and help to maintain well-being and a sense of self. This is particularly important for those suffering from memory loss, either through dementia or through the natural process of ageing. The past and our recollection of it is the story of ourselves, seen and heard from our own personal perspective, and this narrative in relation to our experiences through life, through interaction, defines us in the present. We are all performers, and the performance of the self in differing situations, circumstances and relationships, is part of who we are. The trigger for the relevant performance may often be the sounds with which we are surrounded at any given time, even the acoustics of a room, and the self we perform is rooted in language as music, responding to one another—other performers—in the world around us, but as David Aldridge has expressed most elegantly:

> This performed identity is not solely dependent upon language but is composed rather like a piece of jazz. We are improvised each day to meet the contingencies of that day. And improvised with others, who may prove to be the very contingencies that day has to offer.
>
> We perform our identities and they have to have form for communication to occur. Such form is like musical form. Language provides the content for those per-form-ances.
>
> —[Aldridge: 14]

THE LOST CHORD

In the opening chapter of this book we briefly examined the structures in the brain, and in particular the connections that link to memory. We need now to apply that information to understand the nature of some of the memory-affecting conditions that can touch us as we grow older. Among these, the most familiar term in common usage is dementia; it is important to define this term. Anne Corbett, Research Communications Officer at the Alzheimer's society in the UK, has said:

> It is not a disease in its own right, and it is not a natural part of ageing. It is an umbrella term that describes a group of symptoms that are caused by many diseases that affect the brain. Dementia is caused by loss of nerve cells in the brain. Most dementias are progressive. This is because when a nerve cell dies, it cannot usually be replaced. As more

and more nerve cells die, the brain starts to shrink. Common symptoms include impaired cognition, lack of physical coordination and memory loss.[9]

It is important to underline Dr Corbett's point about the term 'dementia' and the wide range of the conditions for which it is a catch-all title. All treatment specialists, researchers and care institutions stress the importance of the requirement to treat the individual: no two of us are alike, and our needs mirror this in health and sickness. Diagnosis remains crucial to enable appropriate help and care and to ensure that stimuli are appropriate for positive responses to be shared. Alzheimer's disease is the most common form of dementia; most typically it develops in the hippocampus area of the brain and affects memory loss. The hippocampus has an important function in the formation of new memories about experiences, but damage to it does not affect all kinds of memory; for example, a person experiencing Alzheimer's disease may retain the ability to learn new motor or cognitive skills, including the ability to play a musical instrument.[10]

Lack of understanding on the part of the carer can result in inappropriate treatment and support, as with the traumatised children discussed in an earlier chapter; a breakdown in communication can lead to disaster. Little wonder that we may become deeply distressed when a condition robs us of the ability to respond while leaving us with the ability to absorb, in however limited a way. The sound dialogue stops. We are robbed of our performance and we become passive observers, outsiders watching—and perhaps failing to understand—the story of others, unable to continue our own narrative. Professor Anthea Innes, director of the Bournemouth University Dementia Institute, underlines the importance of treating the person rather than the illness:

> People are people, and good dementia care practice should be responding to the individual. The idea is that you compensate for the particular disability and enable people to live well, and that is a social agenda rather than a medical agenda. The important thing is to ensure people are part of society and not ostracised or marginalised.[11]

People with dementia, or others with severe memory or speech problems, such as those who have experienced a stroke, find themselves losing reference points, and can no longer perform their own self in a social sense. Here radio may be able to help, but it is essential that it plays an interactive role in communication rather than transmitting signals one way. If we are in our own home but devoid of company, without a social existence, sound and music can act as a stimulus to memory and imagination. Yet without the right of reply, or a set of circumstances that permit discussion or conversation developing from audio experiences, the flower soon withers.

Likewise within residential situations such as care homes, audio and visual programmes need to be selected carefully, with opportunity for interaction and triggers to positive rather than negative memories. Passive entertainment may help, hinder or irritate; active performance—either on a communal or one-to-one basis—restores something of our place in the world, gives us a sense of two-way communication. The South Yorkshire charity, The Lost Chord, founded in 1999 by Helena Muller, organises musical sessions with professional performers in residential homes 'in an attempt to stimulate responses in the main part from those who can't walk, talk, feed themselves or communicate in any way'.[12] The Lost Chord organisation ensures that its musicians and volunteers develop appropriate skills through training to work in care homes, and understand the impact that music can have on the brain and its application in dementia care. 'The whole idea is to get residents to interact, as much as possible, with the musicians, whether by playing percussion, singing, dancing, or moving in their chair to the beat of the music. At times, when you've got somebody who can hardly move their body at all, a small piece of percussion, enabling them to move to the beat of the music is often all they're able to cope with, but that for them provides a tremendous sense of achievement.'[13]

More than 120 locations are visited across the north of England, including Yorkshire, Derbyshire and Nottinghamshire, and satellite projects are operating in London, Cardiff, Coventry, Bury St Edmunds and Ipswich, with in excess of 1,300 sessions annually. One of the most important aspects of the service provided by *The Lost Chord* is continuity: 'We visit the same homes each month in order to build on the responses achieved in previous successive concerts.'[14] Habit, expectation and memory are all part of our lives, and a song, as we know, can live in the mind beyond other recollections. By providing active involvement in the making of music and a regular development from one session to the next, the regaining of a sense of self can to some degree be achieved. By continuing dialogue between The Lost Chord and carers, it is possible to measure the success of specific sessions and to develop strategies for maintaining the impetus of the music therapy between each one:

> All sessions are reported on by the musicians, the volunteers attending to assist the musicians in their efforts to stimulate responses, and the carers on behalf of the people with dementia. We are quite regularly informed on the reports of how the sessions and the music remain with the residents for longer than we all thought possible. All carers are invited to attend free training on the impact of music on the brain and the importance of music in the care of people with dementia as well as a recommendation of what is expected of the carers during and between sessions.[15]

For many years music therapy has been found to be beneficial to Alzheimer's patients. As long ago as 1991, Carol Prickett and Randall Moore were conducting experiments that indicated ways in which direct involvement in performance could help patients suffering from Alzheimer's-type dementia (AD): 'Patients for whom spoken response is becoming problematic, but who have not completely lost this faculty, may be actively engaged in vocal expression through singing, especially singing long-familiar songs.'[16] Prickett and Moore went on to conclude that 'staff interactions [at the time], both in formal Reality Orientation sessions and in informal contact, are almost always spoken, and if music is a part of ward life, it is most frequently in the form of a mass group singing or listening activity with little personal attention.'[17] More beneficial is a direct engagement: 'Singing is an appropriate component of the treatment plan for patients, but . . . it is probably most effective on an individualised basis.'[18] While in an ideal situation this might always be the case, logistics and funding often prohibit such direct personal contact. In the case of The Lost Chord, sessions are based predominantly on a group experience, but 'musicians are encouraged to perform to each person with dementia on a one-to-one basis during the sessions, kneeling down and singing or playing their instruments individually to everyone present'.[19]

The Lost Chord is a charity and relies heavily on public support to pursue and develop its work; in some areas performance therapy using sound and music is an adjunct of research into ageing disorders within academic institutions, although here too ongoing development of understanding and treatment often remains reliant on gift-aid support. The Comprehensive Centre on Brain Ageing at New York University (NYU) is specifically devoted to research and clinical advances towards the treatment and cure of neurodegenerative diseases affecting cognition. Within the department, Dr Mary Mittelman, director of the Psychosocial Research and Support Programme, has been working on research in support of the belief that music and social interaction can be of significant benefit to people with dementia and their families. To this end a pilot study was started in 2011, in which she and colleagues formed a unique choir which they have called The Unforgettables, made up of people recruited through outreach and involving a number of local organizations, including the New York City chapter of the Alzheimer's Association and NYU support groups. As part of the programme, choir members meet once a week to practice and are led by two conductor-directors, by whom they are taught standard techniques to enhance breathing, vocalization and performance, just like any other choir. A typical rehearsal period lasts for thirteen weeks in preparation for a concert that usually includes nearly twenty songs. Concerts have been given at regular intervals. The results for Mittelman and her team were self-evident: it has been clear from the start that there is joy in this process, a place of equality where no one feels stigmatized. The aim of the programme is to explore non-drug therapies in dementia care for those with the illness and their carers, and the choral group has been a vehicle with which to study the value of such interaction. There is also a process of education for the wider public, using the concerts as catalysts for changes in attitude and as exemplars for replication in other areas and communities. Music, involvement in its creation and the mutual sharing of an experience based on memory and interaction are shown to help many disorders, including depression. The great value of such projects is that they involve both the person with dementia and the carer together in physical activity, singing in a group as part of a mutual and equal partnership. There remains more work to do; Mittelman recognises that a qualitative and quantitative evaluation of the outcomes with a larger number of participants is essential to develop a stronger evidence base for its effectiveness. As is so often, this is reliant on funding to enable further research. Dynamic as the project is, this is only a start; funding would lead to more research, and there would be rigorous proof positive of the effectiveness of a normative activity such as rehearsing in maintaining function for people with dementia, and providing an effective alternative to available drugs. Radio and other forms of pure audio is, like performance, mentally interactive; the cliche of pictures in the mind being best in imaginative terms remains valid, and the connections discussed earlier have the potential for actively engaging and stimulating ideas and memory. Schools Radio, in which programmes created for classroom consumption were supplemented and augmented by written material and teachers' notes, is almost as old as broadcasting itself. The author recalls sessions in which teaching staff and pupils alike shared material led by broadcasters through a communal classroom receiver, in programmes such as *Singing Together*, a long-running series aimed at infant and primary schoolchildren across the UK, which featured catchy songs that would often remain with pupils for the rest of their lives. Words and music were frequently learnt between broadcasts when only the teacher had a copy of the the supplied book that accompanied the programmes, but *Singing Together* booklets were produced in sufficient quantities for most classes to have multiple copies. Likewise, from 1940 to 1970 the BBC ran a series of twice-weekly schools broadcasts under the title *Music and Movement,* consisting of various dramatic and descriptive exercises, led, as with *Singing Together*, by studio-based presenters, and remembered with a variety of emotions by those who experienced them.

Such programming has had a long and illustrious history; BBC Schools Radio began on 4 April 1924, when the BBC was still the British Broadcasting Company. The School Broadcasting Council for the United Kingdom was set up in 1947, and from the 1960s to the 1980s, a period often considered as a 'golden age' for British schools radio broadcasting formed an active part of education. By the early 1970s, around ninety per cent of schools were using the School Radio service, with the BBC producing eighty series per year for School Radio, which amounted to around sixteen hours per week. From the autumn of 1996 came a shift in policy, with all programmes broadcast overnight during BBC Radio 3's downtime, when they could be pre-recorded, before policy changed again and overnight broadcasts on the digital version of BBC Radio 4 were made available in the autumn of 2003. Since 2003 all school radio programmes have been available on the Internet, and the arrival of download technology has opened up a whole new avenue in audio for schools. It would seem to be a small shift in policy and thinking to apply such an idea to care homes and specialist support for the elderly and those with memory or cognitive problems. As always, funding is an issue, but in order to address this the fundamental question of attitude and will must be addressed. If the value of music and the benefits of interaction that comes with being part of a choir is proven, then this is surely an investment through sound that can we can ill afford to ignore?

It is frequently a point of discussion—and often of some wonder—that as we move into extreme old age our long-term memory develops sometimes seemingly miraculous powers of recall, while our short-term memory fails us completely. On reflection, this is not surprising. We are struggling to maintain the performance of ourselves within the present tense, and—if we accept that the historical narrative of our self is stored complete and in infinite detail within the memory, back to our beginnings—the mind offers us a mechanism for reconstructing that story. This is a profound concept: that long-term memory is a part of our being's survival instinct, from which it may follow that its developing power as we grow older is a device to preserve the essence of who we are and have been, enabling the continuing construct of our personal narrative. Here interactive media, in whatever form, plays a crucial role. Music, even passively experienced, as well as other forms of reminiscence therapy will open the door; however, it is active stimulation to communicate our memories that enables us to become content providers using those recollections, of value to ourselves and to to others as witnesses to a shared continuum, and providing ourselves—and the world—with new memories. Performance—in every meaning of the word—is key.

*

In October 2010, Emilie Gossiaux, a young art student from New Orleans studying at The Cooper Union School of Art in Manhattan, was struck by a truck whilst riding her bicycle in Brooklyn. Her injuries were terrible; as well as multiple fractures in her head, pelvis and left leg, she experienced resuscitated cardiac arrest, stroke and traumatic brain injury. Doctors and surgeons at Manhattan's Bellevue Hospital fought to save her life, but the prognosis was not good. Although her condition stabilised after some six weeks, she was blind and showed little sign of mental functioning or response, and medical staff came to the conclusion that her future lay in long-term nursing home care rather than rehabilitation. Emilie was in a dark, seemingly unreachable place. Before the accident, she had suffered from hearing loss that had begun as a child and had deteriorated throughout her teens. Now she was, seemingly, almost beyond communication. Day after day, night after night, her family and her boyfriend, Alan Lundgard, sat by her bedside, looking for ways to help her demonstrate some form of cognition.

The initial breakthrough came when Alan began spelling out words on the palm of her hand, to which, after some time, she began to respond, thus proving high-level cognitive functions were present. She was, in ways that had seemed once impossible, able to communicate, and pain, frustration and bewilderment came back. Through it all she had resisted the introduction of a hearing aid, and due to the distress such attempts caused her, and the delicacy of her physical situation, she remained in her silent, dark world. Finally, one day Alan persuaded Emilie to allow the insertion of the hearing aid, and immediately she came back to the world, enabling her to be transferred to a neuro-rehabilitation programme at another New York hospital. During some of the time of her most intense treatment, Alan Lundgard recorded his attempts to communicate with Emilie on his smartphone, and these sounds, combined with his recollections and those of Emilie's mother, Susan, formed the basis of a radio documentary made by WNYC's *Radiolab* programme from New York City. The programme prompted much international response when it was placed online. As well as the moving witness of recollection from Alan and Susan, there were interesting details of sound memory; for example, as Emilie began to respond, she showed intense irritation at hospital staff and others moving or even touching her, cursing and shouting 'Dashwood'. Alan was able to explain this by the fact that before the accident, they had seen the film of Jane Austen's novel *Sense and Sensibility*, and Emilie had clearly carried a memory of the rather flighty and irritating character of Mrs Dashwood, mother of Elinor and Marianne, whose decision-making powers left much to be desired.

At the time of writing, Emilie Gossiaux's story continues; as it does, sound, helped by artificial aids, becomes of increasing significance in her rehabilitation and sense of self, just as her struggle, and that of those around her, was chronicled through a remarkable audio documentary, in itself made possible partly by recordings created in hospital on a mobile phone.[20]

PERSONAL SOUND MAPPING

While the proactive exploitation of music memory has a major role to play in preserving identity, the identification and reproduction of sounds that relate specifically to a time and place in a person's life is harder to introduce into therapy. We come from diverse backgrounds and places, and each of our personal histories evokes a unique set of sounds that may have little or no meaning to many others, but that for ourselves can open important vistas of recollection. Music is universal, whereas a singular sound event that is part of an environment—a fog horn that was site specific to a particular part of coastline for instance—may not be widely available as a recording, but may be the key to an individual past for a person or community for whom it was once a daily occurrence. Likewise, that sound offers both a communal memory to those who lived within range of it, and at the same time an individual memory, given the particular circumstances of each hearer. The audio signals of factories, dockyards and shipyards echo across whole communities, just as air-raid sirens sent their chilling sound of warning into the homes and streets of diverse social classes. These sounds link the memories of a populace, but within that shared experience lies a myriad of personal recollections. Many towns and cities share sounds that ring at the same time with a sense of the communal and the personal. In Harrow, Greater London, for example, a common sound for many years was the hooter at the Kodak factory, summoning workers at the start of a shift. Everyone heard it—it became a collective memory—but it also lodged in the private memory of residents, embued with a layer of meaning specific to the individual circumstances of each person and family from an emotional and cultural point of view, at the same time powerfully enhancing a sense of Place. Were a number of people from Harrow to discuss the sound of the 'Kodak hooter', they would share a community of recollection, tempered by variation of volume, distance, direction and so on, while retaining the capacity to individualize the sound and its meaning within their own lives, in the process recalling details that were apparently long forgotten until stimulated by collective memory.

Richard Ranft, director of Sound and Vision at the British Library, points out that sounds often become significant when they are no longer part of our lives; we may not consciously remember them, but when they are reintroduced to us, memories and often imagery flood back, triggered by the sound stimulus. It may be loud sounds like a factory siren, or more subtle reminders such as the ambience of street conversation and the background noise of traffic:

> One sound we have in the archive is of a London Routemaster bus, a familiar sound to Londoners who used to travel on that form of transport. It has a very distinctive sound that's not something people might have been conscious of when they were sitting on the bus at the time, but there's obviously something that's preserved in the memory, because when you play that sound, people will suddenly remember the bus, smells, colour, shape, images, aspects their daily journey: so much is evoked through sound.[21]

It is often in the very normality of such material that its personal importance can lie, and within this fact is part of the problem regarding accessability; that is to say, we take sound so much for granted, we may overlook its role in our lives, to the extent that we do not consider it worth recording consciously in our mind. Here is where the democratisation of sound recording has a major role to play; there are more recording devices in use today than at any time in history, be they audio or video or both, and public dissemination media such as SoundCloud and YouTube are increasingly ubiquitous.

In July 2010, the British Library launched a one-year project called the *UK Soundmap*, inviting members of the public to record the sounds of their personal environment. The project produced more than two thousand recordings made in a geographical spread from the Shetland Islands to the Channel Isles, eighty per cent contributed from mobile phones.[22] The importance of such initiatives lies in the fact that even the most enlightened archivist and professional sound recordist cannot be everywhere, and it is impossible to know the unique role a particular sound may play in memory. Equally, the everyday audio that informs daily life will become more key to memory *because* it is ordinary and ephemeral. A Nokia mobile ringtone, the sound of a certain check-out till, or the dial-up sound of a modem from the 1990s will in time be superceded by new sounds, and be largely forgotten on a concious level. They *will*, however, become significant because they represent symptoms of a particular time and place, although not sounds we would recognise now as being of long-term significance: 'That's why working with the public to find what is significant to them is so important to us. For example, we received a recording of a warning siren from a chemical works on the estuary near Bristol. It was tested once a week, and when the sound went onto the website, we had a lot of responses, with memories of living in the area, beyond the direct recollections of the sound itself. So these sounds can be very colourful in evoking memories, but not necessarily the sort of things we would think of or systematically record ourselves.'[23]

Likewise, technology has increasing capacity and potential to help us preserve the sounds we hear, the matter of sonic memory. Earlier in this chapter we discussed the implications of the loss of hearing on our cognitive powers. One scenario suggested was that of remembering sounds no longer audible, and by an imaginative leap recreating audio inside the mind. For the writer and naturalist Richard Mabey, the experience has been the opposite of this. 'When it came to missing—or mishearing—birdsong, I certainly didn't fill in the gaps; rather I didn't recognise, so cognitively "erased", the bits I *could* hear. I ended up projecting onto the birdworld a collapse in song (and therefore of singers) that was in fact happening in my head.'[24] Mabey had begun to lose high frequency hearing during his thirties: 'Grasshoppers were the first to vanish, then the scream of swifts, then many of the warblers' songs.'[25] For a naturalist, the increasing loss of sound was both serious and depressing. The average frequency of birdsong is about 4,000 Hz, which in terms of pitch is close to the highest note on a piano keyboard. Many warblers, sparrows, waxwings, kinglets and a number of other birds produce sounds that reach 8,000 Hz and beyond, and so hearing loss in the 3,000–10,000 Hz range has a major impact on the sonic world of birds, not to mention insect sound, which typically occupies frequencies above 4,000 Hz.

For Richard Mabey, help—if not a cure—came in the form of the Song-Finder, an American invention that transposes birdsong down several octaves and that is under the user's control.[26] This works on a frequency-dividing principle, by which incoming sounds above 3,000–4,000 Hz are converted into digital signals that are then processed to split the frequency, enabling high bird sounds to be lowered to a frequency range where the user still has normal hearing. In adopting the device, Mabey had to overcome certain personal prejudices towards enhancing technologies that take experience beyond what is normally humanly possible, such as night-vision binoculars, bat detectors and so on: 'These devices are extensions of human senses rather than compensations for their failings, and I used to feel uncomfortable about what I felt was a kind of unnaturalness, the privileged access they gave to worlds and sensoria that were not properly ours.'[27] The SongFinder changed his mind, giving him back voices, albeit changed, lower and deeper, but with their song patterns preserved and—at last—audible to him again.

Valuable as this is, as Mabey suggests, can the purist amongst observers of the natural world come to terms with a representation of sound that is not as the human ear had once represented it to the brain? 'I now think these sensory extensions are most valuable precisely *because* they *do* disrupt our usual, anthropocentric perceptions.'[28] For Mabey, in coming to the SongFinder and regaining sounds he had thought lost forever, 'the greatest revelation was the extraordinary soundscape it revealed, a low, sonorous, intricately detailed symphony quite outside my usual experience'.[29] To step beyond our human sense systems, to occupy worlds of sound and vision that are not native to us, can both enable us to regain memory-feeding experiences from the past, and at the same time facilitate unexpected imaginative journeys offering new and spectacular memories for the future.

NOTES

1. Angel Radio, report and information document, April 2013.
2. Ibid.
3. Soo Williams, Ofcom Manager, Community Radio and RSLs.
4. Michael Berkeley, *The Guardian*, 7 September 2010.
5. Ibid.
6. Dr Jonathan Peelle, Assistant Professor, Department of Otolaryngology, Washington University at St. Louis, USA, personal communication with the author. See also Peelle et al: 'Hearing Loss in Older Adults Affects Neural Systems Supporting Speech Comprehension' in *The Journal of Neuroscience*, August 31, 2011, 31(35): 12638–12643, http://jpeelle.net/reprints/Peelle-2011-Hearing_loss_in_older_adults_affects_neural_systems_supporting_speech_comprehension.pdf (accessed July 2013).
7. Ibid.
8. *Research Works* survey, quoted in Angel Radio report and information document.
9. Dr Anne Corbett, Research Communications Officer, Alzheimer's Society, UK: *Dementia Brain Tour*: www.alzheimers.org.uk/braintour (accessed June 2013).
10. One specific type of Alzheimer's disease is Posterior cortical atrophy, affecting the back of the brain. This was the condition the author Terry Pratchett experienced. Other forms include Vascular dementia, associated with blood supply to the brain, Dementia with lewy bodies, a condition that prevents cells from communicating properly, and Fronto-temporal dementia, sometimes seen in younger people, in which language and behaviour are affected. Dementia can also be caused by HIV, Huntingdon's disease, Prion diseases such as CJD and excessive alcohol consumption. See the link in note 6 for further clarification.

11. Professor Anthea Innes, Director, Bournemouth University Dementia Institute, interviewed by the author.
12. Helena Muller, interview, *The Lost Chord* website www.lost-chord.org.uk/ (accessed July 2013).
13. Ibid.
14. Ibid.
15. Helena Muller, correspondence with the author.
16. Carol A. Prickett and Randall S. Moore, the University of Alabama and the University of Oregon, 'The Use of Music to Aid Memory of Alzheimer's Patients', *Journal of Music Therapy, XXVlli (2)* 101–110, 1991, National Association of Music Therapy Inc.
17. Ibid.
18. Ibid.
19. Helena Muller, communication with the author.
20. *Finding Emilie*, WNYC, *Radiolab*, www.radiolab.org/2011/jan/25/finding-emilie/ (accessed 10 August 2013). A website for Emilie Gossiaux may be accessed via this link: www.emiliegossiaux.com/ (accessed 10 August 2013).
21. Richard Ranft, Director, Sound and Vision, British Library, interview with the author.
22. Information can be found about the UK Soundmap through this site: http://britishlibrary.typepad.co.uk/archival_sounds/uk-soundmap/ (accessed July 2013).
23. Richard Ranft, interview with the author.
24. Richard Mabey, personal communication with the author.
25. Ibid.
26. More information on this device may be found by following this link: www.nselec.com/ (accessed August 2013).
27. Richard Mabey, personal communication with the author.
28. Ibid.
29. Ibid.

10 The Future Sound of Memory

Memory makes us human because it is a major symptom of our existence. We cannot remember not being here, and the idea of not being able to remember, whether it be the mystery of pre-existence or a darkening of consciousness either through illness or death, gives us the sense of an island of cognition bordered by the pre-natal and the post-sentient, and provides riddles that have fuelled science and art for as long as the human species has existed. Memory is part of the sense of our selves. It is the context in which we live our present and consider our future. Sound surrounds us whether we hear it or not, whether we are conscious of its presence or whether—either through a hearing defect or other medical issue—we are unable to consciously react to it. The role of sound in memory is under-researched and underappreciated, even within ourselves.

We know music to be of huge significance in memory. As we have seen, from childhood and teenage years it registers sonic landmarks in our lives that can be immensely valuable if we can reinvest in its memory as we grow older. Yet other sounds, and even the voices of loved ones, seem harder to hold. The memory of them must be there within us—we recognise a voice when we hear it—but calling up the recollection of a voice as we would a melody seems sometimes, although not always, distressingly difficult.

We need our recordings, as much as—or more than—we need our photographs and diaries in the evocation of memory, but we have less of a habit in this area, and domestic spoken recordings do not find a place in family archives in the way that pictures and movies traditionally do. With the increase in appetite for commercial speech recordings such as talking books, perhaps this will change. Certainly, as Karin Bijsterveld has pointed out, there is the capacity for both recorded and unrecorded sound to help stimulate and foster memory; musical memory is often remarkable, but 'actively remembering everyday sound and voices seems to be much harder'. [Bijsterveld & van Dijck: 13]

Developing technology enables the calling up of archive material, creating the possibility for radio stations to be at once commentators on the present day and libraries of memory through online access to past programmes. For example, successive controllers of BBC Radio 4 have long been aware of the fund of material accrued by the UK's leading speech-orientated broadcaster, and in 2013 the network's controller, Gwyneth Williams, took the step of making a large amount of these programmes available via the station's website on a permanent basis.

> Radio 4 as it unfolds each day is a chronicle of British life. The nature of the network, offering the opportunity for encounters across different subject areas, is a unique way to evoke the state of the nation. Now the evolving digital side of Radio 4 and the deployment of our unique archive allows us to travel through time and evoke in an unprecedented way the feel, sound and dominant influences of periods from the past. The imaginative world of Radio 4 provides a powerful trigger for memory and can immerse us in personal or political times gone by. So listeners can experience episodes of some of the network's most iconic programmes from the past, such as of *Desert Island Discs*; Alastair Cooke in a distant *Letter from America*, or, say, the *Reith Lecture* series given by Edward Said in the 1990s.[1]

Through the first decade of the twenty-first century and beyond, the development of technology for broadcasters and individuals alike continually opened new possibilities for dialogues between the present and the past. As we have seen, the capacity and fascination with home recording has been present for almost as long as sound preservation has been technically possible. The coming of miniaturisation in the form of the first the transistor radio and subsequently the audiocassette ushered in the concept of both portability and—with the advent of the Sony Walkman in 1979—also privacy and control over recorded audio; we acquired the ability to choose the sounds through which we moved, rejecting, if we so wished, the 'found' soundscape of the world and replacing it with a selected personal soundtrack.

By so doing of course, we become divorced from the real sound world and therefore retain no memory of it for our future. For example, we may hold a visual memory of a walk past the waterfront bars and restaurants of Singapore while having no sense of the sonic character of the place, replacing it perhaps with a song or instrumental tune heard on our personal stereo that may or may not contain any relevance or context to the place in which we find ourselves. With the development of MP3 players and the playlisting of past musical memories, this sense of disengagement has increased, separating us in auditory terms from the currency of place-experience through a separate created nostalgia. As Michael Bull has written, the users of MP3 players 'often report being in dream reveries while on the move—turned inward from the world—and living in an interiorised and pleasurable world of their own making, away from the historical contingency of the world, and into the certainty of their own past, real or imagined, enclosed safely within their own private auditory soundscape. Nostalgia bathes these experiences in a warm, personalised glow'. [Bijsterveld & van Dijck: 83–93]

Traditional modes of media consumption have changed enormously since the turn of the century, and today's infants are growing into a world where technologies with which their parents were familiar will be of historical interest rather than of day-to-day use. Electronic media will always provide sound memories, but like language itself, the means of communication will change. The same intense emotional engagement of the sound experience that radio provided before television for generations, will continue to shape future listening through new and yet unimagined carriers. In the end it is the message, not the messenger, that counts. The makers for young children are already adjusting to how their audiences will absorb these messages. In August 2013, BBC Children's, the department handling dedicated programming for the young, launched its CBeebies' *Playtime* app, designed to share the experience of its television programmes on mobile devices. The move recognised, as the director of BBC Children's, Joe Godwin, said at the time, that 'technology is firmly embedded in children's lives and has opened up opportunities to inform, educate and entertain them in new ways. The CBeebies *Playtime* app is a great example of this, allowing our youngest audiences to learn through play and get even closer to the characters and shows they love, safely, whenever and wherever they want. We've also introduced several innovative features that let parents share in the fun with their little ones'.[2] This latter point is a crucial one; as we have seen in our discussion about the influence of media on the young in Chapter 4, efforts need to be maintained to ensure that memory and experience are not developed in isolation. The challenge is to gain the most positive aspects of mobile interaction while preserving security, and at the same time enabling, wherever possible, interaction also at a human level.

Technical interaction can take us into alternative worlds; in the appendix to this book memories of radio listening are linked to the environment in which those programmes were heard, and in turn this stimulates memory of personal histories and relationships. What, then, of a world of entertainment that excludes the surrounding world and creates an alternative existence? Gaming can involve, in some instances, placing a helmet on the head, switching on, and moving into a virtual place that may or may not relate in some way to the environment in which we physically find ourselves. This kind of immersion may provide powerful memories, but how will these memories twenty, thirty or forty years on relate to the *real* time and place in which they were experienced? The American sound designer David Sonnechein has developed games using current technology, and considers the sense of ownership in these cases—as in a song—to be potentially significant. At the same time, in recent decades, circumstances have changed, with the earlier onset of puberty on one hand, and a later development of adulthood and the adoption of fuller responsibility on the other. For producers making new generation creative materials, more than ever the factors come to a confluence that is at one and the same time neurological, cultural and technological:

The speeding up of technology, information and audio-visual media certainly is affecting everyone's consciousness and memory. There is so much more to absorb, and the filters and attention span are working at a very different rate than a generation ago. Although things are moving much faster, I'm not sure how much more is being absorbed and retrievable as memory in later years. It could be just a blur. It might depend on the individual. The digital repository (i.e. Google) makes access easier, but it's not clear how this affects personal memory.[3]

The potential risks to peripheral memory of immersive listening was identified in an earlier chapter. Nevertheless, Gill Davies, working on programmes for young children, sees the evolution of media consumption as overall highly positive; with the exponential increase in bandwidth in homes and educational establishments, 'future generations will have the ability to communicate with their peers in other parts of the world to a far greater extent than is possible now, and therefore will be exposed to sounds not only from their own environments, but from different cultures'.[4] Davies sees these proactive developments in her personal relationships as well as in her professional work, and notes how the fusion of experience between media leads towards a sharper interactive memory:

My 10 year-old son is quick to identify music or sound effects he has heard in computer games when he hears them in another context. Similarly, he can identify music he hears on the radio that has featured in a film or TV programme. I asked him and a group of his friends if they would prefer to play games on their tablets with the sound turned down, or wear headphones, and they unanimously declared that they would prefer to wear headphones as the sound is such a vital part of the gameplay.

Some console-based games allow players to choose which sounds they would like to use (in the same way that mobile phones offer a choice of ring tones), but the children of Davies' son's generation belong to an era in which becoming part of the process is increasingly important. For earlier generations, imaginative interaction with radio broadcasts created memories; Davies has noted that the desire for modern youth to be a part of the experience is developing in a more proactive way. 'They would like to be able to make their own sound effects and compose music—something that games manufacturers should perhaps consider, given the availability of cheap recording and editing equipment!'[5]

✳

The pocket technology at the heart of mobile entertainment and communication has the capacity to revolutionise the gathering and preservation of daily life, a factor that could have a potentially far-reaching impact on archiving the memory of the sounds with which we surround ourselves. Here may exist a key to a greater understanding of the power and value of sound as human memory. The British Library has explored projects using mobile telephones, most of which carry built-in cameras and sound recording facilities, to engage the public and enhance interest in sound as a document, as in its crowdsourcing initiatives such as *The UK Sound Map*,[6] discussed in an earlier chapter, and *Map Your Voice*.[7] Richard Ranft, director of Sound and Vision at the British Library, believes that at public events and in situations of conflict such as protests and riots, a mobile device in the hands of what might be termed as 'citizen journalists', together with the ability to store and email audio files instantly around the world, represents a recording tool of great potency.

> People always carry their 'phones, so recording devices are now absolutely everywhere. Looking back, how interesting it will be to hear these sounds; we'd love to hear the sounds of a London Street at the time of Charles Dickens, but we can't. In 100 years time, people will KNOW what Britain sounded like now. We want to document contemporary life, sounds of the weather, sounds of the everyday, not just special occasions. Mobile 'phone projects are democratising the recordists' and the curators' role.[8]

The latter, while often led by institutional initiatives, can also develop independently through the enthusiasm of an individual or group. The success of the *UK Sound Map* project has prompted the development of similar schemes in other countries, such as the *Sound of the Netherlands* initiative across Holland, and may inspire further Europe-wide developments to map environmental sounds over several countries, moderated locally.[9] Certainly the sophistication of smartphones lends them to crowdsourcing for material, further enhanced by the metadata that is contained in the phones' software. Within the first five years of the twenty-first century, organisations such as OhmyNews in South Korea and Bayosphere and KYOU in the United States were exploiting user-contributed audio linked to the Internet, and Ranft sees such initiatives as important for the future: 'It's very good for the Library to be involved with. It brings a whole new range of audiences into contact with us, many of whom perhaps had not used the Library before.'[10] For institutions funded from the public purse, it is not only good practice to provide as wide a sense of ownership of collections as possible, but it is also an investment in that audience, empowering it as it does not only to use but also to contribute to collections in an interactive way. Historically, public usage of mobile communication and social media has tended to adapt and even at times subvert available facilities to often unexpected ends, as with the early adoption of texting amongst the young, which quickly grew to a major form of communication in its own right.

The appendix of this book, based on an online survey of radio memories, is a simple example of how Internet communication has been used to explore the memory of sound, specifically delving into recollections of radio from childhood. Expanding the question of sound memories beyond radio, Stijn Demeulenaere, the Belgian sound artist and radio maker, has created an art installation called *Soundtracks*[11] that seeks out sound memories in written form, specifically *handwritten* hard copies. Thus new technology links with a fundamental communication form to share the memory of sonic experience.

Demeulenaere is the curator, producer and presenter of the free-form radio show *Radio Eliot* on Radio Scorpio.[12] He was a member of the improvisation collective *Karen Eliot* and his wide experience has included work as dramaturge for Archipel, editor for Jan Fabre and radio journalist for a number of European radio stations. With his art installation *Soundtracks* he is building an archive, not of sounds themselves, but of memories of sounds. The motive is to draw attention to sound; with mobile technology, millions of people are taking photographs to bear witness to their lives every day, so why not chronicle and document sound experiences in the same way? The concept and the facility is there, but it is not yet instinctual. This is perhaps changing, led by sound practitioners and such apps as *Soundcloud, Mixcloud* and others, but meantime:

> The only way most of us retain sounds is by remembering them . . . Our memory of sound becomes infused with where we were and who we were in the moment we heard the sound. Thus the remembered sound becomes a little piece of personal history. A remembered sound can be powerful. Sometimes when we hear a particular sound, we are catapulted back to the moment we first heard it.
>
> I'm interested in this phenomenon, and in the stories that cling to those sounds, and therefore I started an archive of sound memories. I have asked people to write me a letter describing the sound they remembered, and to tell me why they remember this sound, why it struck them, why it is important to them. The archive now counts over a 1,000 letters, in about 15 languages. The longest letter is 12 pages long. The shortest is a 5 word sentence in German.[13]

This is a brave and interesting initiative, particularly given the fact that letter writing is an increasingly lost form of communication; (where will all the memories contained in emails go?) A personal sound archive, either recorded or based on written memories of sounds, may help to fill the void created by our virtual interaction with one another.

The question that relates to all memory—not only sound—is how it may change as a result of instant Internet access to the vast array of information and facts at our fingertips; the verb 'to Google' has entered world language, and we encounter knowledge on an instant basis of desire and requirement. This culture of instant gratification of curiosity leaves out the process of considered searching and acquisition, and the implications on memory may be profound. In research conducted by Betsy Sparrow of the Department of Psychology at Columbia University, it becomes clear that within a relatively short space of time, computer access and the 'need to know' culture of immediate information has already changed its character to be less of an add-on to our absorption of facts, but to become, an extension of ourselves:

> The result of four studies suggest that when faced with difficult questions, people are primed to think about computers and that when people expect to have future access to information, they have lower rates of recall of the information itself and enhanced recall instead for where to access it. The internet has become a primary form of external or transactive memory, where information is stored collectively outside ourselves.[14]

An analogy might be this: if I am driving on an unfamiliar route, I am concentrating, and striving to recall directions I have been given, but when I am being driven to my destination by someone who knows the way, I relax and pay little heed of the process of negotiating the journey. (Satellite navigation systems can have the same effect.) What is particularly interesting in the study by Sparrow and her colleagues is that we are applying this relationship to computer technology in the same way as we would to human interaction, 'depending on several of the same transactive memory processes that underlie social information-sharing in general'.[15] Also, we are training ourselves to be selective in what we remember, so we do not remember things we believe we can access on our computer, while retaining memory of things we think we may not be able to reach through technology. In the former, the memory is of where we are likely to find an item rather than a detailed memory of the item itself. The results of the research conducted by Sparrow's team suggest that 'the processes of human memory are adapting to the advent of new computing and communication technology . . . We are learning what the computer "knows" and when we should attend to where we have stored information in our computer-based memories'.[16] The conclusion of this is that computer access to information is treated as an extension of our own memory; we are interconnected systems.

What the long-term implications for human memory are due to this reliance is hard to conceive, but it is clear that in order to function at the level of intellect and memory as they currently do, computer-literate people need to remain connected at all times. It is a part of our societal interaction, and functions in the same way as our knowledge-acquisition relation with the wider human world. As Sparrow says, 'the experience of losing our Internet connection becomes more and more like losing a friend. We must remain plugged in to know what Google knows'.[17] The old saying, 'I don't know the answer, but I know a person who does' still applies; in the new culture however, the difference is that the 'person' is a computer. This may seem shocking to some, and yet we have really not come far since the ancient world debated the controversy engendered by the coming of the written word and the transfer from oral culture to a 'fixed' text on a page. The fear then was that the art of memory, said to have been created by the poet Simonides, would disappear; indeed things *did* change, and they continue to do so. The ability to archive in print or in any other form subtly changes the mnemonic strategies we call up to access our past and the essentials of our context for living. As we devise aids to the symptomatic preservation of our existence, we become more dependent upon them because they remove the necessity for us to carry that information with us mentally.

In terms of accessing sound memory, this dependence may well actually aid our ability to reach significant sonic prompts to past experience. Being guided as to how to reach a destination can in some cases trigger other mnemonic responses, including sound. Even the act of typing a certain set of digits in a certain order engrains itself and can open new pathways. Creatively, there is a significant link between the physical body and memory and in the performing arts; this becomes most tangible through sound, because we hear not only through our ears but also through our whole body. Thus a profoundly deaf person will feel vibrations and frequencies of sound that the mind can 'listen to' and interpret. So both hearing and memory are linked to the physical while retaining the mystery of invisible forces. For an actor, characterisation goes beyond the process of thought to put the mind in the right place to enter a fictionalised world. This may be a physical place, a part of a stage 'inhabited' by the character at a specific time, or it can be an imagined environment (although none the less real within the context of the role being interpreted). When an actor 'dries'—forgets his or her lines—it is often because the connection has been lost between understanding and speaking, in other words, the performer no longer knows why he or she is saying what they are saying. We remember in sequence; given the first line of a familiar poem, we may be able to remember the rest, but if something interrupts that sequence, or if we become mentally disturbed, distracted or affected by, for example, stage fright, or a concern outside of the context of the immediate act, the sequence breaks down. In a play, the prompter is there to provide the clue that resets the rhythm of memory. A rehearsed move from one side of the stage to the other may be enough to trigger the next line, because of its association with a mood or an idea. The word does not begin as a word, but as a thought and an emotion; it is perhaps very significant that we speak of 'learning by heart'.

The future sound of memory, subject to new and ever-developing media-led objects and lifestyles, bewilders one generation as it liberates and exhilarates another. Faced with predictions, the trap is to be dazzled by technology without its application to content, and therefore to see only a partial picture. There are some reverberations back into silence—that most profound of all sounds—and the silent sound of learning by heart, and there is the sense also that new forms are not actually new at all, but in themselves memories and reinventions of eternal human forms of communication. As

Piers Plowright says, 'in some ways, fast culture—RAP for example—calls on and stimulates aural memory, just as ballads and songs used to'. On the other hand: 'I do think the difficulty of/resistance to standing and sitting still and listening to silence or the small sounds of the world, must be making it more difficult to reverence and remember.'[18]

As a species, we are slow to give up the objects of habit, and while new generations may adopt new habits, they will perhaps find themselves clinging to them as they grow older, just as their parents and grandparents did with the technology that accompanied *their* formative years. At the time of writing (late 2013) on-demand radio—or 'audio' listening, via online players such as the BBC iplayer, the commercial Radioplayer or through podcasts, is still relatively small. However, as the radio futurologist, writer and consultant, James Cridland points out:

> It is growing: and the future trend is for more time-shifting into radio listening. Why wait until next week, when your favourite programme is available at the touch of a few buttons online?
>
> I think the growth of on-demand audio means a subtle, imperceptible change in our relationship with radio or audio. Slowly, it will feel less 'connected' and more solitary. In the 1980s, I remember, on motorway trips, seeing other people singing along to the same song I was. I don't think that happens much now. As we continue making our audio a more on-demand experience (with *Pandora*-like services, too), it'll happen even less.[19]

That said, the capacity for the radio as an object to feature in memory will remain because the simplicity of the medium in its basic form makes it in some ways impervious to change. Earlier in this book, the sense of nostalgia for the object was discussed, and the appendix explores this aspect further. Although this object nostalgia will alter for a number of generations, radio sets will still retain the curious quality of physical friends, and for this reason will tend to stay with us and around us much longer than other technologies, partly because of their timelessness and partly because of the habit they form with us.

> Very few of us actively switch stations. The user interface is, for most of us, one button—press it, and your radio makes noise, press it again, and it's quiet. If you have a favourite radio station, there's no reason to change your radio, since a new one will get the same station and sound roughly similar. That's a drawback for technologists, who want us to constantly upgrade, and a drawback for those single-mindedly backing DAB, who are frustrated with the rate of change: but it is, I believe, why radio has been so resilient to changes. Another reason? By and large, most families these days don't have a radio in their living room

and therefore have no fashion-related reasons to change the radio set—they're normally in more intimate places like the bedroom, bathroom or kitchen.[20]

In other words, if the technology still works, and does not offend the decor, why change it?

MEMORY, SOUND AND TIME

Without memory, we would live in a profound mental darkness, with no chronology. We have seen in earlier chapters the torment this can produce. Through history we have used art—in whatever form—as one way of explaining our identity, and in the process of that defining, however we choose to do it, memory is the key factor, and that key is turned in different ways. Just as for the actor the physical and the mental are linked, so it is for a dancer, learning and relearning the relationship between music and movement until the sound enters the body and finds expression. Likewise for a musician, the memory of sound in sequence is linked to the physical placement of the fingers on the instrument. A spiritual logic takes over, memory is no longer the issue, because it is so deeply engrained in expression; just as for a painter such as Howard Hodgkin, making a physical object out of memory opens profound doors of human understanding. To know this is to come to terms with the responsibility, as our world of technology develops, for the continuing use of that technology at the service of sound in the preservation of experience.

When we seek to find a beginning to modern media, we come to no clear single moment. A number of names come up from the memory of history, each having played a part in the birth of electronic communication; the German physicist C. A. Steinheil experimented with railway tracks as conductors of telegraph messages as early as 1838, and in 1842 Samuel Morse found that wires laid alongside a canal utilised the adjacent water as a conducting medium. Later players in the drama included Alexander Graham Bell, Thomas Edison, Oliver Lodge, Heinrich Hertz, J. A. Fleming, David Sarnoff, Reginald Fessenden and of course Guglielmo Marconi. Yet perhaps the fundamental father of the modern world of the transfer of thought should be considered to be James Clerk Maxwell, whose 1864 paper to the Royal Society, 'The Dynamic Theory of the Electromagnetic Field', explored the existence of electromagnetic waves and their ability to travel at differing rates through air and water. Twenty-three years later, in 1877, Maxwell wrote a work intended as an introduction to Newtonian dynamics for students and informed lay readers, called *Matter and Motion*. Early in the work, he gives us an elegant and concise picture of his conception of the idea of time: 'The recognition of an order of sequence in our state of consciousness.' [Maxwell: 11]

He speaks of memory, the difficulty of comparing intervals of time between events and the placing of experience within a chronology. In the end, he concludes, it is through human interaction with one another and the world that the structure of our existence is best measured:

> By our intercourse with other persons, and by our experience of natural processes which go in a uniform or rhythmical manner, we come to recognise the possibility of arranging a system of chronology in which all events whatever, whether relating to ourselves or to others, must find their places.
>
> —[Ibid.]

Because sound and experience are temporal, our relationship with the world around us is a continuing journey in which the senses interpret life and make memory of it. Because sound is always present as it happens, always fading as it passes, it is a potent link between ourselves as we are and ourselves as we once were, as well as a metaphor for our own transience. This makes it the gift it is, something, whether we have the facility to play it back on a machine or to recreate it in our imagination, that we try so hard to preserve and revisit as we move forward. The idea of voluntary and involuntary memory has its mirror in the way radio and downloadable audio provides us with the sounds that accompany our day-to-day life and help to form the fabric of recollection. Listening to a familiar song or poem or voice held on an MP3 player has the capacity to blend surprise and familiarity: 'Oh, I had forgotten this was part of the mix!' or 'I hadn't remembered she sounded like that!' On the other hand, live, traditional radio, coming out of the *æther* and returning to it, touching us as it passes, can truly surprise and offer the potential for an involuntary—yet hopefully nonetheless welcome—auditory experience that will be added to our own playlist of sound memories. John Reith, the first Director General of the BBC, believed in the serendipity of broadcasting; his is still a valid view today. In both cases, whether it be electronic or natural, we must be ready for and receptive to the messages as and when they come.

As the German sound artist Christina Kubisch has written, 'listening is, in itself, an activity that must be consciously learned and developed'. [Lander & Lexier: 72] The same could be said for committing sound to memory. We can learn a song and call its melody back from the past, just as we can recognise a bird's voice because it is part of our experience. We already navigate the world through the recognition of sound, so it is a simple expansion of this subconscious act to exercise our sonic memories deliberately and consciously. Just as we are able to commit a speech from a play, a verse from a poem or a multiplication table to memory by an act of will and concentration, so we can 'learn' a sound and call it back to memory, part of a cognitive 'library' that enriches existence. Too often we hear with inattentive ears and listen with indifferent minds. To truly listen to the sounds of the world around us would be to enhance both our past and our present, so we should learn how to remember sound. A still greater gift to ourselves would be to learn a sense of practiced recall, to listen to sound in the memory, as if for the very first time, regaining the wonder in the same way a good poem, in Jane Hirshfield's words, 'flenses the dull familiarity from words, allowing them to gleam as they did when first made.' [Hirshfield: 35]

Earlier chapters discussed the role of place in audio memory and ourselves as history; taking these two ideas, we may see ourselves as recording devices, absorbing and preserving our personal witness of the world through the senses.

While this ideal may appear to have the potential for vastly expanding the sense of self and enriching our lives and history, the problems of sonic overload increasingly mitigate against us. Because our ears never shut, we too often take sound memory for granted. Worse, we may actually be losing the skill of listening, so Christina Kubisch's exhortation becomes more urgent and important as we find ourselves more surrounded by the world's cacophony, the sonic equivalent of fast food, mixed with diverse messages, some relevant and some not, requiring more processing and filtering by our mind than ever before.

The problem becomes twofold: firstly we become bewildered by the sheer volume of material; we have moved from a place where we had too little access to our history, to a situation where there is so much that we need extra memory to retain what we have access to. As Francesca Panetta says, 'we need to be librarians to store everything!'[21] The second issue is related to the 'Google problem' discussed earlier in this chapter: because we have the capacity to store so much, will our listening change as a result? 'Because we can record sounds of our life and access them at will, is there a danger that we won't listen as well or with the same concentration as we did when we had to rely on retaining more in our memory? Our attention has changed, is different now, so if we are checking our phones at the same time as talking and doing a dozen other things, are we listening as carefully and imprinting these sounds in a deep neurological way? With our focus switching all the time, does sound have the same space in our head that it used to?'[22]

The sound that reverberates around a giant sacred building is a metaphor for the temporal experience of listening, because an echo is the memory of the sound that produced it. Our ancestors, entering the relative security of their cave-homes, sensed the acoustic change as they walked deeper into the earth. At first they may have thought they heard voices answering theirs; in time they came to understand that the walls sent back to them an instant sound memory of themselves, and the concept of a sonic past may well have been born at that moment. We have seen throughout this journey how Place memory can engage us through sound; and of course, because we inhabit life in terms of a series of places, be they office blocks, tent cities, condominiums or caves, we carry their memory and—if we can focus our minds—their sounds with us ever after. The poet Percy Bysshe Shelley wrote:

> The curse of this life is, that whatever is known, can never be unknown. You inhabit a spot, which before you inhabit it, is as indifferent to you as any other spot on earth, and when, persuaded by some necessity, you think you leave it, you leave it not; it clings to you—and with memories of things, which, in your experience of them, gave no such promise, revenges your desertion.
>
> —[Peacock: 123]

Certainly we carry our past with us, but its presence may lie dormant until a trigger releases it from its silence—spiritual and physical. Much has been discussed in these pages relating to voluntary and involuntary memory and the relative attributes of both. When considering these two forms in relation to sound, given a choice, which would we choose to retain, were such a choice to be offered? In some future state of mind, would we opt for perfect recall, or the option of being surprised by sound? Samuel Beckett considered that Marcel Proust had a bad memory; moreover, Beckett viewed this as an attribute, a source of the writer's genius. 'The man with the good memory does not remember anything because he does not forget anything. His memory is uniform, a creature of routine, at once a condition and function of his impeccable habit, and instrument of reference instead of discovery.' [Beckett: 29–30]

If we hear the same old song—that melody that once meant so much to us so long ago—too often, it ceases to shock us with its memory. The sound of a Routemaster bus becomes significant because we had forgotten it until the recording reminded us of the place it once occupied in our daily life, as it took us to our place of work or school, just as the factory hooter, which was part of a daily routine once upon a time, opens a new door now when heard again after a lifetime. Any training of the body's aural system and mind's mnemonic receiver should seek to preserve and enhance our sense of Self, but it should not prevent the ear from being innocent, from retaining the capacity for wonder at the retrieval of a sonic experience and the joy of rediscovery. Absorb the unexpected in sound, recall a forgotten voice, a voice we might believe to have been lost to us; hear the space rocket take off at the start of a long-gone radio drama from childhood, let the audio sepia of a forgotten song unlock its meaning once again, and the past seeps through like colour on paper. It was there all the time, but the glory is in the rediscovery of it, the surprise of its regained place in consciousness and the added dimension this offers the senses and the spirit. Sound is both tangible and intangible at one and the same moment, an emotion as well as a sense. It begins its communication with the mind even before physical birth, and whether or not it be, as some say, the last sensory link we have with our earthly life, the dialogue between sound and memory, while it exists echoing off the walls of our world, is the most significant and precious symptom of—and witness to—the self we possess.

NOTES

1. Gwyneth Williams, communication with the author.
2. BBC Media Centre Press Release, www.bbc.co.uk/mediacentre/latestnews/2013/cbeebiesapp.html (accessed August 2013).
3. David Sonnenchein, communication with the author.
4. Gill Davies, communication with the author.
5. Ibid.
6. http://sounds.bl.uk/Sound-Maps/UK-Soundmap
7. www.bl.uk/evolvingenglish/maplisten.html (accessed Augsut 2013).
8. Richard Ranft, director, Sound and Vision, the British Library, interview with the author.
9. Details of the *The Sounds of the Netherlands* project and other European initiatives can be accessed through this link: www.soundsofeurope.eu/eblog/the-sound-of-the-netherlands/ (accessed August 2013).
10. Richard Ranft, interview with the author.
11. www.stijndemeulenaere.be/soundtracks.html (accessed August 2013).
12. www.radioscorpio.be/ (accessed August 2013).
13. Stijn Demeulenaere, communication with the author.
14. Betsy Sparrow, Jenny Liu and Daniel M. Wegner, 'Google Effects on Memory: Cognitive Consequences of Having Information at Our Fingertips', in *Science 5*, August 2011, Vol. 333, pp. 776–778, www.sciencemag.org (accessed August 2013).
15. Ibid.
16. Ibid.
17. Ibid.
18. Piers Plowright, communication with the author.
19. James Cridland, communication with the author.
20. Ibid.
21. Francesca Panetta, interview with the author.
22. Ibid.

Appendix
Radio in the Context of Memory

While this book has explored the relationship between sound and memory in broad terms, a case has been made for the potential for radio in particular to stimulate recollection; it has been suggested that from this the power of subliminal connections to produce cognitive responses may in turn open up lost avenues of our personal histories. In the first chapter I attempted an exercise imposed on myself, in which I used the remembrance of a radio broadcast heard in my childhood as a form of time machine to unlock other experiences and peripheral sound memories from a time in the early 1950s. It became clear through further analysis and discussion with oral history experts that these may not have been the memories of the actual sounds but the recollection of circumstances in which the sounds were first experienced. On the other hand, it is difficult to prove objectively that the aural witness carried in my mind from the time I was seven years old is *not* that of the *actual* audio moment; a chicken clucking, a train shunting and so on. It is not just the sound itself, which could be generic, but the acoustical environment in which it is heard—internal walls, the placement of buildings affecting echoes and weather conditions—that create a unique context for a sound to be preserved from the past. We are capable of retaining a phrase from a beloved song exactly, the tone, pitch and general delivery of a famous speech or an advertising jingle, so it follows that we have the capacity to carry with us the sounds that surround us at key times of our lives.

I was interested, having carried out this experiment on myself, to learn something of the experience of others, and to this end an online survey was set up during the month of May 2013, in which respondents were invited to offer the following:

- Place of the memory
- General age range: (18–30, 31–50, 51–70, 70+)

Specific questions in the survey were as follows:

- What is your earliest memory of listening to radio?
- How old were you at this time?

- What do you remember about the set on which you listened to the radio?
- What were the programmes you listened to regularly?
- Did you normally listen to radio on your own, with family members or both?
- What can you remember about your listening environment?
- What other sounds were going on immediately around you at the time you were listening?
- Spreading the sound circle, can you recall peripheral sounds outside of your immediate environment?
- How does recalling these sound memories make you feel now?

Respondents could answer or pass over questions by choice, although almost all chose to answer all questions. The survey, conducted over the period of one month and disseminated through social media, dedicated online radio interest discussion groups and the author's website, produced one hundred responses, some of the contents of which are discussed in this appendix. Of these responses, 55% came from the UK, 15% from Australia, 10% from Ireland, 10% from the United States, 7.5% from Canada and 2.5% from China. In terms of gender, responses broke down approximately as 70% male and 30% female. The exercise did not seek to provide definitive answers to the question of the power of radio within the context of living through formative years, nor did it set out to examine national differences in listening habits, but more the aim was to explore something of the emotional link between early listening and its human context. Responses came from all strata of society, and it was notable how radio from the earlier eras shared its light and 'highbrow' content, largely due, one suspects, to an overall lack of choice. Whatever the content, the power of the medium, particularly pre-television, was extremely strong, and this strength has imprinted itself on memory and time. Certainly the responses show overall involuntary memories evoked by recalling the listening experience and often a deep nostalgia that in many correspondents was largely unexpected. I am extremely grateful to those people who took the time and care to respond to this survey, and am gratified by the number who have expressed what a pleasurable and interesting exercise it has been for them.

A significant number of respondents, principally male, recalled in some detail the technology used to receive programmes and the physical appearance and presence of the object itself. Even if the brand and model had been forgotten with the passing of years, the character of the set often remained firmly entrenched in memory. One Australian correspondent in an older age group recalled 'a large brown model with valves, the glow of which fascinated me. Later (early 1950s), a Pye "portable", (huge batteries—portability compromised accordingly).' Other older listeners also recalled how cumbersome radio listening could be in its early days, particularly in the years between the wars: 'It used a lead-acid battery that often had to be taken to the garage (about three miles from the farm where we lived) for re-charging.' Early radios as developed in the 1920s were pure technology—machines—and it was the development of this technology to blend into the home living environment that was the first social breakthrough, enabling the entertainment systems as they evolved to become easier on the eye and therefore more acceptable to a wider range of family members. Thus young listeners in the immediate pre- and post-war years recalled the apparatus as 'a piece of furniture' that became the first objects to earn the title of 'music centres', embellished 'with a deep veneered finish that also incorporated a record player (78 r.p.m.) as well as stored records in the base. When you opened the doors it had a picture of Nipper, the HMV dog.' Other memories could be less specific, but equally evocative: 'Biggish, about one foot high, two feet wide, a glowing yellow ochre dial. You twiddled knobs and the pointer moved along, fizzing from station to station.' The light from sets and the dial itself fascinated many children. One respondent from the south-west of England recalled 'the glow of the valve radio, and the intricate pattern with double-ended needle pointing to wavelengths and station names in green and yellow writing on a black background ("Hilversum, Paris, Vienna, Home, Light, Third," etc)'. The detailed remembrance of the physicality of the object, as here, is often remarkable.

Equally memorable for many of this generation was the coming of transistorised radio technology, for UK listeners initially imported: 'I remember my father returning from Singapore in the early 1960s with one of the first ever Sony transistor radios as a birthday gift for my sister.' It is hard for later generations to comprehend the revolution in listening caused by the transistor, and the sense, almost of wonder, at the resulting miniaturisation and portability that was linked to a more private listening experience. This moment of change is captured vividly in the memory of this UK listener, brought up on heavy, cumbersome Bakelite listening devices: 'I remember being amazed and astonished, as the whole family was, when we went to America for a year, about 1960, and bought our first little transistor radio. It was about the size of a pack of cards, came in a little leather case, and was branded "Royce."' The transition from fixed-point listening to portable was often more gradual, as this Australian respondent recalled of a New Zealand childhood in the 1950s and early 1960s:

We had an old Philips mantle model radio on a shelf in the corner. Later, when I was about seven or eight, I was given my own radio and I listened to it in my bedroom. This was one of those valve radios with a carrying handle which slotted into a place in the car. Essentially it was a "portable" car radio of the time I guess. It plugged into the electricity and took a while to warm up after being switched on. It also hummed a lot in the dark. Later, when transistors were invented, my sister and I were given identical Pye portable radios in leather covers by our parents. Mine was brown and my sister's was green. These were just the best ever! How proud we were.

As implied by this recollection, the 1960s saw a cross-over from communal to individual listening, with the presence of the larger furniture-type music centres (radiograms) still present within the home. With the coming of the audio cassette, a further variation emerged for younger music enthusiasts, combining the attributes of the portable radio with the multifunctionality of the home music centre. Thus, for the generation born between 1960 and 1980, the solution was, as for this Canadian respondent, brought up in Britain:

> The "ghetto blaster", silver, "modern". It had a single tape-cassette deck on the front and a large radio tuner section, FM, MW and SW. I explored the tuning on the Short Wave dial for a long time; it was an amazing experience to slowly turn the dial from one end of the bandwidth to the other, finding stations in between stations. I suppose it became a kind of travel experience. I recall trying to "hear" transmissions from UFOs, and convincing myself that some of the beeps and morse code I heard was indeed a nearby crashed alien spacecraft—which I and my friends would go out searching for in the safety of daylight.

This recollection in itself recalls similar imaginative responses to the power of radio suggestion from previous generations, in particular the infamous Orson Welles CBS *War of the Worlds* broadcast of October 1938, after which the residents of the named town in New Jersey, Grovers Mill, chosen as the fictional landing place of the Martians, searched the area in vain for alien invaders.

From the 1980s onwards, the physical presence of the technology becomes less memorable, mirroring the move towards an era when the artefact as carrier was less a part of the experience. The exception both to this and to the individualised consumption of audio was the car radio, and a number of respondents from younger generations carried memories of their families listening on the move, on the way to school or on family daytrips or holidays. Prior to this, there were strong recollections of family rooms in which, post-war, the radio was still the communal focal point, a place later to be occupied by the television set. Clear visual memories of these rooms were common: 'A bit crowded, with a dark heavy oak table and chairs, a sideboard, a mirror over the fireplace, bookcase and radio to the left of the fireplace, Mum's sewing box and table lamp to the right.' This clear picture of a 1950s living room shows an environment little changed from the 1930s and 1940s, and the listening fare also retained a quality that was slow to change. Radio Luxembourg brought back many of the programmes that had been familiar before the war, such as *The Ovaltineys*, and on the

BBC radio serials such as *Mrs Dale's Diary* and *Dick Barton, Special Agent*, remained popular.

Another similar set of images of the time conveys a picture that confirms how we lived in the domestic context for radio listening:

> The living room was a typical 1950's setting, three piece suite, coal fire, three-quarter length curtains, net curtains, two large bookcases, small table stacked with books and magazines, a black cocker spaniel often asleep on my father's chair. There was another table that often had tea cups and plates etc. A glass ash tray that held my father's pipe. A bay window that allowed me to sit and look down the road each way.

There was still in 1950s Britain a clear divide between the family room, where most of the living, listening, eating and reading took place, and the 'best' room, seldom used exept on Sundays and for guests; descriptions almost always placed the radio in the family room. The detail in these answers was largely produced by beginning the questioning with the programme itself. Thus the sound of the content has evoked the context in which it was listened to. For instance, memories came back of the selective listening of a young teenager:

> Family listening in the lounge, around the fireplace, shouting answers during *Take Your Pick*. Charles Chilton serials alone, in the bedroom, profound concentration and energetic imagination. In teenage years, bedroom listening to pop music from Radio Luxembourg (Pete Murray). School exams suffered somewhat was a result, but I can still recall a lot of the song lyrics.

As in my own experience, many 1950s young people cite *Journey Into Space* as a key radio memory, and interestingly, as in that example, the concentration with which such programmes were listened to. The strength of the medium, being both primary and secondary, is a theme, as is the commitment to favourite programmes; 'appointment to listen' experiences and marked and highlighted programmes in such journals as the *Radio Times* in the UK remind us of the place in life a single mass home entertainment medium held. This fact is underlined by an Irish listener: 'We listened both passively and actively, doing things and not sitting down with 100% attention but in the busy heart of a big family. It was the soundtrack of our lives.' Respondents asked to remember peripheral sounds around radio listening often cited the sense of concentration and an awareness of often very small sounds surrounding it:

> There wasn't much sound in the house. Everyone listened attentively to the radio, and rarely spoke because others were listening. I can still hear

the clicking sound of my mother's knitting needles while we listened to the radio. She would also often bring us our evening meal on a tray, while we listened to the radio round the fire (or electric heater). Thus, the sounds of clinking china and food being eaten.

From the period between the 1960s and 1980s, much of the memory moved from the living or family room to the bedroom, often with an equally detailed recollection of the environment; headphones would be frequently used, and the visual focus was often heightened by its sense of becoming secondary to the audio content:

A tiny room with a single bed, a wooden wardrobe smelling of mothballs, dominating the room. Later on, my brother's bedroom. The blankets on the single bed, which I usually got into to listen on headphones, were very heavy and warm. A yellow carpet with an orange repeating pattern. All curtains, carpet, blankets, impregnated with the smell of smoke. I recall now a crockery and glass cabinet on the landing which shook and rattled when I walked (or usually ran) past. In there were teacups and saucers that we never used.

Some 1980s teenagers brought up in a rural environment recalled radio as a relief from silence and country sounds. Some would find this an idyll, but growing up required the stillness to be broken, and pop music provided a solution:

Wind in the tree outside, birds. I would open the window and blast music radio outside. My room faced over a path to a field, a stream, and high trees, further on, a sleepy road of bungalows. It was a very dull suburban village and very quiet; walking around, you rarely heard a sound—you could hear bees buzzing.

Radio listening and the sounds that surrounded it moved in and out of focus. Headphones shifted the concentration hub and placed the sensual centre on the internalised sound with an unrelated external visual commentary. When the listening was on a speaker, the experiences blended and interwove. As we have noted previously, the memory is often evoked of a time and a place in general terms rather than specifically recalled actual sounds. Nonetheless, the sound world as it is remembered now is valid and real, as in this picture from an Australian respondent:

There must have been a pesky younger sister babbling. A pekinese snuffling around, bell tinkling as it flopped downstairs, following Granny through the swish and jangle of the green bead fly curtain on the back door as she stomped down to her garden.

Detail of sound memory is consistently remarkable: 'The crackling of Dad's paper' from a seventy-year-old, the whirring of a fan heater in winter, recalled by a sixty-five-year-old, the strikes of a distant church clock, again from a respondent in their mid sixties, as well as intruding sounds that registered through their significance, such as the tinkling jingles of ice cream vans as they moved around neighbourhoods.

As to the programmes themselves, these of course varied according to location, although commonwealth countries such as Australia and Canada shared many radio memories with the UK, such as *The Goon Show* and other comedy shows. It is notable that most radio memories from childhood did not relate to children's programmes specifically, although in the UK *Listen With Mother*, aimed at the very young, was memorable for many, mostly through its theme music, the 'Berceuse' from Fauré's *Dolly Suite*, a tune that, heard out of context, would for many immediately evoke that fifteen-minute programme, while the actual content would usually be forgotten. Likewise the theme from *Dick Barton, Special Agent,* and Radio Luxembourg's *The Ovalitineys* could be recalled and hummed at will. For some, themes such as 'With a Song in My Heart' from the Sunday lunchtime BBC/BFBS (British Forces Broadcasting Service) record request programme *Two Way Family Favourites* was so evocative as to actually produce the sensory memory of the smell of Sunday lunch being cooked. The 1940s and 1950s—a golden age of radio comedy—was often evoked in recollection through catchphrases, and the fun of 'trying to beat the wireless by a couple of seconds: "A good idea, son!" (*Educating Archie*), "He's fallen in the water!" (*The Goon Show*) or "Oh, Ron!"/"Oh, Eth!" (The Glums in *Take it From Here*) and so on'. Likewise, the opening of the BBC Light Programme's *Billy Cotton Band Show* evoked the memory of the opening sequence, 'Wakey Wakey!' followed by the theme tune of 'Somebody Stole My Gal', another Sunday lunchtime recollection from the early to the late 1950s in the UK. In particular listeners of the 1940s, 1950s and 1960s from almost anywhere in the world will be able to summon similar archived sounds from their own pasts.

For many respondents, the exercise evoked a feeling of nostalgia. Recurrent phrases in the survey were 'warm and relaxed', 'loved', 'very happy, comfortable, but a little sad that those times have long-since gone', 'security and stability' and 'enormous nostalgia and recollection of times which were very simple and relatively safe'. Central to most of these feelings was the association of radio listening with the family unit, and the formative nature of that rooted sense of the presence of radio, where it existed in this context. Thus listening habits acquired in childhood were retained and have frequently informed later life and experience. Often there was a subjective regret expressed that later generations would not share the same mode of listening within a social context, but a common theme was a continuing appreciation of sound and radio that most respondents felt gave their lives an enrichment. As one listener from the older age range expressed it:

> It goes beyond nostalgia, which, so we are led to believe, is a treach-erous set of emotions. Radio was central to the life of my family: we enjoyed it together, discussed it, and respected the medium as a supplier of culture as well as entertainment. The richness of language it brought surely had an effect on the quality and amount of language used in our domestic circle, while the music we listened to, the tastes I started to develop in those years, has stayed with me through life.

Bibliography

BOOKS

Aldridge, David. *Music Therapy in Dementia Care*. London: Jessica Kingsley Publishers, 2000.

Alter, Nora M., and Koepnick, Lutz. *Sound Matters: Essays on the Acoustics of Modern German Culture*. Oxford: Berghahn Books, 2005.

Baddeley, Alan. *Human Memory: Theory and Practice*. Hove: The Psychology Press, 1999.

Baddeley, Alan, Eysenck, Michael W., and Anderson, Michael C. *Memory*. Hove: The Psychology Press, 2009.

Baily, Leslie. 'The Blattnerphone.' *The Sunday Referee and Entertainment Supplement* 15 January 1933: 12.

Beckett, Samuel. *Proust: And Three Dialogues with Georges Duthuit*. London: Calder Books, 1949.

Benjamin, Walter. 'Unpacking My Library: A Talk about Book Collecting', in *Illuminations: Essays and Reflections*. New York: Schocken Books, 2007.

Bijsterveld, Karin, and van Dijk, José, eds. *Sound Souvenirs: Audio Technologies, Memory and Cultural Practices*. Amsterdam: Amsterdam University Press, 2009.

Bitner, Jason. *Cassette from my Ex*. New York: St. Martin's Griffin, 2009.

Boym, Svetlana. *The Future of Nostalgia*. New York: Basic Books, 2001.

Breton, Andre. 'Introduction to the Discourse on the Paucity of Reality.' *What is Surrealism? Selected Writings*. Ed. F. Rosemont. New York: Monad, 1978.

Chion, Michel. *Audio Vision: Sound on Screen*. New York: Columbia University Press, 1994.

Dickens, Charles. *David Copperfield*. London: Penguin, 1985.

Ellison, David. *A Reader's Guide to Proust's 'In Search of Lost Time'*. Cambridge: Cambridge University Press, 2010.

Fuller-Maitland, John Alexander. *Brahms*. London: Methuen, 1911.

Giles, John Allen. *The Works of Gildas and Nennius*. London: James Bohn, 1841.

Gioia, Diana. *Daily Horoscope*. Saint Paul: Graywolf Press, 2002.

Gopnik, Alison. *The Philosophical Baby*. New York: Farrar, Straus & Giroux, 2009.

Hardy, Thomas. *The Life and Work of Thomas Hardy*. London: MacMillan, 1984.

Harvey, Jonathan. *Music and Inspiration*. London: Faber & Faber, 1999.

Hirshfield, Jane. *Nine Gates: Entering the Mind of Poetry*. New York: Harper Collins, 1997.

Howard, Deborah, and Moretti, Laura. *Sound and Space in Renaissance Venice*. New Haven: Yale University Press, 2009.

Johnson, Stephen. *Mahler: His Life and Music*. Redhill: Naxos Books, 2006.

Jones, David. *The Anathemata*. London: Faber and Faber, 1972.

Jones, Ernest. *The Life and Work of Sigmund Freud*. Vol. 2. London: Hogarth Press, 1953–57.

Krause, Bernie. *The Great Animal Orchestra*. London: Profile Books, 2012.

Lander, Dan, and Lexier, Micah. *Sounds By Artists*. Mississauga: Blackwood Gallery, 2013.

Lester, Julius. *To Be a Slave*. New York: Puffin Books, 2005.

Lockwood, Annea. Insert note to *A Sound Map of the Housatonic River*. 3Leaves, 2012. CD.

López, Jay-Dea. Insert note to *The Great Silence*. 3Leaves, 3L020, 2013. CD.

Marek, George R. *Toscanini*. London: Vision Press, 1975.

Maxwell, James Clerk. *Matter and Motion*. New York: Dover Editions, 1991.

Milner, Greg. *Perfecting Sound Forever—The Story of Recorded Music*. London: Granta, 2009.

Muller, Carol Ann, and Benjamin, Sathima Bea. *Musical Echoes: South African Women Thinking in Jazz*. Durham: Duke University Press, 2011.

Murch, Walter in Chion, Michael, *Audio Vision, Sound on Screen*. New York, Columbia Press, 1994.

Murdock Jr., Bennett B. 'Auditory and Visual Stores in Short-term Memory.' *Acta Psychologica* 27 (1960): 316–24.

Olick, Jeffrey K, Vinitzky-Seroussi, Vered, and Levy, Daniel. *The Collective Memory Reader*. Oxford: Oxford University Press, 2011.

Peacock, Thomas Love. *Peacock's Memoirs of Shelley*. Ed. H.F.B. Brett-Smith. London: Henry Frowde, 1909.

Peddie, Ian., ed. *Popular Music and Human Rights, Volume ll: World Music*. Farnham: Ashgate Publishing Company, 2012.

Piette, Adam. *Remembering and the Sound of Words*. Oxford: Clarendon Press, 2004.

Pikes, Noah. *Dark Voices: The Genesis of Roy Hart Theatre*. New Orleans: Spring Journal Books, 2004.

Proust, Marcel. *In Search of Lost Time, (The Captive)*. Trans. C. K. Scott Moncrieff and T. Kilmartin. Rev. D. J. Enright. London: Vintage Books, 2000.

———. *In Search of Lost Time*. Ed. Prendergast, C. London: Penguin Classics, 2003.

Robinson, Rony. *Who's Been Talking?* Sheffield: ALD Print, 2010.

Sacks, Oliver. *The Man Who Mistook His Wife for a Hat*. London: Picador, 1986.

———. *Musicophilia*. London: Picador, 2008.

Salaman, Esther. *A Collection of Moments: A Study of Involuntary Memory*. London: Longman, 1970.

Schnupp, Jan, Nelken, Israel, and King, Andrew. *Auditory Neuroscience: Making Sense of Sound*. Cambridge, MA: The MIT Press, 2011.

Scott, Robert Falcon. *Journals: Captain Scott's Last Exhibition*. Oxford: Oxford University Press, 2008.

Simon, Scott. *Below Sea Level: An Exploration of the Subterranean Fenland Environment*. Cambridge: 12k, 2012. CD.

Sonnenchein, David. *Sound Design: The Expressive Power of Music, Voice, and Sound Effects in Cinema*. Studio City, CA: Michael Wiese Publications, 2001.

Spence, Jonathan D. *The Memory Palace of Matteo Ricci*. London: Penguin Books, 1985.

Street, Seán. *Crossing the Ether: British Public Service Radio and Commercial Competition, 1922–1945*. Eastleigh: John Libbey Publishing, 2006.

———. *The Poetry of Radio: The Colour of Sound*. Abingdon: Routledge, 2013.

Tipp, Cheryl. Insert note. *Waves: The Sounds of Britain's Shores*. London: British Library, 2011. CD.

Upton, Clive, and Davies, Bethan L. *Analysing 21st Century British English: Conceptual and Methodological Aspects of the 'Voices' Project*. Abingdon: Routledge, 2013.

Wearing, Deborah. *Forever Today: A True Story of Lost Memory and Never-Ending Love*. London: Doubleday, 2005.
Wordsworth, William. *The Poetical Works of William Wordsworth (Oxford Edition)*. Ed. Thomas Hutchinson. London: Oxford University Press, 1909.
Wörner, Karl. *Stockhausen: Life and Work*. Trans. and ed. Bill Hopkins. Rev. ed. Berkeley: University of California Press, 1973.
Yates, Frances A. *The Art of Memory*. London: Pimlico, 2012.
Zuckerkandl, Victor. *Sound and Symbol: Music and the External World*. Princeton, NJ: Princeton University Press, 1956.

JOURNALS

Landau, Carolyn, and Topp Farjeon, Janet. 'We're All Archivists Now: Towards a More Equitable Ethnolmusicaology'. *Ethnomusicology Forum* 21.2 (2012): 130.
Brinkhurst, E. 'Archives and Access: Reaching Out to the Somali Community of London's King's Cross', *Ethnomusicology Forum* 21.2 (2012): 243–58.
Conn, S. 'Fitting between Present and Past: Memory and Social Interaction in Cape Breton Singing.' *Ethnomusicology Forum* 21.3 (2012): 354–73.
Journal of the American Medical Association, 261(13)
Prickett, Carol A., and Moore, Randall S. 'The Use of Music to Aid Memory of Alzheimer's Patients.' *Journal of Music Therapy* XXVlli.2 (1991): 101–10.
Peelle, Jonathan, Trolani, Vanessa, Grossman, Mary, and Wingfield, Arthur. 'Hearing Loss in Older Adults Affects Neural Systems Supporting Speech Comprehension.' *The Journal of Neuroscience* 31.35 (2011): 12638–43.
Sparrow, Betsy, Liu, Jenny, and Wegner, Daniel M. 'Google Effects on Memory: Cognitive Consequences of Having Information at Our Fingertips.' *Science* 5. Vol. 333 (2011): 776–78. www.sciencemag.org
Watts, Cecil. Interview. Rec. LP26453 Jan. 1961. Developments in Recorded Sound, Oral History Collection, British Library Sound Archive.

AUDIO CDS

Lockwood, Annea. *A Sound Map of the Housatonic River*. 3Leaves 3L018, 2013.
López, Jay-Dea. *The Great Silence*, 3Leaves 3L020, 2013.
Ruhlmann, Mathieu. *This Star Teaches Bending*. 3Leaves 3L021, 2013.
Scott, Simon. *Below Sea Level*, 12k 12k1071, 2011.
Tipp, Cheryl. *Waves: The Sounds of Britain's Shore*. British Library, NSA CD 84, 2011.

ONLINE REPORTS, PAPERS, WEBSITES AND OTHER RESOURCES

'After the Day of Infamy: "Man-on-the-Street" Interviews Following the Attack on Pearl Harbor.' http://memory.loc.gov/ammem/afcphhtml/afcphhome.html
Angel Radio. A full report and further station information can be obtained by clicking on the 'Station Information' button on the Angel website: http://angelradio. co.uk (accessed April 2014)
Audiology online: Understanding Hearing Loss and Alzheimer's, www.audiologyonline.com/articles/remember-me-guide-to-alzheimer-1008 (accessed August, 2013)
Batmanghelidjh, C. 'Oxford TED Talk.' 2012. http://tedxoxford.co.uk/camilabatmanghelidjh/ (accessed July 1013)

'BBC Launches CBeebies App.' BBC Media Centre Press Release. www.bbc.co.uk/mediacentre/latestnews/2013/cbeebiesapp.html (accessed August 2013).

Berkeley, Michael, *My Beethoven Moment*, www.theguardian.com/music/2010/sep/07/beethoven-deafness-music-composition, (accessed July, 2013)

Corbett, Anne., 'Dementia Brain Tour.' www.alzheimers.org.uk/braintour (accessed June 2013).

Demeulenaere, Stijn, Le Petit, Alexandre, and Andersen, Tawny. 'Soundtracks.' http://versonatura.org/sound/soundtracks.htm (accessed July, 2013).

'Finding Emilie.' *Radiolab*. WNYC. www.radiolab.org/2011/jan/25/finding-emilie/ (accessed August 2013).

Gobnik, Alison. 'Amazing Babies.' http://edge.org/conversation/amazing-babies (accessed June 2013).

Hough, Stephen, *Maria João Pires: the panic, the miracle. The Daily Telegraph*, 26 October, 2013 (Accessed October, 2013) http://blogs.telegraph.co.uk/culture/stephenhough/100071203/maria-joao-pires-the-panic-the-miracle/

'Landscape Stories.' www.landscapestories.net/interviews/65-2013-annea-lockwood?lang=en (accessed June 2013).

'The Lost Chord.' www.lost-chord.org.uk/ (accessed July 2013).

Marredo, Jorge. 'De Ópera a la Plaza de San Jerónimo Pasando Por Sol.' http://satisfaccionlab.bandcamp.com/album/de-pera-a-la-carrera-de-san-jer-nimo-pasando-por-sol (accessed April 2013).

Moon, Christine, Lagercrantz, Hugo, and Kuhl, Patricia. 'Language Learning Begins in Utero.' Pacific Lutheran University. December 2012. www.plu.edu/news'2012/12/infant-language/ (accessed June 2013).

Ofcom Report, 'The Reinvention of the 1950s Living Room, July, 2013: http://stakeholders.ofcom.org.uk/market-data-research/market-data/communications-market-reports/cmr13/uk/ (accessed July, 2013)

'Psychosocial Research and Support Programme at the Comprehensive Centre on Brain Ageing.' New York University. http://aging.med.nyu.edu/frontpage (accessed July, 2013).

'Radio and Ad Avoidance: You Can't Close Your Ears.' Radio Advertising Bureau Report. December 2005. www.rab.co.uk/archived-pages/Ad-Avoidance (accessed May 2013).

Reilly, Jamie, Westbury, Chris, Kean, Jacob, and Peelle, Jonathan E. 'Arbitrary Symbolism in Natural Language Revisited: When Word Forms Carry Meaning.' www.plosone.org/article/info%3Adoi%2F10.1371%2Fjournal.pone.0042286

'The September 11, 2001, Documentary Project.' http://memory.loc.gov/ammem/collections/911_archive/

'Turning Art into Science: New Insights into Radio Creativity.' Radio Advertising Bureau Report. April 2013. http://rab.co.uk/turning-art-into-science (accessed May 2013).

'Understanding Hearing Loss and Alzheimer's.' Audiology Online. www.audiologyonline.com/articles/remember-me-guide-to-alzheimer-1008 (accessed August 2013).

Watson, Chris, *The Echoes of Benjamin Britten's 'Composing Walks'*, www.theguardian.com/music/2013/jan/30/benjamin-britten-composing-walks (Accessed May, 2013)

WNYC, *Radiolab, Finding Emilie*, www.radiolab.org/2011/jan/25/finding-emilie/ (accessed August, 2013)

Radio Broadcasts

'The Annotated Jack.' Narr. Chris Brookes. Battery Radio for Radio Telefís-Eireann, Radio 1. September 2009. Radio. Programme note.

'Endangered Sounds.' *Sound Stories.* Series 2, Episode 1. Produced by Kevin Brew. RTÉ Radio. 11 August 2006. Radio.

'Home Recorded Voices.' Narr. Seán Street. Soundscape Productions for BBC Radio 4. Produced by Andy Cartwright. 20 December 2008. Radio.

'I Remember, He Remembered.' Produced by Barbara Crowther. BBC Radio 4. 13 July 1979. Radio.

'Marie Slocombe and the BBC Sound Archive.' *Archive on 4.* BBC Radio 4. 1 September 2007. Radio.

Index